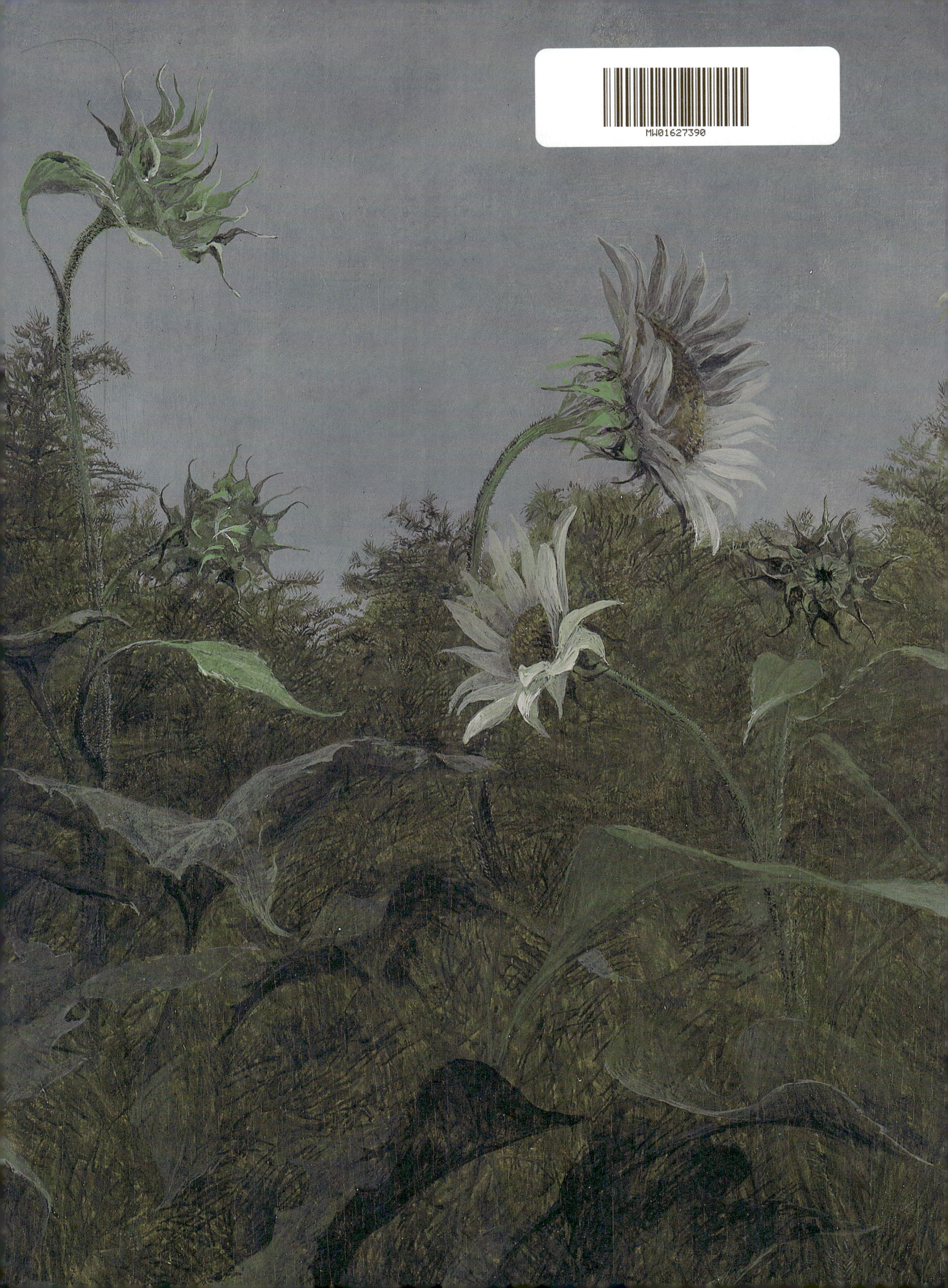

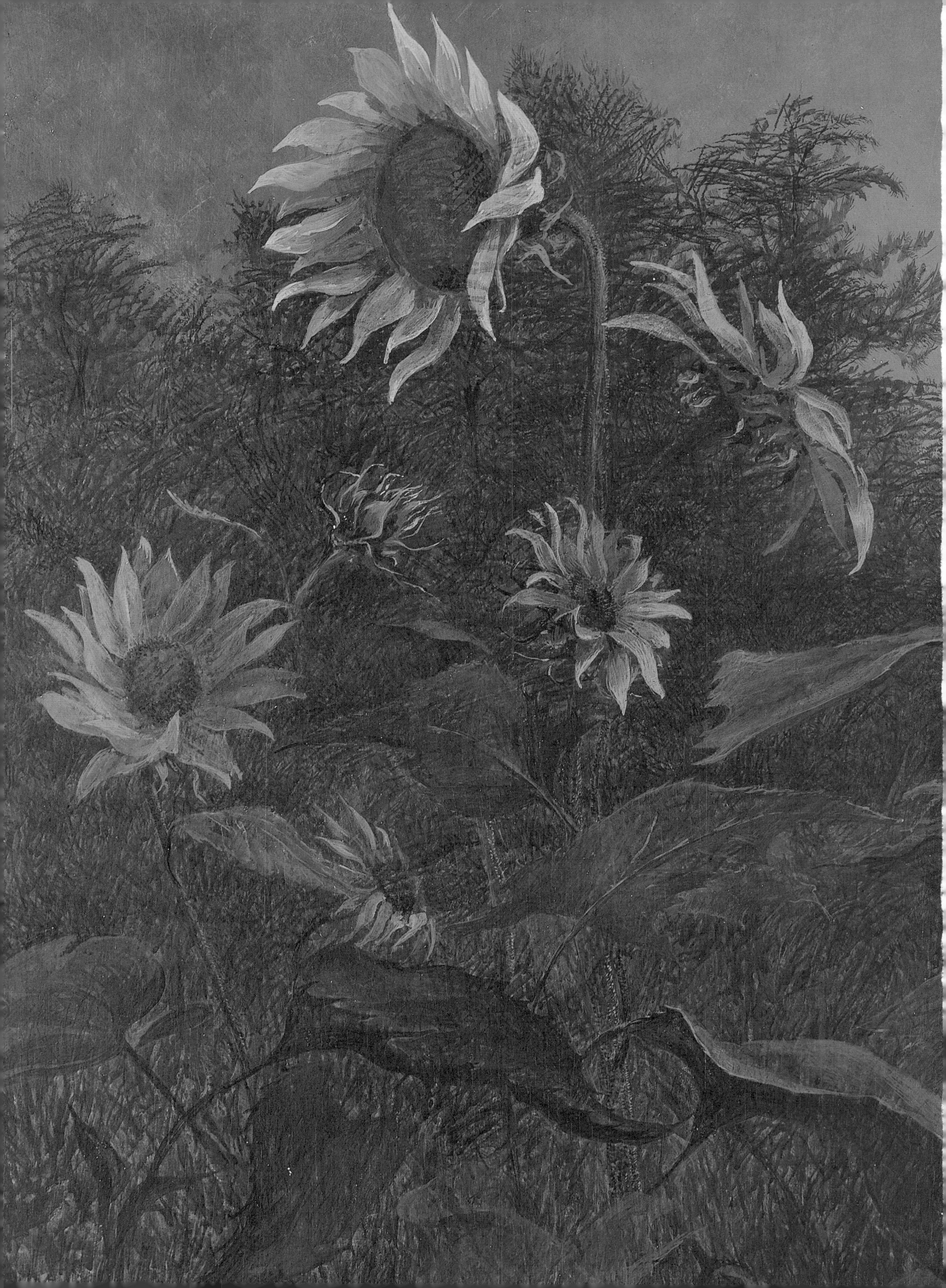

THE WAY BACK: THE PAINTINGS OF GEORGE A. WEYMOUTH

A BRANDYWINE VALLEY VISIONARY

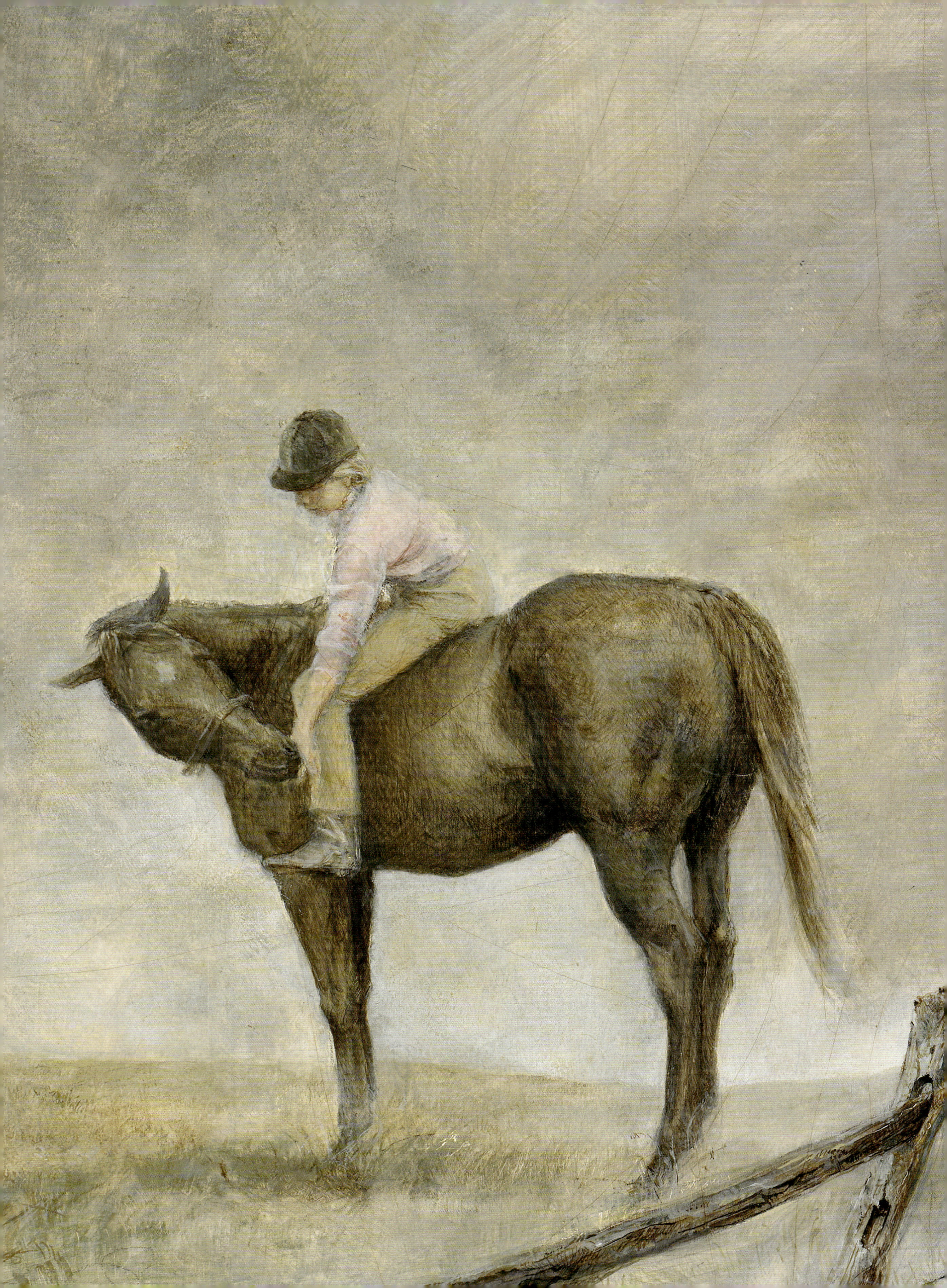

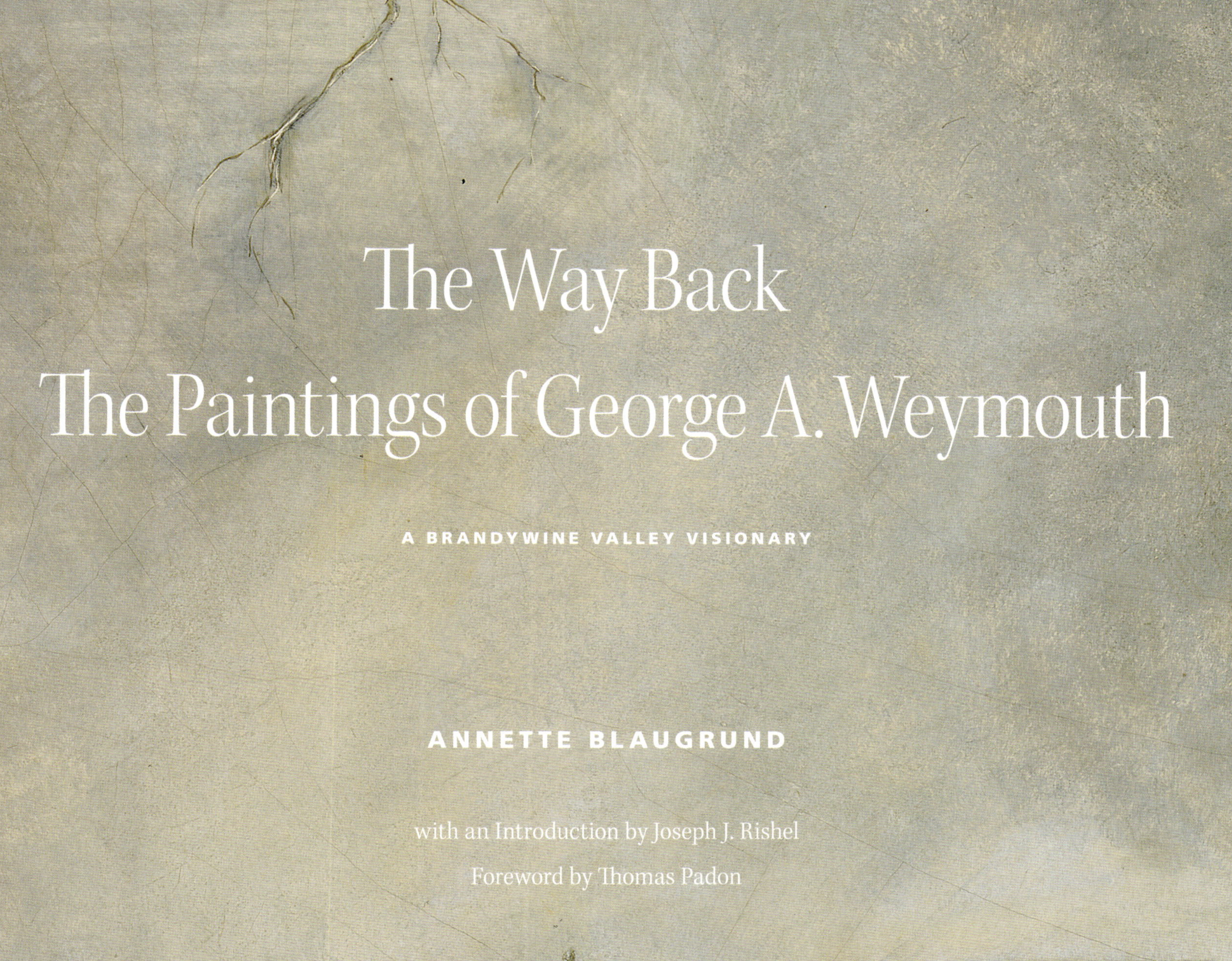

The Way Back
The Paintings of George A. Weymouth

A BRANDYWINE VALLEY VISIONARY

ANNETTE BLAUGRUND

with an Introduction by Joseph J. Rishel

Foreword by Thomas Padon

BRANDYWINE RIVER MUSEUM OF ART

Rizzoli Electa

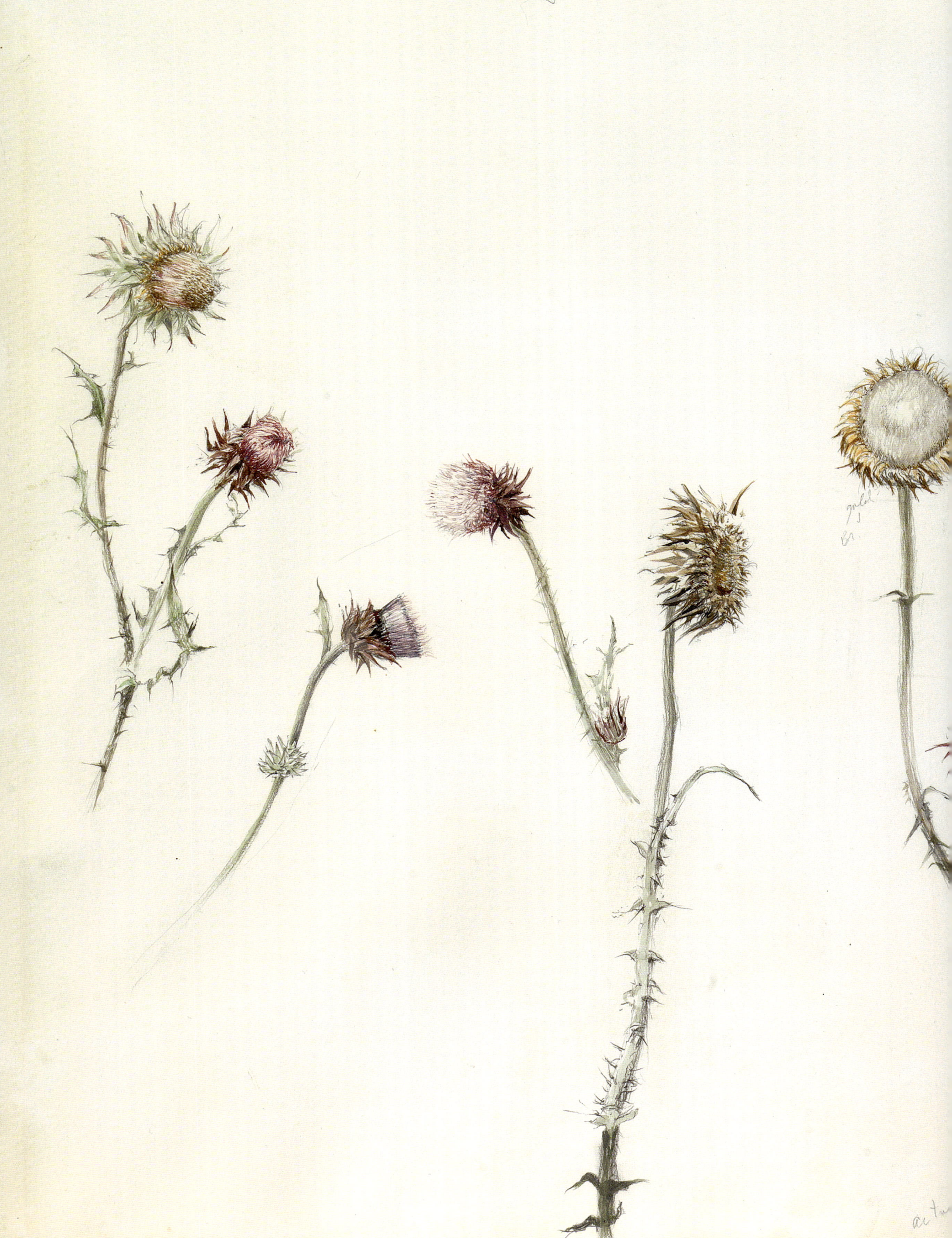

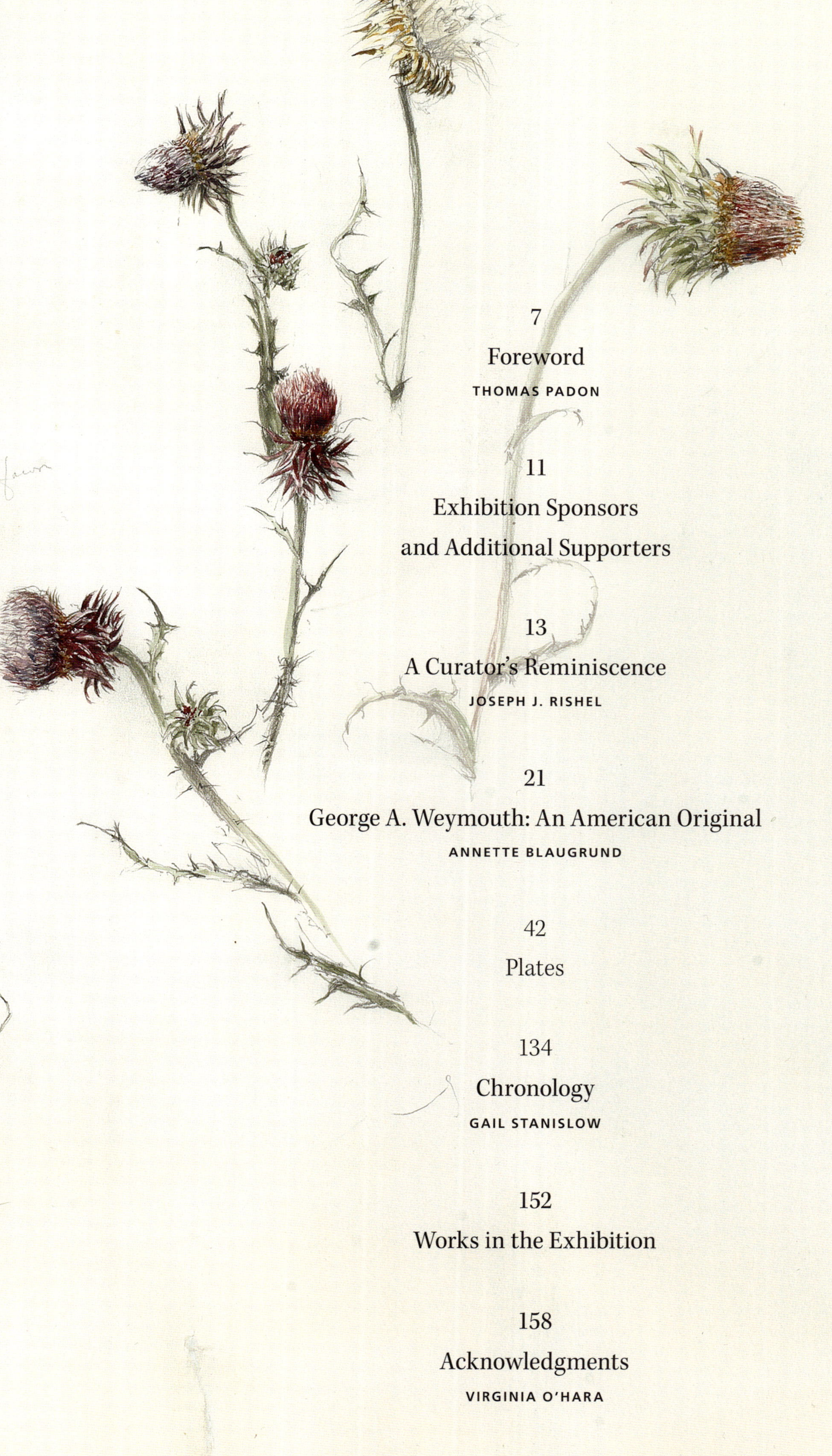

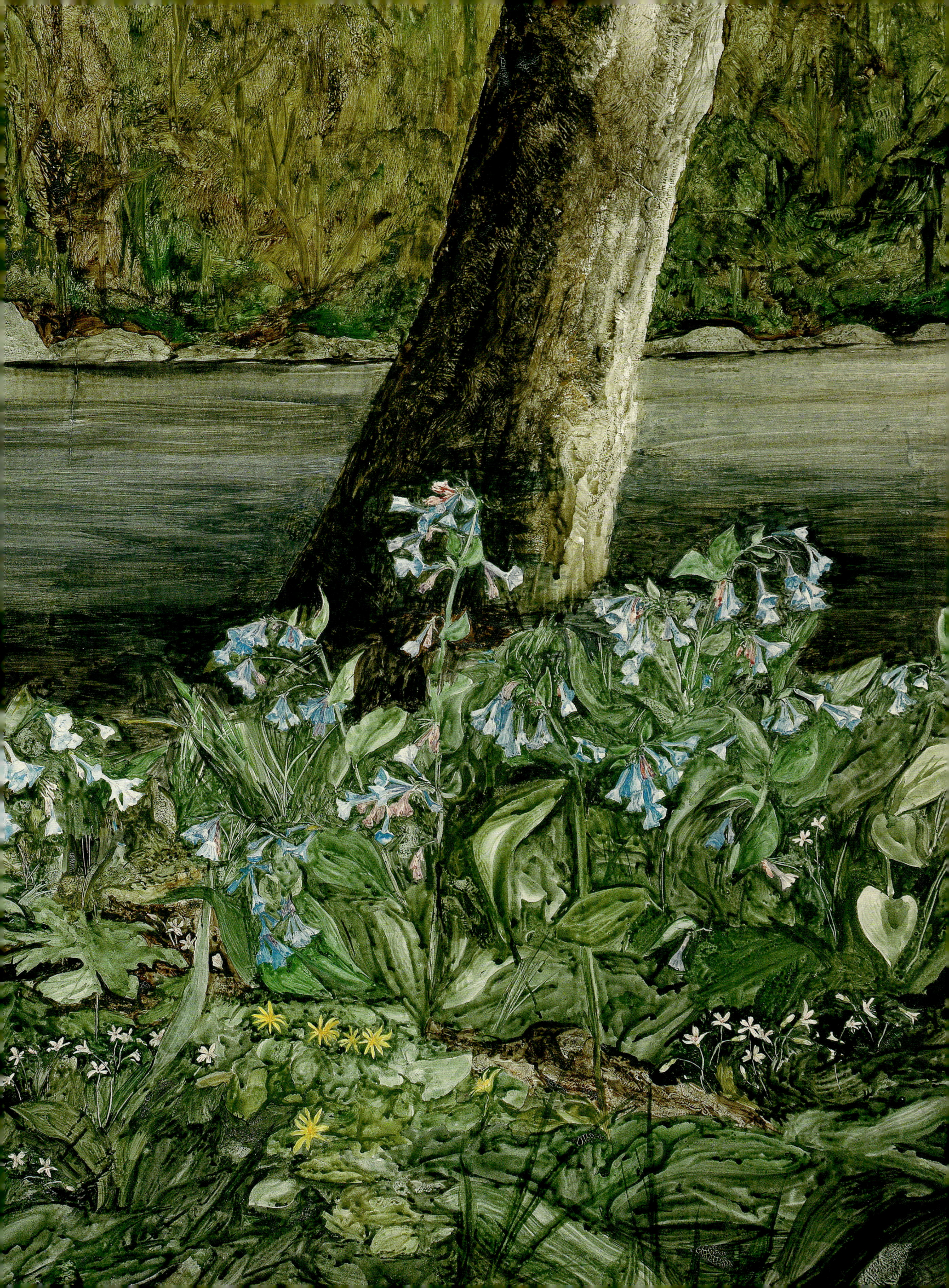

FOREWORD

THE IMPORTANCE OF GEORGE A. WEYMOUTH ("Frolic" to everyone who knew him) to the Brandywine Conservancy & Museum of Art in Chadds Ford, Pennsylvania, cannot be overstated. He is interwoven into every story in the fifty-year history of the Conservancy and the Museum. Together with two other founding board members, Weymouth had a vision for the protection of the natural and cultural heritage of the Brandywine Valley that has resulted in an organization that is—without hyperbole—unique. As Brandywine's chairman for almost five decades, he inspired those around him with his relentless and infectious passion for art and nature and his optimistic belief that the two are the wellspring of inspiration and connectedness. Because of his efforts and those of a remarkable group of generous supporters over decades, the Brandywine Conservancy & Museum of Art now has over sixty thousand acres of land under permanent protection and four thousand works of art in its collection.

There are many remarkably accomplished facets to Weymouth's life. In his philanthropic endeavors he devoted much of his adult life to the Brandywine Conservancy & Museum of Art and Winterthur Museum, Garden & Library. As a sportsman he grew up riding and mastered the game of polo, becoming head of Yale University's formidable team in the late 1950s and later one of the country's leading figures in the four-in-hand horse driving coaching world. His success in any one of these areas would be impressive. What you would not necessarily predict from such an accomplished life was the humility of the person: Weymouth made it seem as if he had no other option than to do the things he did. When you add to these achievements his extraordinary talent as an artist—the subject of this exhibition and publication—you gain a sharpened sense of the exceptional person that Frolic Weymouth was and of the determination, passion, and interconnectedness that undergirded all his efforts.

Much like his friend and artistic mentor Andrew Wyeth, Weymouth was very private about his painting. Also, as they were for Wyeth, his subjects tended to be friends and family and the scenery that surrounded him daily—in Weymouth's case the bucolic landscape of his estate in Chadds Ford. Artists going back to the nineteenth century, among them Jasper Cropsey and William Trost Richards, have celebrated the beauty of the region. Weymouth both carried on that tradition and created its next chapter. It is especially fitting, then, for the Brandywine River Museum of Art to organize the first comprehensive exhibition of Weymouth's career and examine his contribution to American painting.

I wish to thank esteemed art historian Joseph J. Rishel, who selected the works for this groundbreaking exhibition that establishes Weymouth's bona fides as a major contributor to what has become known as the Brandywine School of artists. Rishel also conveys a very personal

Indian Hanna, 1990 (detail)
Watercolor on panel,
39 × 59 inches
Brandywine River Museum of Art. Anonymous gift, 2005

perspective born of a three-decade friendship with the artist. Annette Blaugrund, one of the leading scholars of American art, brings Weymouth's career vividly to life in her astute essay. For the first time, she considers Weymouth's paintings in the context of the American realist canon.

At the Brandywine, I wish to thank the Museum staff for all they did to organize this project, a labor of love for all of us who had the privilege to know Weymouth so well. In particular, I want to recognize Virginia O'Hara, manager of the Museum's Walter and Leonore Annenberg Research Center, whose knowledge of Weymouth's painting was invaluable to the entire project team. To her we extend our deepest gratitude.

In producing the handsome publication that accompanies the exhibition, I would like to recognize Margaret Rennolds Chace, associate publisher, and Ellen Cohen, senior editor, at Rizzoli/Electa, who shepherded the project with unerring intuition and skill. Thanks are also due to Eileen Boxer at Boxer Design, with whom the Brandywine has the pleasure of again working, for the luminous design of these pages that so perfectly foreground the directness of Weymouth's artistic vision. For the catalogue I would also like to highlight the contribution of Sandra Klimt and Lucie Teegarden.

A major project such as this could not be possible without the generosity of numerous individuals. I would first like to thank Anson and Debra Beard, Jr., Richard and Sheila Sanford, Mac and Toni Weymouth, and Phyllis and Jamie Wyeth for their leadership gifts that were instrumental in realizing this ambitious exhibition. I would also like to recognize the many other individuals, foundations, and businesses that gave essential support for this project. Special thanks are due to Mac Weymouth and Claire Reid for this fundraising effort. Finally, my appreciation goes to the board of trustees of the Brandywine Conservancy & Museum of Art, in particular Morris Stroud and Virginia A. Logan, for their unwavering support. Our deepest gratitude goes to all those who have lent to this exhibition. Their generosity ensures that Weymouth's vision is brought to life fully.

It is fitting to place George A. Weymouth firmly in the firmament of the Brandywine School of artists. He inherited a storied American landscape tradition yet made it his own. His art is indelible, poetically stating his love of place. This publication is dedicated to Frolic Weymouth with the gratitude, respect, and friendship of all the staff of the Brandywine Conservancy & Museum of Art.

THOMAS PADON

THE JAMES H. DUFF DIRECTOR
BRANDYWINE RIVER MUSEUM OF ART

Website, 2003 (detail)
Tempera on panel,
40 x 28 inches
Private collection

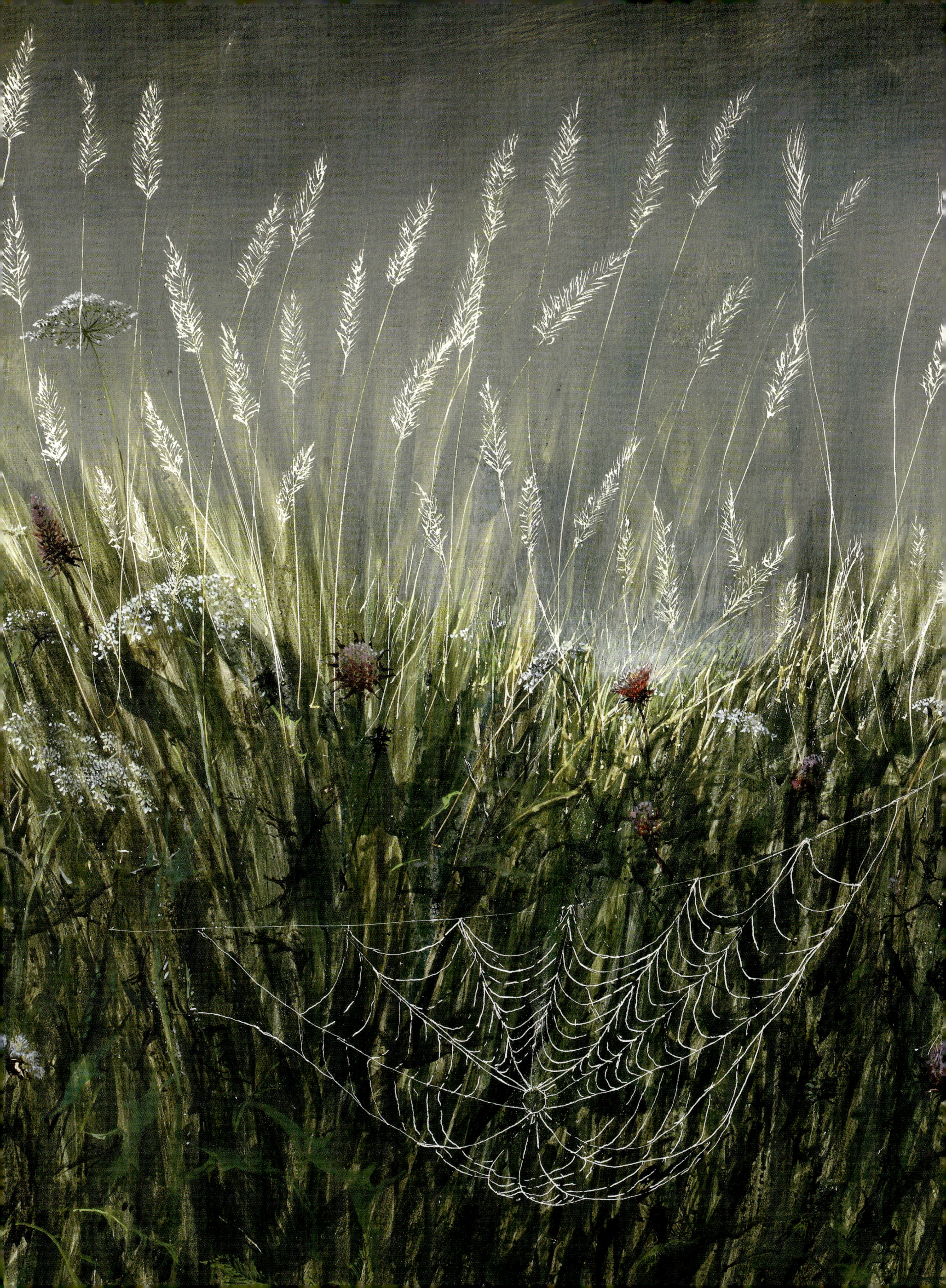

EXHIBITION SPONSORS

Anson and Debra Beard, Jr.
Richard and Sheila Sanford
Mac and Toni Weymouth
Phyllis and Jamie Wyeth

Additional support provided by:

Mr. and Mrs. Robert V. Duprey
William and Katharine Gahagan
Glenmede
The Stephen Philibosian Foundation
Elizabeth "Lisette" Prince

Ritchie Battle
Jean J. Beard
The Davenport Family Foundation
Sophie and Lance Derrickson
Freeman's
Otto Haas Charitable Trust
Dr. Benjamin F. Hammond
David Harrington
Marguerite and Gerry Lenfest
Bill and Renée Lickle
Dan and Missy Lickle
Virginia A. Logan
Mr. and Mrs. Michael R. Matz
Laurie and John McBride
Mr. and Mrs. Frederick L. Meserve, Jr.
The Nor' Easter Foundation
Susan Bissell Parker
Claire Reid
Suzanne F. Roberts
David and Lisa Spartin
Mr. and Mrs. George Strawbridge, Jr.
Morris and Boo Stroud
Hope H. van Beuren
J. Robinson West and Eileen Shields West
Jack Wetzel
Mr. and Mrs. John P. White
Young Friends of the Brandywine
Mr. and Mrs. Hugh J. Zimmer

Jim and Sally Duff
John and Elizabeth Fawcett
Casey and Martin Fenton
John and Marlou Gregory
Nathan and Marilyn R. Hayward
Hillary K. Holland
Sherry Kerstetter
C. Victoria Kitchell
Mary Alice Malone
James and Misdee Miller
Beth and Ran Miner
Jeffrey and Annie Nielsen
Thomas Padon and James Melançon
Mr. and Mrs. Louis G. Piancone
Gail and Joe Pitone
Dr. M. J. Potter and Mr. Chadwin Walker
Barbara Cushing Riegel
Sascha Rockefeller
Geoff and Sheryl Rogers
Jim and Jocelyn Stewart
David Thalmann
Kelly Valdes
Ms. Douglas Walker
Gene Weymouth
John and Libby Winthrop

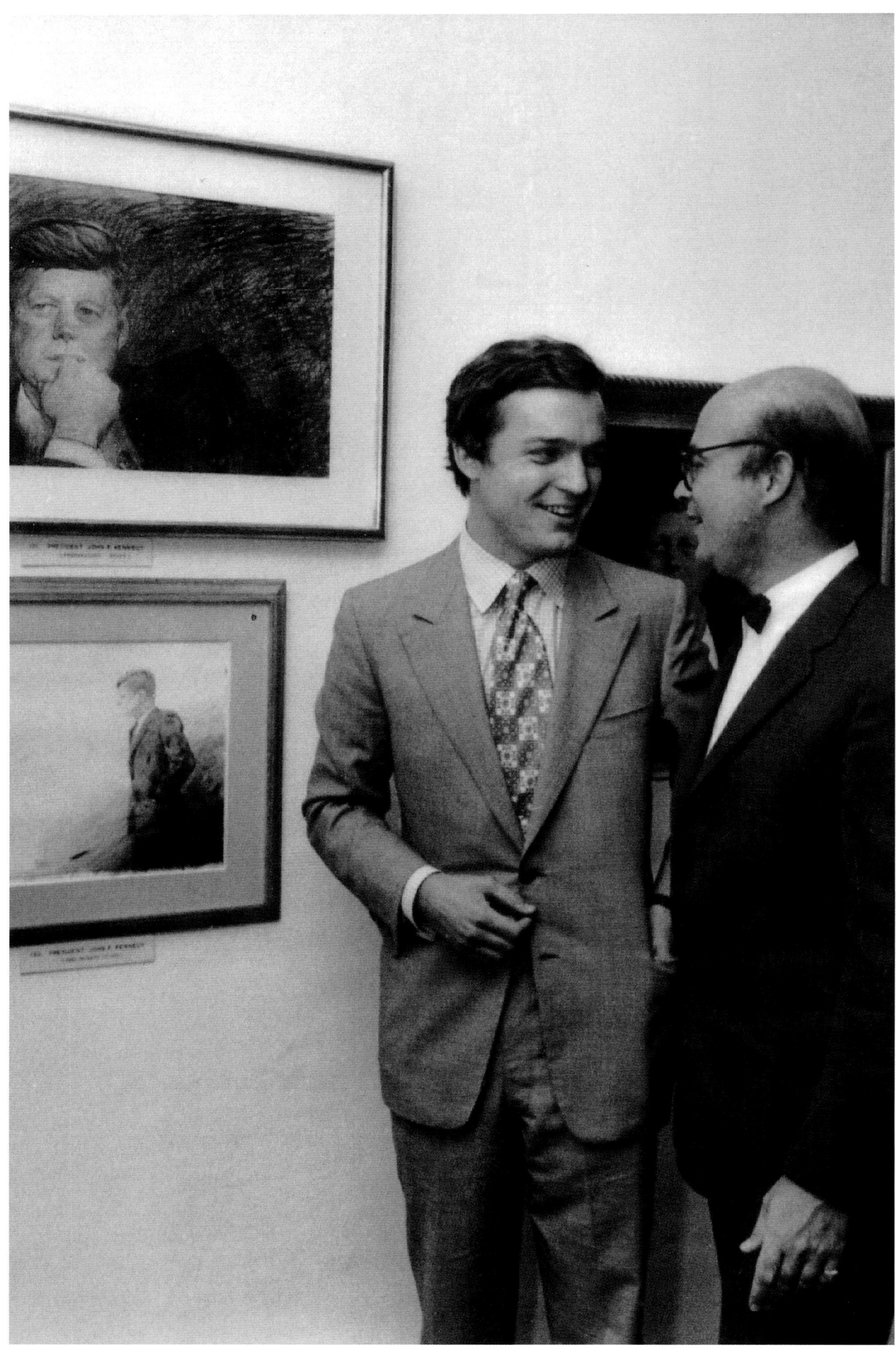

A Curator's Reminiscence

JOSEPH J. RISHEL

WHEN GEORGE ALEXIS ("FROLIC") WEYMOUTH died on April 24, 2016, press coverage celebrated his career as a conservationist, coachman, and accomplished painter who was instrumental in the founding of the Brandywine River Conservancy & Museum of Art.[1] Sadly, Weymouth died just as we were in the early phases of preparing a major retrospective of his art at the Museum. We had just been interviewing friends and colleagues and the artist himself to deepen our understanding of his process and inspiration as well as his relationship to his own art.

Not that literature about Weymouth is lacking. Richard J. Boyle's essay for the 1991 catalogue accompanying the exhibition organized by the Brandywine River Museum of Art is an invaluable source of information,[2] as is the catalogue for the 2001 exhibition at the Haggerty Museum of Art at Marquette University in Milwaukee.[3] A more intimate account of the artist's attitudes and feelings is found in the documentary film *The Way Back: A Portrait of George A. Weymouth*, made in 2004 by Renée Harrison Drake, the artist's cousin.[4] The film's interviews of the artist capture his famous spirit and bonhomie and reinforce our intention to explore Weymouth's critical involvement in the Brandywine circle defined by the three principal artists of the Wyeth family—N. C. (1882–1945), Andrew (1917–2009), and Jamie (b. 1946) (fig. 1). Frolic was deeply involved with Andrew Wyeth and his family both as a friend and fellow artist and as a relative through his marriage to Anna Brelsford McCoy, a painter, and through their son, McCoy ("Mac").

Frolic Weymouth was a sixth-generation member of the du Pont family, whose forebears settled in the Brandywine Valley in the early 1800s. Members of the family owned numerous notable properties in the area: the Winterthur Museum, Garden & Library, which opened its gardens and collections to the public in 1951; Longwood Gardens, purchased by Pierre du Pont in 1906 and now a world-famous destination for garden lovers; and the Nemours Mansion, owned and developed by Alfred I. du Pont. Frolic grew up on his family's estate, which they named "Doggone." Frolic acquired his own home in the area through his purchase in 1961 of an abandoned eighteenth-century stone farmhouse, which he named "The Big Bend" after the Lenape name for the sharp curve of the Brandywine River flanking the property. He would spend years restoring the house and treasuring its historic character.

FIG. 1
Weymouth with Jamie Wyeth at the Museum's first exhibition, *The Brandywine Heritage*, 1971. Brandywine Conservancy Archives

Weymouth has said that he cannot remember any moment in his life when he was not painting. His interest and talent were actively supported by his mother, Dulcinea ("Deo") Ophelia Payne du Pont, herself a painter. Weymouth's early aptitude for art, recognized even in elementary school, was reinforced by his study with two noted art teachers, Kleber Hall at St. Mark's School in Southborough, Massachusetts, and Deane Keller at Yale.[5] In her essay, Annette Blaugrund provides a carefully researched summary of Weymouth's high school and college art studies.

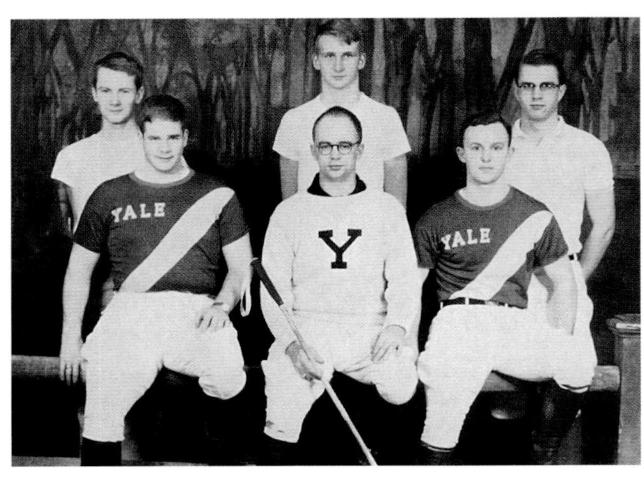

FIG. 2
Weymouth, front row, center, as captain of Yale's polo team, 1958.
Yale University Archives

Captain of the polo team at Yale (fig. 2), Weymouth spent the summer after his graduation in Europe, where he was a member of the U.S. Intercollegiate Polo Team (see Chronology). The team was defeated by one goal by the team of the Maharaja of Cooch Behar in the Pimm's Cup competition, but was able to defeat the Cambridge University team. After the official tour, the U.S. team entered the tournament for the Gloucestershire Cup and won.[6] Returning home that fall, Frolic moved into a room over the barn on his father's estate, near his beloved horses, and was able to spend time painting. His love of horses and of coaching, detailed in the Chronology, would become a lifelong passion, as would his work to conserve the landscape of the Brandywine region.

At this time, he also reestablished contact with Andrew Wyeth, to whom he had been introduced by his aunt while he was still a student. Wyeth was a well-established painter in egg tempera, a medium that was widely practiced in the fifteenth century and was experiencing a major revival in the 1930s. (Daniel Thompson's *The Practice of Tempera Painting*, a carefully honed instruction on method, was originally published by Yale University Press in 1936.)[7]

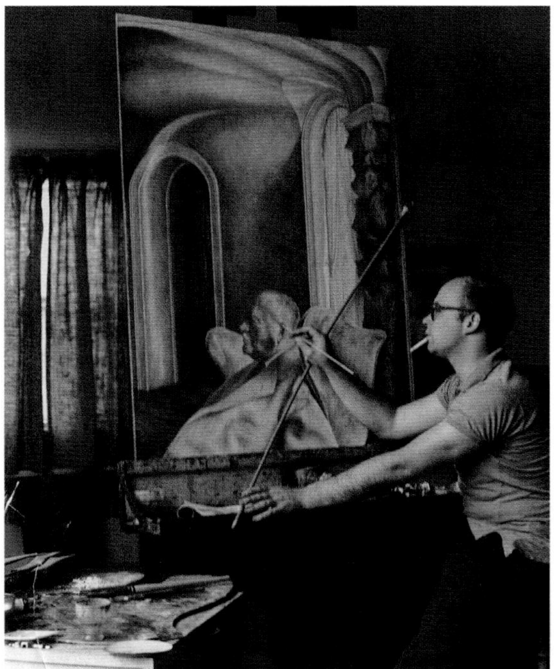

FIG. 3
Weymouth painting the portrait of Eugene Eleuthère du Pont, 1958.
Ann Wyeth McCoy Archives, Brandywine River Museum of Art, the Walter and Leonore Annenberg Research Center

Weymouth was then working largely in thinned oil paint, a technique described by Annette Blaugrund in her essay. When Andrew Wyeth and Peter Hurd visited Weymouth at his studio, they observed that his approach to painting was well suited to tempera in its attention to detail and exacting brushstrokes (fig. 3). Weymouth's deliberate execution of his early works is illustrated by his depiction of his grandfather Eugene du Pont's herringbone jacket in a 1958 portrait (plate 10),

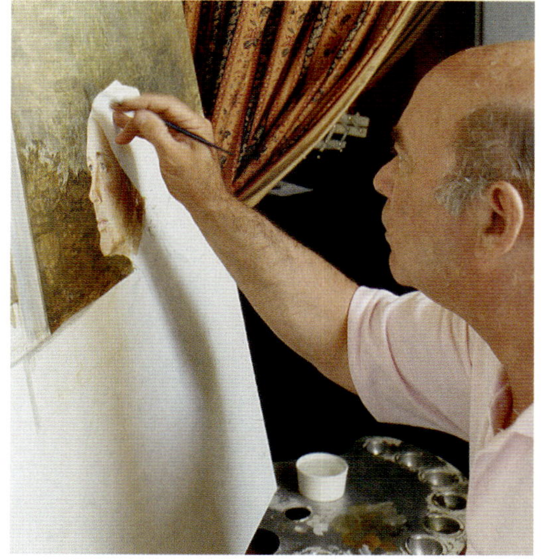

FIG. 4
Weymouth painting a tempera portrait titled *Margaret*, 1986. Photograph by Susan Gray © susangrayart.com

a touching memory of his grandfather. It is a notable achievement by the twenty-year-old Weymouth, equaled the next year by *Pete*, 1959 (plate 6), a painting that suggests the luminous effects of tempera while remaining an oil on panel. His first work in tempera was the small equestrian portrait *Charfoot*, 1959 (plate 4). Within a few years, his ambitious embrace of tempera is seen in the 1963 portrait of his friend Will Farish (Blaugrund essay fig. 19) and again in a commissioned portrait of a close friend, Joy Valentine, resulting in a panel with sky and rider (*Mrs. E. Miles Valentine*, plate 14) that is as affecting and fond as any work he would ever do.

Portraits constituted much of Weymouth's output, ranging from "boardroom portraits" commissioned by wealthy entrepreneurs (*Edgar Bronfman*, 1980-81, plate 21), to friends in the museum and horse worlds (*Margaret*, 1986, fig. 4), and public figures including Pennsylvania's Governor William Scranton (1969, plate 40), culminating in the portrait (1995) of H.R.H. Prince Philip, Duke of Edinburgh (Blaugrund essay, fig. 1). The recordings of the grand and the good have their equivalent in equally pensive and admiring perceptions of childhood friends and workers at his estate. Closer to home—showing the diversity of Weymouth's portraits—is a wonderful pencil drawing of his son, Mac, dated 1990 (plate 28), a rendering that is both sensitive and descriptive.

We must also mention here *The Way Back*, 1963 (plate 17), a painting of great charm that is to some extent both a portrait and a landscape. According to Weymouth's son, Mac, the artist depicted himself in a cart pulled by his first driving horse, providing a literal record of himself returning to the house after an excursion into the extensive fields at The Big Bend (fig. 5), and reflecting the exhilaration and pride he felt about this historic property.

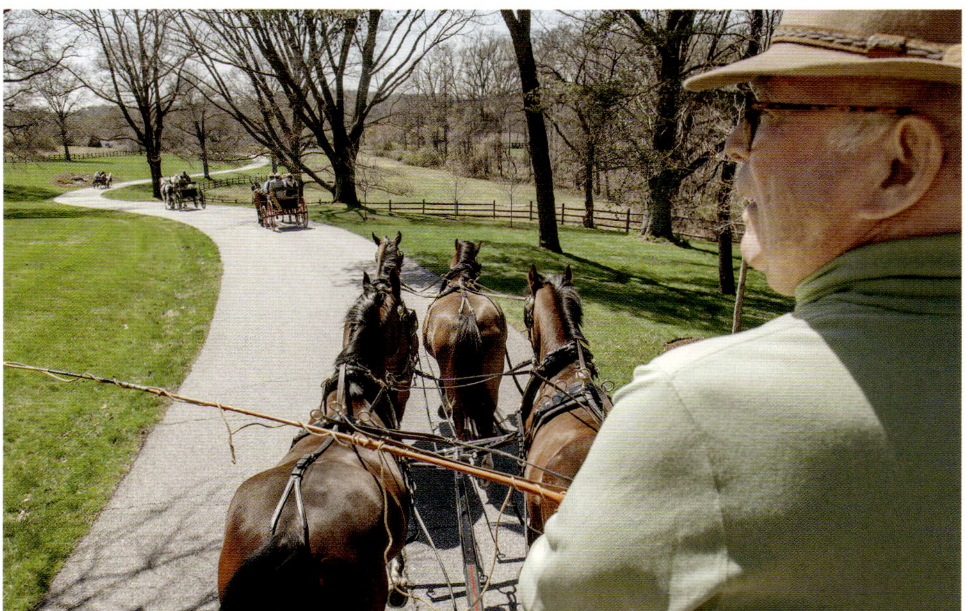

FIG. 5
Weymouth driving his carriage, 2006. Photograph by Jim Graham ©Jim Graham

Although he took great delight in company, it was Weymouth's landscapes that were more closely geared to his interests, both in relation to his bucolic life at home and his notable achievements in conservation. His interest in the landscape goes back to his early childhood. As he has said, "When I was young, if I said I was bored, my mother said, 'Go outside and look at nature.'"[8]

His landscapes celebrate the natural wonder that Weymouth preserved to a remarkable degree and that carried him most deeply into contemporary formal exploration, particularly in his portrayals of cornfields, snowdrifts, and ascending hills of blooming flowers. Early on, he was exploring the crisp, papery quality and textural delicacy of dried cornstalks up close (*Cornfields*, 1962 (plate 11); the remote and lonely vista of a shed in winter (*The Shelter*, 1964, plate 22); and a beckoning view of Brandywine topography in a painting that depicts a historic house snuggled within sloping snow-covered hills (*Robin's House*, 1972, plate 26).

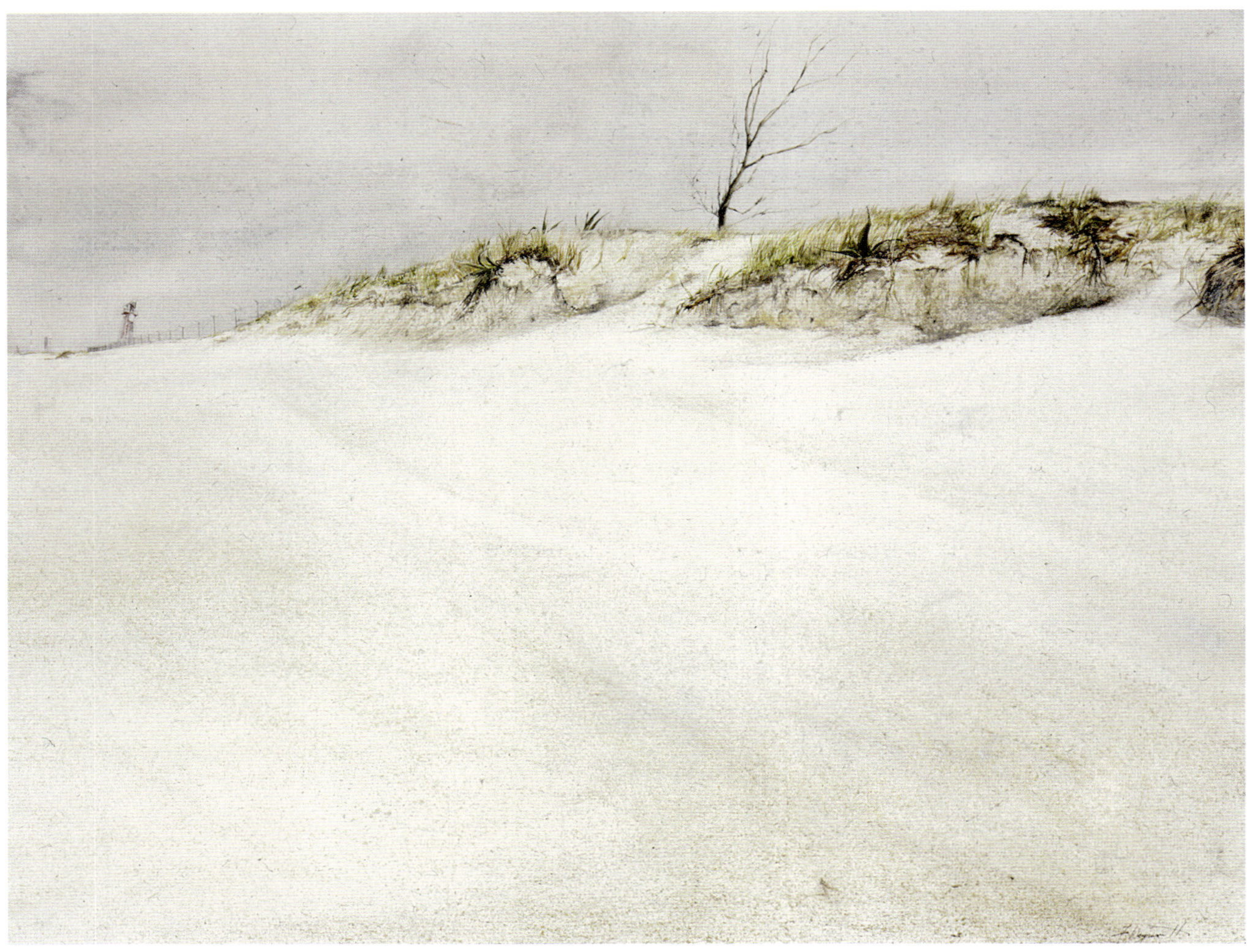

FIG. 6
George A. Weymouth
On the Beach, 1963
Watercolor on paper,
21½ x 27½ inches
National Aeronautics and Space Agency (NASA) Art Program, Kennedy Space Center, Florida

Living on the banks of the river in his restored eighteenth-century house, pursuing landscapes, Weymouth completed what is arguably the greatest and most loved painting of his career, the tempera *August*, 1974 (plate 30). In this painting, the highly descriptive details of grasses and flowers add up to create veils of color that ascend in white and yellow into a deep green peak in a way that recalls a vaporous day at Mont St. Michel painted by Cézanne (an observation not completely accepted by the artist but one that did elicit a rather satisfying grin). Like his mentor Andrew Wyeth, Weymouth often relied on studies to develop the concepts for his landscapes. The tempera's watercolor companion, *Study for August*, 1974 (plate 31), never before exhibited, presents a completely different tenor. It is loose and abstract and full of energy reaching into the sky, contrasting with the final exacting tempera. These two works are an outstanding pair and say much about Weymouth's process.

THE NASA ART PROGRAM

In 1962, Weymouth was invited to become one of the first members of the NASA Art Program, which sought to garner support for the country's intense competition with the Soviet Union in space exploration. The program involved a noted group of artists, from Robert Rauschenberg to Norman Rockwell, with Weymouth among the first commissioned, followed soon thereafter by Peter Hurd, John McCoy, and Jamie Wyeth.[9] Today, all of the works of art completed through the program are the property of the National Air and Space Museum.

Weymouth completed two landscapes *en plein air* at the launching site, one of which, *The Start*, 1963, is a direct view of an abandoned tower already wasting away on a rusty track. *On the Beach*, 1963 (fig. 6), features the natural dunes with a minuscule view of a launching tower in the far distance, nearly offstage, reflecting what one cannot help but assume is the artist's choice to prioritize nature over human invention. These are perhaps his only landscapes of consequence done away from the Brandywine.

The fiftieth anniversary of the founding of the NASA Art Program was celebrated with an anthology that included images of Weymouth's two paintings. In 2009, he received a copy of the book with a personal letter from James Dean, founding director of the program, offering his sympathy on the recent death of Andrew Wyeth as well as thanking Weymouth for his participation in the program.

I think the first time I met Frolic Weymouth was in the 1970s at The Big Bend. Several members of the family were there, including Andrew Wyeth, who at one point I believe asked my wife, Anne d'Harnoncourt, director of the Philadelphia Museum of Art, if he could do her portrait, which made her very happy through the long ride home. This first meeting inaugurated a lifetime affection between their family and ours that culminated in retrospective exhibitions of works by Wyeth held in Philadelphia in 2006 and Washington in 2015. I have many happy memories of our interactions, both at the Philadelphia Museum of Art and in other settings. On one occasion, Andrew and Frolic had joined us for lunch at the museum restaurant. We were sitting in the corner nicely protected by the luncheon audience, which was very aware of the artists' presence. It was only when we got up to leave, when Andrew put on his long coat, that the entire room cheered. Andrew made a stately departure, but I couldn't help but notice that it was Frolic, the lover of people and cheering rooms, who enjoyed himself the most. We sometimes received a spontaneous invitation to bring friends for afternoon tea at his home and would end up leaving at ten. If you were lucky, you might see a new picture of his brought down from the studio upstairs.

I remember another day when Weymouth took us up to the top of the hill to see the newly completed chapel, which he described with such affection and deeply moving love for his son. The chapel is inscribed with the words: "This chapel was built to thank God for a wonderful life filled with fun, humor, work, sport and beauty. A close loving family; loyal and unique friends; and a fabulous son, Mac."

One of the delights for me of working on this exhibition was the occasion to talk with some of those closest to Weymouth who helped to clarify (or helped me understand why one *could not*) the artistic motives and pleasures that would have motivated his selections, which of course led to more discursive discussions about this complex and delightful man. In one of these conversations, Jamie Wyeth emphasized his admiration for Weymouth's attention to detail in his paintings. Jim Duff, longtime director of the Brandywine Conservancy & Museum of Art, said that while Frolic was never happier than when home at The Big Bend, if he did go abroad, such as with the 1987–88 tour of Wyeth family art to England and then Russia, on which Duff accompanied him, he took advantage of any opportunity to visit museum and private collections. Duff also reminded me of Weymouth's time given to acquiring eighteenth-century furniture as well as his creation of a major garden at The Big Bend. Toward the end of his life, he had the advantage of making short trips with friends to see specific works of art.

As I mentioned at the beginning, the loss of Frolic as our "source" was difficult to handle. However, the one happy development is the many drawings that have come to light with the settlement of the estate. It has been particularly rewarding to have the occasion to go through these with Virginia O'Hara.

Weymouth's evolution as an artist is due partly to his confidence in his own creation, remarkable to those who knew him best. The making of this exhibition is a celebration of that gift as well as an opportunity to explore his work more deeply and to reflect anew on the depth of Weymouth's contribution to art and how much more there is to be learned. We celebrate our delight in the complexity of a man who was so remarkably disciplined in the making of art from his early days straight through to his late glorious output.

1. "George Weymouth, 79, Conservationist, Horse Enthusiast and Bon Vivant, Dies at 79," *New York Times*, April 29, 2016. "Brandywine Conservancy founder 'Frolic' Weymouth dies," *Wilmington News Journal*, April 25, 2016. "Point-to-Point's carriage procession leader Frolic Weymouth remembered Sunday," *The News Journal*, May 5, 2016.

2. *George A. Weymouth: A Retrospective* (Chadds Ford, PA: Brandywine River Museum of Art, 1991).

3. *George Weymouth: Landscapes and Portraits of Brandywine* (Milwaukee: Haggerty Museum of Art, Marquette University, 2001).

4. *The Way Back: A Portrait of George A. Weymouth*, directed by Renée Harrison Drake (Rainmaker Films, 2005) DVD.

5. Keller is perhaps best known today as an international hero for his critical work with the "Monuments Men." This was a group of more than three hundred men and women recruited for their expertise in the arts to save Europe's cultural treasures from the ravages of World War II. Keller and his team entered Italy on the heels of the Fascists to protect works of art, notably in Florence and Pisa. Monuments, Fine Arts, and Archives Program. See Monuments Men Foundation. http://www.monumentsmenfoundation.org/the-heroes/the-monuments-men/keller-capt.-deane.

6. Horace A. Laffaye, "International Polo in England," in *Polo in the United States: A History* (Jefferson, NC: McFarland, 2011).

7. Daniel V. Thompson, Jr., *The Practice of Tempera Painting: Materials and Methods* (New York: Dover Publications, Inc., 1936).

8. J. F. Pirro, "Old Man River," *Main Line Today*, May 2009, 117.

9. Julie F. Codell, ed. *The Political Economy of Art: Making the Nation of Culture* (Madison, New Jersey: University Press Copublishing Division/Fairleigh Dickinson University Press, September 2008).

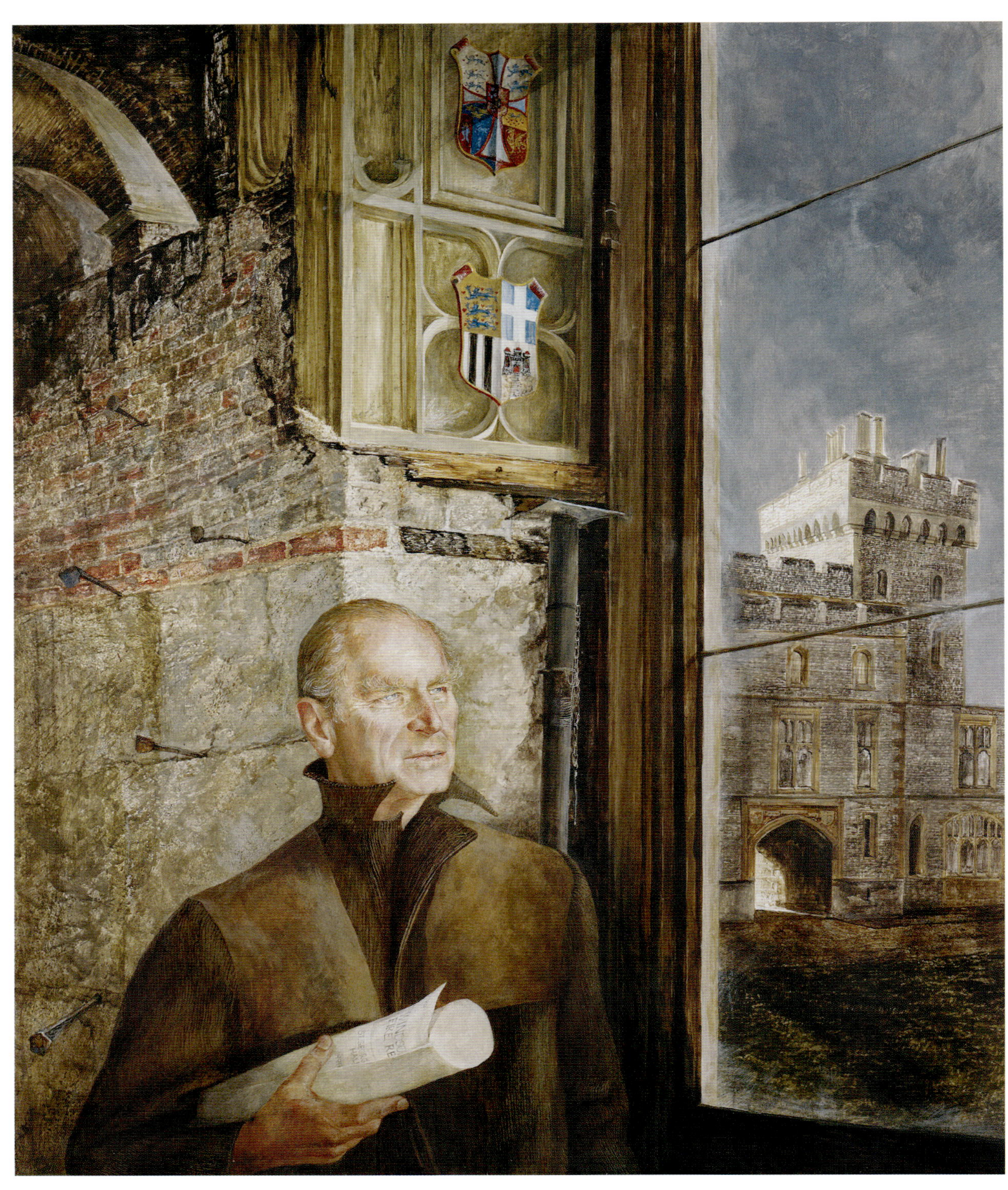

George A. Weymouth: An American Original

ANNETTE BLAUGRUND

GEORGE A. WEYMOUTH (1936–2016), a Renaissance man, was first and foremost an accomplished, internationally recognized artist and visionary.[1] A true American original, he had a genuine appreciation for beauty and nature that is expressed not only in his landscapes of the Brandywine Valley that he helped to preserve but also in his portraits. His candid love of people and the region in which he lived is conveyed in his work. His myriad interests are articulated in his paintings and drawings; his style of realism derived from earlier painting traditions and evolved over a career of nearly sixty years.[2]

BACKGROUND AND INFLUENCES

Weymouth grew up in and spent almost his entire life within a few miles of Pennsylvania's beautiful Brandywine Valley, near Wilmington, Delaware. His mother, Dulcinea du Pont (1909–1981), was an artist who trained at the Art Students League in New York. She encouraged her son's talent, exposing him to art books and museums early on, and instilled in him a love for old masters such as Hans Memling, Hans Holbein, Rembrandt, and Jacques-Louis David, whose works he saw during his travels abroad. Most certainly he was privy to the collections of decorative arts and paintings at the Winterthur Museum, Garden & Library, founded by his cousin Henry Francis du Pont (1880–1969).

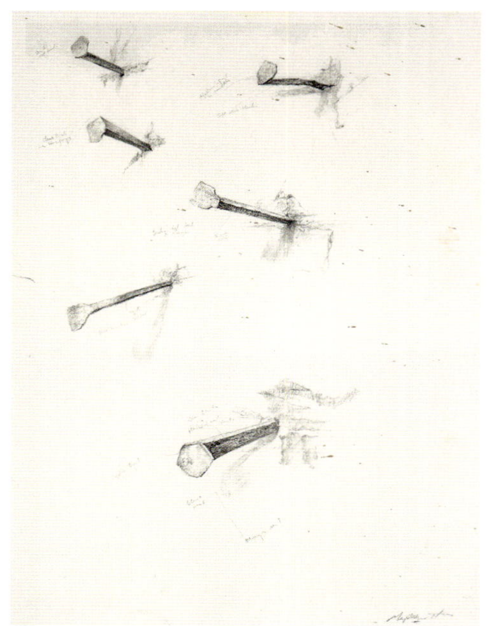

After attending public school in Wilmington, Weymouth spent the years 1950 to 1954 at St. Mark's School, a boarding school in Southborough, Massachusetts. Weymouth was dyslexic and did poorly in his academic subjects, but was lucky to have as one of his teachers Kleber Hall (1882–1967), a sculptor and painter (fig. 4), who took a special interest in Weymouth and developed his innate ability. Hall was trained in the rigorous academic traditions of Paris, where drawing

Fig. 1
H.R.H. Prince Philip, Duke of Edinburgh, 1995
Tempera on panel, $46^{3}/_{8}$ × $38^{15}/_{16}$ inches
Royal Collection Trust/All Rights Reserved

Fig. 2
Detail of Six Stanchions Jutting from the Wall of St. George's Hall, 1995
[Study for *H.R.H. Prince Philip, The Duke of Edinburgh*]
Pencil on paper, $23^{5}/_{8}$ × $18^{1}/_{8}$ inches
Royal Collection Trust/All Rights Reserved

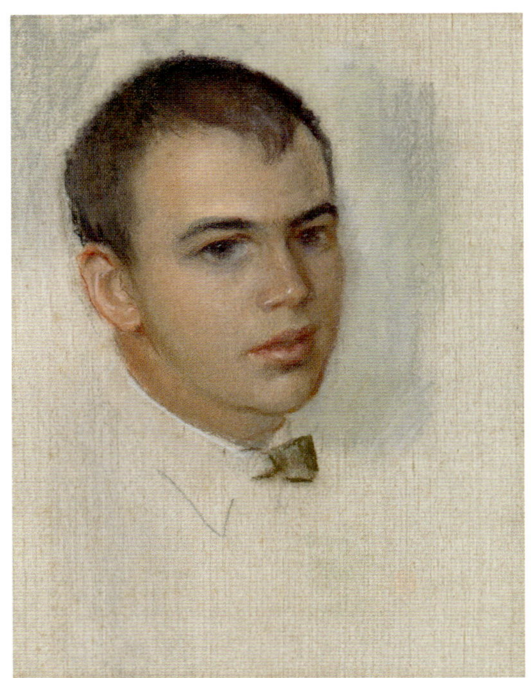

FIG. 3
George A. Weymouth (1936–2016)
Self-Portrait, ca. 1954
Pastel on canvas, 17 × 13⅛ inches
Brandywine River Museum of Art, Gift of Mac Weymouth, 2017

was the foundation of painting. He was a dedicated teacher who taught twice a week in the school's basement studio, selecting gifted students for extra classes and trips to Boston.[3] He believed in developing his students' technical skills and taught Weymouth the basics of drawing and painting in watercolor, pastel, and oil. An early pastel self-portrait reveals Weymouth's talent (fig. 3). Hall taught at the school for more than forty years and was an exacting teacher who urged Weymouth to work hard and strive for excellence. Weymouth's father, George T. Weymouth (1904–1990), stressed that, in addition to hard work, the three pillars of a successful life were honesty, generosity, and a sense of humor.[4]

From St. Mark's, Weymouth went to Yale University, where he joked that, although he was dyslexic, he was accepted without being able to read and write because of the du Pont family name. At Yale, Weymouth endeavored to attain a liberal arts education and majored in American Studies while taking life-drawing classes with Deane Keller (1901–92), and in his spare time doing some anatomical drawing at the medical school, with Keller's encouragement. Weymouth said in an interview in 1993: "I wasn't technically at the art school—I was just using the models and courses with Deane Keller; then I would go to the medical school and do the drawings for anatomy."[5] These exercises served him well, since he would develop a process whereby most of his paintings began with multiple detailed pencil studies that allowed him to refine his compositions without the distraction of color. The drawings often formed the basis of watercolors, and early in his career, were followed by finished oil paintings. By the 1960s he had mostly switched to egg tempera.

Keller, a Yale alumnus (see Chronology), taught at his alma mater for more than forty years, with a hiatus during World War II when he was an officer with the Monuments, Fine Arts, and Archives (MFAA) program. After the war, he returned to Yale as professor of art and as Yale's unofficial portraitist; he painted faculty portraits (fig. 5) as well as presidents William Howard Taft and Herbert Hoover. He taught life drawing in the Department of Art and was a staunch supporter of traditional painting techniques and styles.[6] Although Weymouth's focus was on his American Studies major, in a continuation of his work at St. Mark's with Kleber Hall he pursued his interest in studio art, in particular following what was considered Keller's conservative

FIG. 4
Kleber Hall (1882–1967)
Self-Portrait Study, 1954
Oil on canvas, 18 × 14 inches
Mac Weymouth

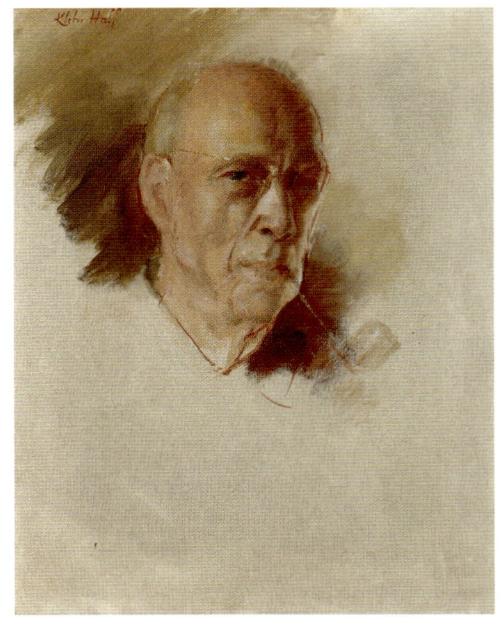

approach to art during his four college years, as opposed to the more avant-garde theories of art practice espoused by Josef Albers, director of the Design Department at Yale. Weymouth's decision to study with Keller during this period speaks volumes about the direction he was to follow.

Weymouth's aunt, Murton du Pont Carpenter, his mother's sister, not only encouraged him to pursue a career as an artist but also introduced him to Andrew Wyeth (1917–2009) in about 1957. She and Weymouth took one of his oil paintings, *Frozen Pond*, 1957 (Chronology, fig. 3), for Wyeth to see, and the older artist was impressed. In a letter of February 5, 1991, Wyeth recalled: "I remember we talked for a while about your training under your mentor, Kleber Hall, your determination to study anatomy, to work from life, to improve your drawing, to learn more about egg tempera, to paint the people and places you knew. It was almost as if I was talking to myself or hearing myself talking."[7] When Weymouth met Wyeth during the heyday of abstract expressionism, he found that they had a similar preference for realist art and an analogous aesthetic. During the 1940s and '50s many artists were experimenting with new ideas, different ways of applying paint and other materials to the canvas, and expressing feelings rather than representing reality, which photography was able to capture.

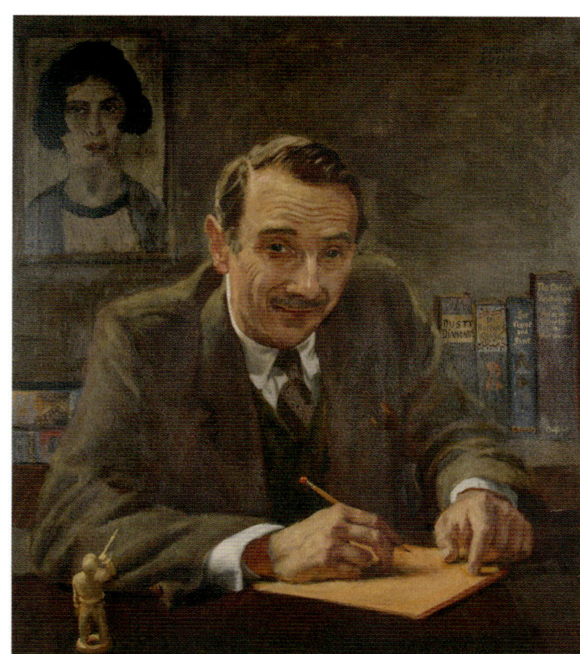

FIG. 5
Deane Keller (1901–92)
Portrait of Norman Holmes Pearson, 1976
Oil on canvas, 30 × 26 inches
Yale Collection of American Literature, Beinecke Rare Book and Manuscript Library

Weymouth and Wyeth became lifelong friends, and while Weymouth did not study with Wyeth, he was obviously influenced by him. He said in an interview about his relationship with Wyeth: "We talk about technique an awful lot and technical questions in terms of composition and color—you know, spotting things that people wouldn't know what you are talking about but he would."[8] And as we shall see, as much as Wyeth influenced the younger artist's work, Weymouth approached painting with subtle differences.

Of all the mediums Kleber Hall introduced to his student, Weymouth preferred oil. He thinned the pigment with turpentine, painting stroke-by-stroke with small brushes to build up the surface with meticulous detail, as seen in the herringbone tweed jacket in his portrait of his maternal grandfather, Eugene du Pont (1882–1966) (plate 10, *Eugene Eleuthère du Pont* [1958]). Although the resulting color was slightly different from its initial application, he was able to obtain a rich effect by layering the paint. Thinning the pigment with turpentine allowed for faster drying and enabled him to complete the numerous layers rapidly. His method was similar to "peinture à l'essence," a technique sometimes used by Edgar Degas, Henri de Toulouse-Lautrec, and others, in which oil is drained out of the paint and the pigment is then thinned with turpentine, resulting in a pastel-like effect.

The compositional structure of this portrait depicts the upper third of the figure seated in a velvet wing chair, centrally placed in the lower third of the canvas. Variations of this format were repeated throughout the artist's career, including one the same year of his paternal grandfather, Clarence A. Weymouth, called *6:59 a.m.* The coloration in the du Pont portrait is subdued and subtle, yet golden tones highlight the man and his chair against the greenish-brown walls and ceiling. Set close to the picture plane, his face dually radiates both strength and tranquility.

Before Weymouth started painting in tempera, he did several other large oil paintings, such as *Field Sparrow*, 1959 (plate 5), an accomplished work with the Japanese-like aesthetic of a branch originating from outside the composition. The branch is set so close to the picture plane that it practically enters the viewer's space and serves to create an illusion of depth. In this sensitive portrait, the woman, Weymouth's lifelong friend "Missy," gazes up at a tiny field sparrow's nest on a leafless branch that cuts the composition in half. Again, as in the painting of his grandfather, the figure is placed in the lower half of the canvas. The placement of the figure, the understated sentiment, and the subdued coloring are harbingers of future compositions.

While Weymouth was painting the portrait of Eugene du Pont, Andrew Wyeth and his brother-in-law Peter Hurd (1904–1984) visited Weymouth's studio and were puzzled by his strange technique of diluting oil paint and then applying it stroke by stroke with small brushes. Hurd, acclaimed for his Western landscapes and portraits, had studied with N. C. (Newell Convers) Wyeth (1882–1945) and was married to Andrew Wyeth's sister, the artist Henriette Wyeth (1907–1997). It was he who had introduced egg tempera to Wyeth in the mid-1930s, and the two now suggested it to Weymouth. Although it was not a technique that he had been exposed to under Kleber Hall, Weymouth decided to try it. Another member of the extended Wyeth family was the painter John W. McCoy, who also studied with N. C. Wyeth and in 1934 married his daughter Ann, Andrew's sister. In 1961, Weymouth married the McCoys' daughter Ann, affectionately called Anna. And so by marriage, Weymouth became part of the extended Wyeth family of artists, and through their influence began using the painstaking medium of egg tempera.

AMERICAN ART TRADITION

Weymouth is part of a long continuum of American realist painters that began with colonial portraitists such as John Singleton Copley (1738–1815), an artist whose work he admired and had probably first seen in the Winterthur Museum collection. Before Copley expatriated to England in 1774, he recreated objects in illusionistic detail and painted clothing stitch-by-stitch, as in *Mrs. Ezekiel Goldthwait (Elizabeth Lewis)* (1771, Museum of Fine Arts, Boston, fig. 6). Realism was found in portraits and landscapes in nineteenth-century America, and many artists studied in England or were influenced by English prints. By mid-century, Hudson River school artists such as Albert Bierstadt (1830–1902) and Worthington Whittredge (1820–1910) went to Germany to study how to achieve exacting details in their paintings. Later in the period, artists favored

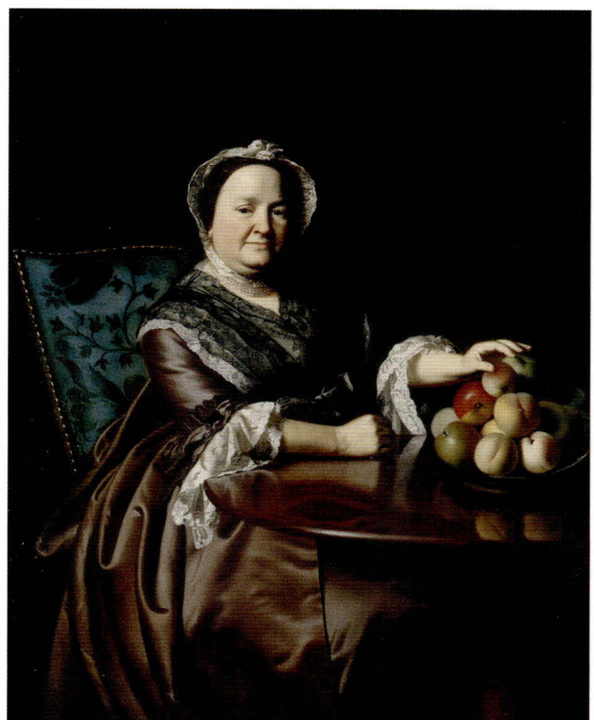

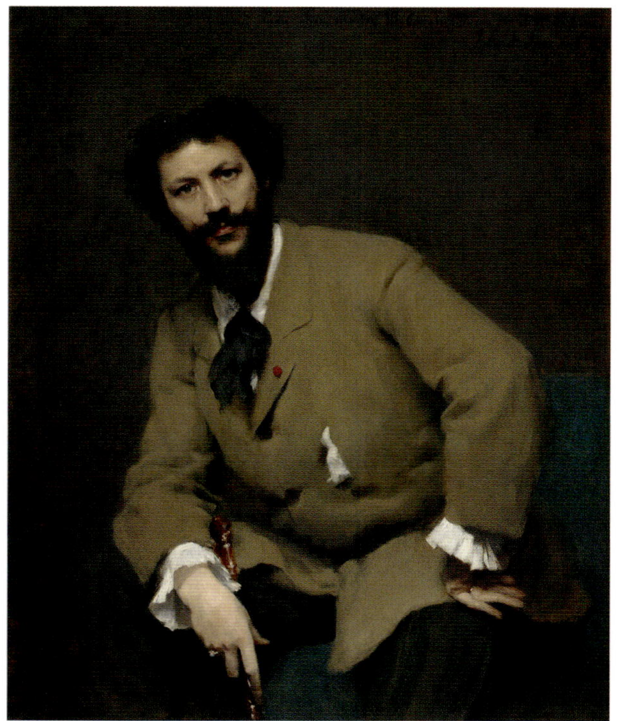

FIG. 6
John Singleton Copley (1738–1815)
Mrs. Ezekiel Goldthwait (Elizabeth Lewis), 1771
Oil on canvas, 50⅛ × 40⅛ inches
Museum of Fine Arts, Boston, Bequest of John T. Bowen in memory of Eliza M. Bowen, 41.84

FIG. 7
John Singer Sargent (1856–1925)
Carolus-Duran, 1879
Oil on canvas, 46 × 37¹³⁄₁₆ inches
The Clark Art Institute, Williamstown, Massachusetts, 1955.14

France, and many were admitted to the private ateliers and academies in Paris veering between academic and impressionist styles, as seen, for example, in the realistic portrait by John Singer Sargent (1856–1925) of his teacher *Carolus-Duran*, 1879 (fig. 7). No matter where they studied, most artists made the obligatory visit to Italy for inspiration from classical ruins and medieval and Renaissance art.

In the American realist group there were artists such as Winslow Homer and Thomas Eakins, whom Weymouth esteemed, followed by Ashcan school artists including Robert Henri, John Sloan, and George Bellows, who kept up the realist tradition by painting the gritty side of life. By the 1950s and '60s, while abstract art was burgeoning in New York, there were always a number of steadfast artists who bucked new modern trends, among them Edward Hopper, and those who in the twenty-first century still maintain a realist approach, such as Lois Dodd, Janet Fish, and Rackstraw Downes, to name just a few.

Weymouth traveled to Europe numerous times and was captivated by fifteenth- to eighteenth-century Dutch, Flemish, Italian, Spanish, and French art. On recent trips, made shortly before his death in 2016, he went to see Rembrandt's *The Night Watch*, 1642, at the Rijksmuseum in Amsterdam; Turner's paintings at the Tate Britain Museum; the Ghent Altarpiece, under restoration in Belgium; and El Greco's paintings in Toledo, Spain. His taste was wide-ranging.

BRANDYWINE RIVER VALLEY ARTISTS

Coming from the Brandywine Valley, Weymouth was exposed to paintings by a group of artists who had worked in the area, beginning with Howard Pyle (1853–1911), a native of Wilmington, Delaware, who founded his School of Art there in 1900. Renowned as a painter and teacher, Pyle

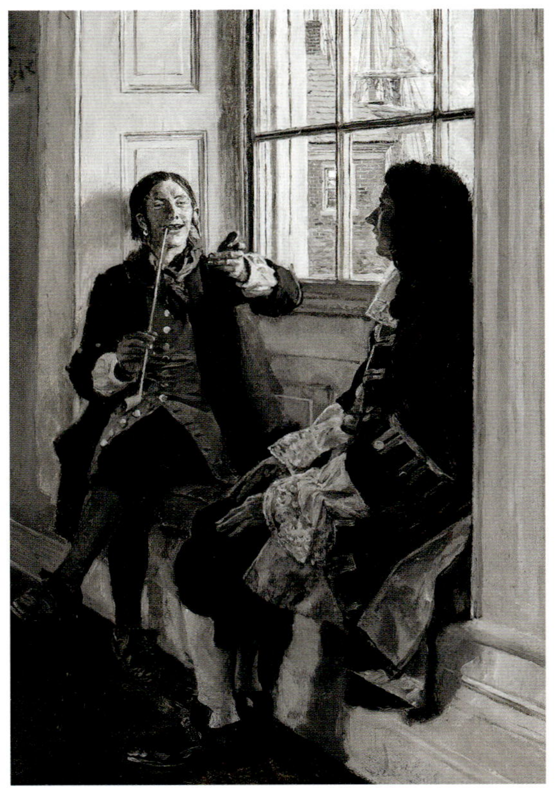

FIG. 8
Howard Pyle (1853–1911)
He Had Found the Captain Agreeable and Companionable, 1894
Oil on board, 16 × 10⅝ inches
Illustration for "The Sea Robbers of New York," by Thomas A. Janvier, *Harper's New Monthly Magazine*, November 1894
Brandywine River Museum of Art, Gift of Mr. and Mrs. Howard P. Brokaw, 2007

created some of the most engaging and unforgettable images found in books and magazines of that time (fig. 8). According to Andrew Wyeth, Pyle taught that an artist must have a deep connection to his subject in order to rearrange it according to his or her imagination.[9] Among his notable students was Frank Schoonover (1877–1972), who was instrumental in organizing what is now the Delaware Art Museum, much as Weymouth later was deeply involved in founding the Brandywine River Museum of Art. Pyle's most famous student was N. C. Wyeth, and ultimately the Brandywine area embraced all of the Wyeths as well as other artists in and around Chadds Ford, Pennsylvania.

N. C. Wyeth was a painter as well as the famous illustrator of *Robinson Crusoe* and *Treasure Island* (fig. 9), and it was he who taught painting to three of his five children but focused on Andrew, the youngest. As a teacher, N. C. was a stern taskmaster who inspired his son's love of rural landscapes. Andrew studied art history by immersing himself in his father's collection of art books and came to admire the work of Winslow Homer, who also painted in Maine, the Wyeths' summer retreat. To Weymouth, Andrew imparted his love for the regional scenery and an interest in the people around him as subjects for his art. The two shared a sense of humor and joie de vivre in a friendship that lasted almost five decades. Thus, Weymouth, along with Andrew's son Jamie, a renowned artist in his own right, carried on the Wyeth family legacy, but each with his own distinct qualities. Over time Weymouth built up a substantial body of work, some of which will be examined here by medium—watercolor and egg tempera—and subject—landscapes and portraits, in more or less chronological order.

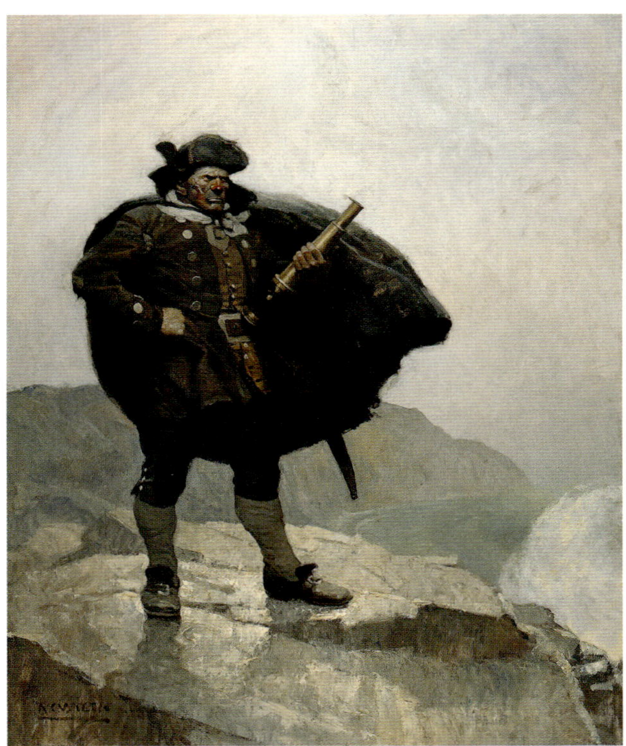

FIG. 9
N. C. Wyeth (1882–1945)
All day he hung round the cove, or upon the cliffs, with a brass telescope, 1911
Oil on canvas, 47¼ × 38¼ inches
Endpaper illustration for *Treasure Island*, by Robert Louis Stevenson (New York: Charles Scribner's Sons, 1911)
Brandywine River Museum of Art, Bequest of Gertrude Haskell Brinton, 1992

EGG TEMPERA TECHNIQUE

Tempera paints are long lasting and were used in ancient and medieval paintings. Around the year 1500, the use of tempera was superseded by oil painting. Tempera is a fast-drying medium consisting of colored pigments mixed with a water-soluble binder such as egg yolk. The pure yolk (without the egg white or the yolk membrane) is the binder that holds the raw pigment together. While the preparation is easy, the mixtures can only be used for a single day because the composition of the egg changes with time and the water evaporates. Because tempera dries very quickly, it is often built up in thin layers. Similar to pastel or colored pencils, the paint is usually applied in small crosshatched brushstrokes to a wood-fiber panel or Masonite (or sometimes to heavy paper), all of which are coated with gesso or a toning material to create an absorbent yet firm ground. The blended linear strokes create values and nuances that result in the smooth matte finish that Weymouth sought in his work. Hurd, Wyeth, and Weymouth were not alone among twentieth-century artists who favored tempera: George Tooker (1920–2011) and Paul Cadmus (1904–1999) are among other realists and surrealists who used the medium to great effect.

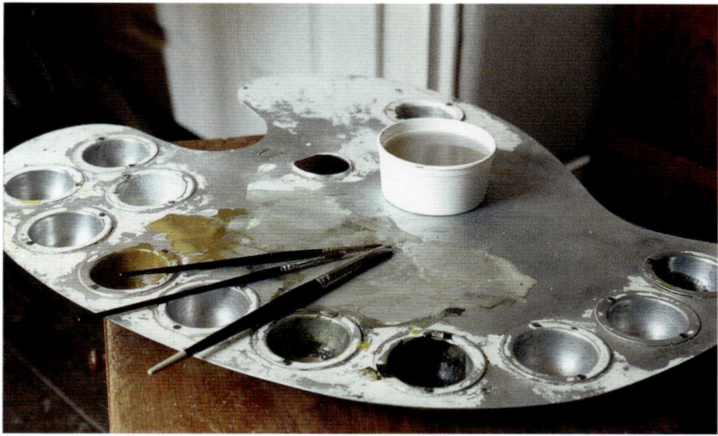

FIG. 10
Weymouth's aluminum palette, a gift to the artist from Andrew Wyeth. Photograph by Susan Gray, 1986 © susangrayart.com

Once he switched from oil paints, Weymouth made tempera his predominant medium and used it skillfully and expressively. A gift from Andrew Wyeth was an aluminum palette with deep individual muffin tin-like cups to separate his colors. It had a flat surface in the middle on which Weymouth could try out colors (fig. 10). When working on a painting, he had to mix fresh colors daily, and he took several months, sometimes years, to finish. He would start with a large board and keep cutting it down as he eliminated sections of the composition. After finishing the exacting process of tempera painting, he would often work on large watercolors of the rolling hills and river's edge outside his house, called The Big Bend because of its location on the bend of the Brandywine River.

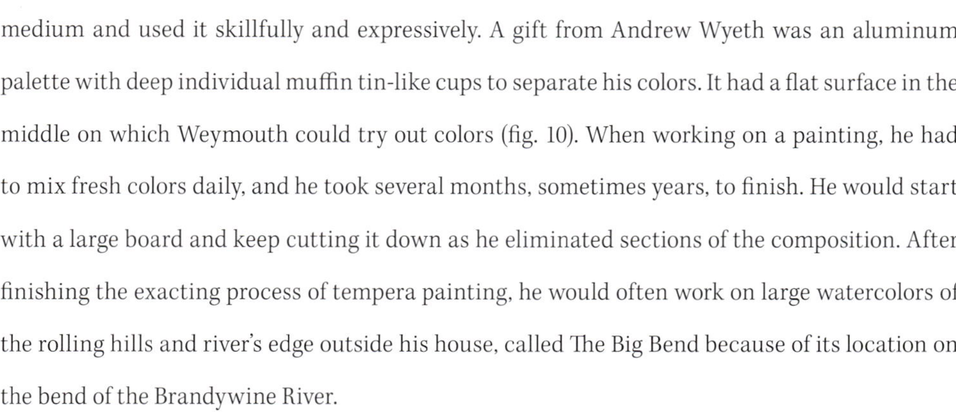

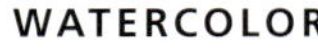

WATERCOLOR

The process of transforming preliminary sketches into finished egg tempera paintings was a time-consuming and solitary endeavor, a surprising choice for as spontaneous and gregarious a person as Weymouth. Yet the traditional background ingrained in him by Kleber Hall and Deane Keller and his intense desire to capture the land and people he knew imposed a sense of discipline, observation, and focus. Weymouth applied these principles to his work, often by making multiple pencil drawings and watercolors for his finished paintings. Watercolor is a medium in which pigments are dissolved in a water-based solution mixed with the adhesive gum arabic, and it is usually applied to paper. Watercolors can be translucent or made opaque by layering the paint or adding Chinese white (gouache). The technique is as old as egg tempera and has been

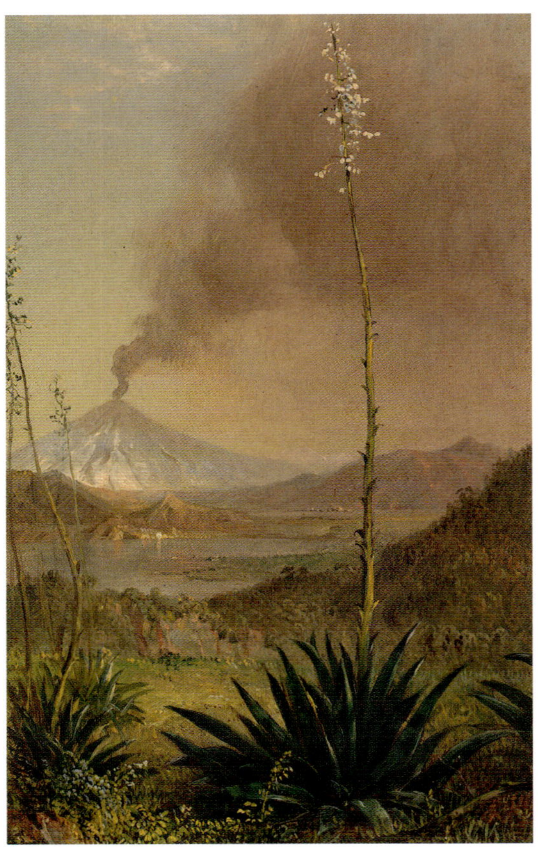

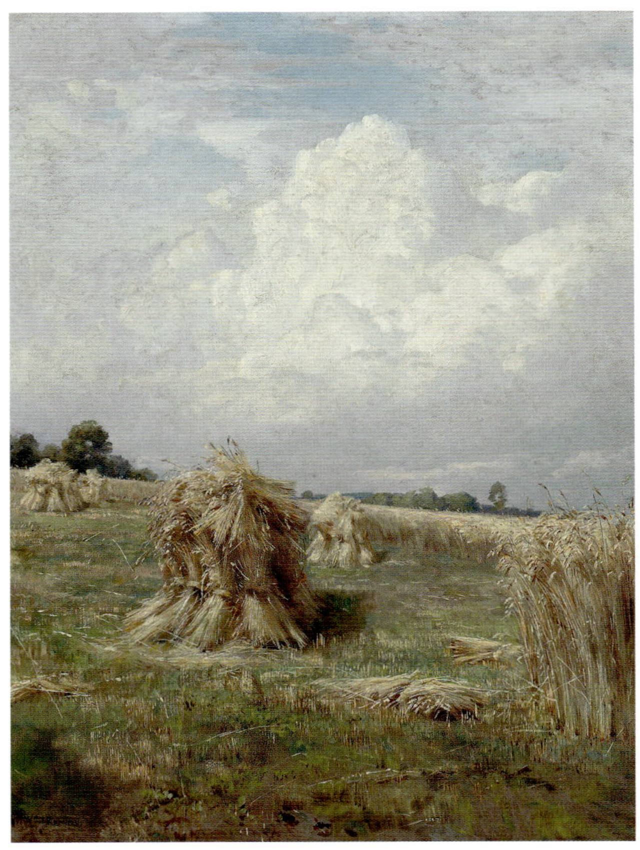

FIG. 11
Frederic E. Church (1826–1900)
A Century Plant at Cotopaxi, Ecuador, 1864
Oil on paper mounted to canvas, 7 5/8 × 4 7/8 inches
The Century Association, New York, William Cullen Bryant Collection, 1908

FIG. 12
William Trost Richards (1833–1905)
Some Fell On Good Ground, ca. 1887
Oil on canvas, 27 × 20 inches
Brandywine River Museum of Art. Purchased in memory of Pamela Cunningham Copeland

used globally by many artists over the centuries. It was promoted in the United States in part by the English art critic and artist John Ruskin (1819–1900), a proponent of the Pre-Raphaelite school of painting that flourished in England and the United States during the mid-nineteenth century. In all of Ruskin's books and articles in American periodicals, he emphasized the connections between nature, art, and society and made detailed sketches and paintings of subjects as varied as rocks, plants, birds, landscapes, architectural structures, and ornamentation. To some extent such meticulous observation is found in small studies in oil and watercolor by Hudson River school artist Frederic Edwin Church (1826–1900) (fig. 11), and by William Trost Richards (1848–1920) (fig. 12), both of whom Weymouth truly admired.

Weymouth used watercolor in his studies for *August*, 1974 (plate 30), a large finished work in egg tempera. There are multiple, detailed pencil and watercolor studies of flowers (plates 32, 33) that reveal his knowledge of the local flora and that resemble the work of the Pre-Raphaelites, who seemed to paint every vein in every leaf. Likewise, in the watercolor for *August* (plate 31), Weymouth painted the wildflowers—thistle, Queen Anne's lace, and various grasses—leading up the hill to a triangular point of vegetation different in coloration from the plants below, more freely than in the tempera painting but still with remarkable detail. Like some of the Pre-Raphaelites, Weymouth built up the surface of the picture plane so that the details subsume the horizon. For him, these exquisite studies for *August* were only preparation for the final painting and were transferred to the resulting tour-de-force egg tempera on panel to be discussed below. While many of Weymouth's watercolors were merely preparatory, he considered others as suitable for exhibition, as the Pre-Raphaelites also regarded their highly finished watercolors.

Tree Trunks, 1968 (plate 37), and *Indian Hanna*, 1990 (plate 55), are watercolors that stand as finished works. Both are devoid of a horizon line. The former fills the canvas with earth, flowers, and tree trunks and reminds me of a similar Wyeth watercolor, *The Virgin Birch*, 1982 (fig. 13), painted much later, indicating that Weymouth and Wyeth mined the same terrain for subjects and had a similar aesthetic. *Indian Hanna* details in the foreground the bluebells that line the banks of the Brandywine River and that were a prominent feature of Weymouth's Chadds Ford property. The trees on the distant bank are cut off at the top edge of the paper. The name of the painting refers to a Lenape woman Hannah Freeman (Weymouth dropped the final *h* in her name), who lived in this area from about 1730 to 1802.[10] These closely observed landscapes disclose the artist's intimate connection to the land and its history, to nature, and to the art of painting in this medium that allows for more freedom and spontaneity than tempera. Nevertheless, watercolor was mostly used by Weymouth in its opaque form, except occasionally in a comparatively loosely brushed transparent work such as *Thaw*, 1962 (plate 38), a grisaille with a hint of green that seems more rapidly painted than most of his watercolors. "I grab several full-size sheets of rough watercolor paper, my paints, a water bucket, and my brushes and I go sit in the field or down by the Brandywine," the artist told a reporter.[11]

Other watercolors of interest that illuminate Weymouth's use of the medium throughout his career are *Cornfields*, 1962 (plate 11), and *Untitled (Pole Beans)*, circa 1990 (plate 36). These two

FIG. 13
Andrew Wyeth (1917–2009)
The Virgin Birch, 1982
Watercolor on paper,
21½ × 29½ inches
Private collection.
© 2018 Andrew Wyeth / Artists' Rights Society (ARS)

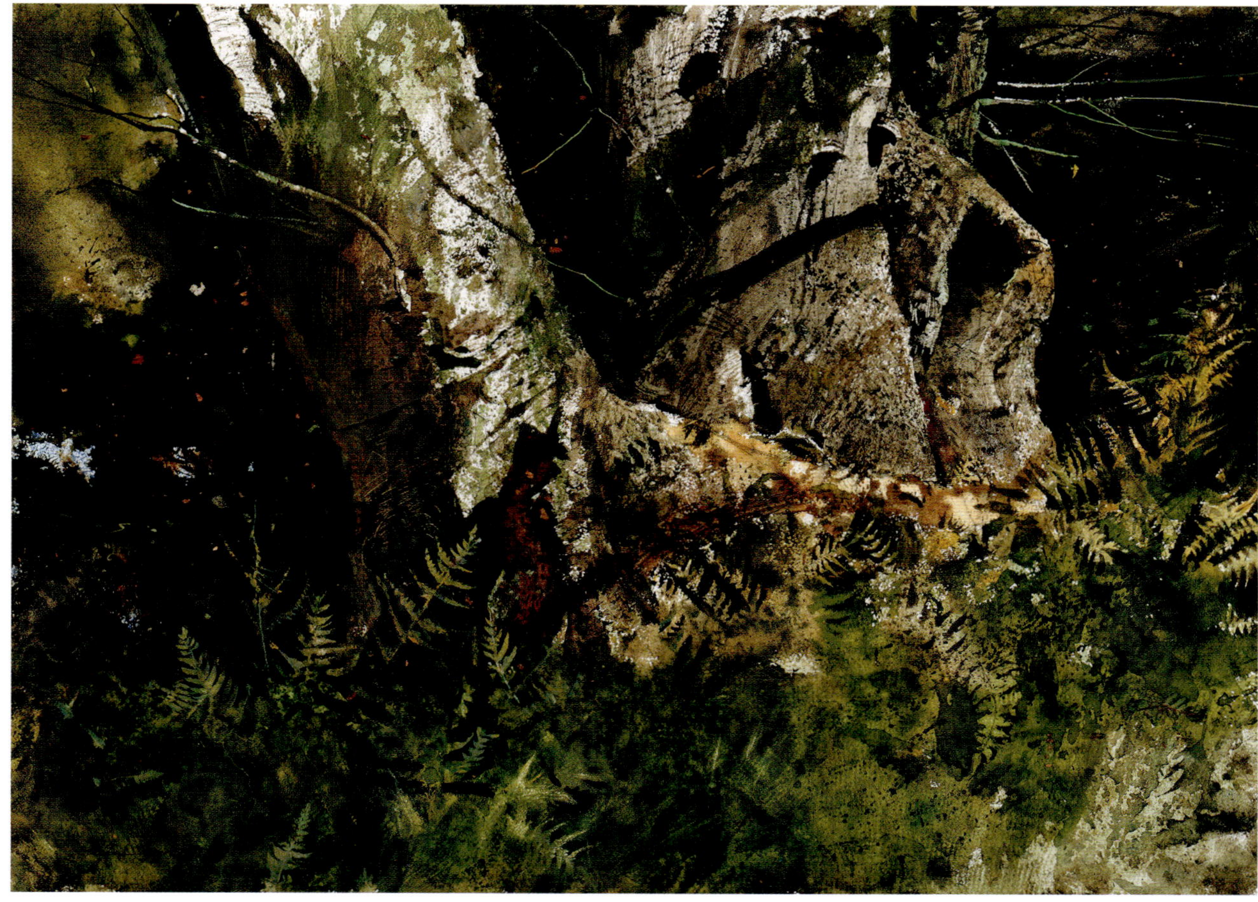

works have a pronounced horizon line and reveal the artist experimenting with compositions different from earlier work. *Cornfields* has a unique vantage point looking through tall cornstalks that partially obscure the house beyond, evoking a sense of mystery through composition and coloration. *Untitled (Pole Beans)* is a more conventional landscape with a broad foreground leading to the large plants staked on posts in the mid-ground and trees on the horizon muted by the grayish sky, similar to French Barbizon School compositions.

EGG TEMPERA LANDSCAPES

The finished landscape of *August*, 1974 (plate 30), is so realistic that you can almost hear the insects buzzing under the bright yet cloudy sky. As in the watercolor study, a burst of white Queen Anne's lace surrounded by yellowed high grasses leads the eye precipitously up the steep incline to a triangle of green vegetation. The artist has included details not seen in the watercolor study in this vertiginous landscape painted entirely in egg tempera on panel. In the distance on the right, he has depicted the cattle guard on the road leading to his house. The triangle of green draws the eye to the hedgerow lining the top of the hill on the left, thereby separating the hill from the sky. The square format is one that Weymouth repeated in several watercolor and tempera paintings.

A particularly intriguing tempera landscape is *Party Line*, 2001 (plate 54). If I had not myself seen these vultures flying overhead and landing on wooden posts lining the long drive to The Big Bend, I might have thought their presence in the picture was a figment of Weymouth's imagination. But the artist was a realist and painted these turkey vultures with their red featherless heads from life. These birds of prey, with their enormous wingspread of over five feet, are native to the Brandywine Valley. In *Soaring*, 1950, Andrew Wyeth portrayed three vultures, seen from above, circling over a lone farmhouse in a parched Pennsylvania landscape. In Weymouth's *Party Line*, however, a row of vultures stretches across the picture, the birds drying their raised wings while surveying the artist's personal domain, a sunny, bucolic setting of tall grasses and mist rising over the river.

When looking at Weymouth's later tempera paintings, in *Requiem*, 2010 (plate 50), I think that he could have been referencing Thomas Cole (1801–1848), leader of the Hudson River school of landscape painting. In *Requiem*, Weymouth focuses on a dead tree trunk reminiscent of Cole's storm-ravaged tree trunks within a wilderness scene, symbolizing nature's cycle of death and regrowth. In *The Crossing*, 2009–10 (plate 46), the fence forms an obvious cross. Both of these paintings were completed soon after the death of Andrew Wyeth in January 2009 and as such could be considered elegies to Weymouth's close friend and mentor. Conceivably, Weymouth was also expressing his own sense of mortality with the dead stump in the foreground that he purposely moved there and then highlighted against a dark background.[12] These paintings and his 1995 design for a chapel in the woods (fig. 14) certainly speak to his awareness of the transience of life and the relationship of man and nature. Nature was a sanctuary from which he could draw strength and communicate his passion for the region. Even more important, they are a confirmation of a spiritual quality in his work.

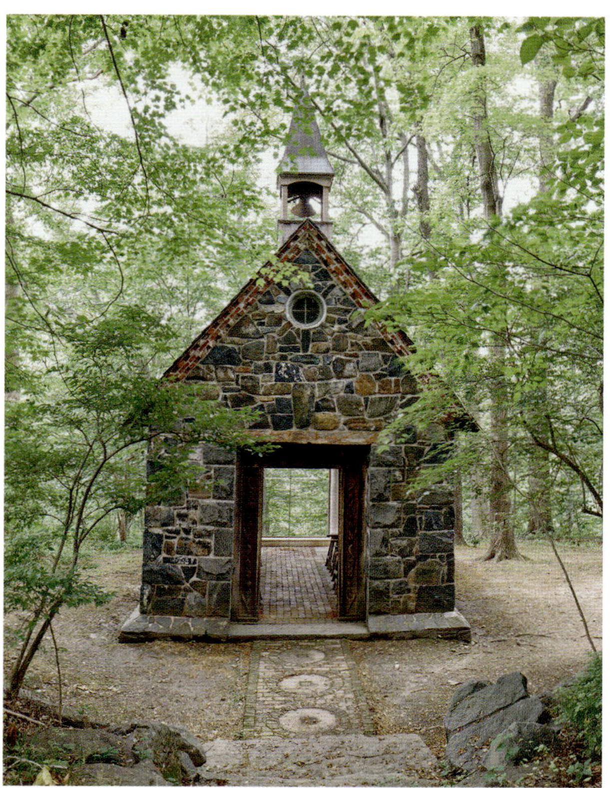

FIG. 14
Weymouth chapel on The Big Bend property
Photograph by Jim Graham.
© Jim Graham

Occasionally Weymouth might move something, as he did with the blasted tree stump of *Requiem*, but mostly he painted things as he found them. "I'm a realist painter," he said, "and that's frustrating since you can never improve on reality."[13] Wyeth, on the other hand, might eliminate objects from a scene to achieve a simpler, stronger composition. Again, Weymouth's extraordinarily detailed depiction of the untamed grasses below the principal vulture in *Party Line* (plate 54) is in sharp contrast to the impressionistic middle ground and sky. "I can never get away from knowing that what is out there is always so much better than anything I can paint."[14]

An interesting horizontal composition that combines foreground visual detail with a high horizon line as seen in a number of impressionist and post-impressionist paintings is *WWW*, 2002 (plate 59). The golden color differentiated by the outline of individual grasses dominates most of the picture except for a sliver of bluish sky above. This artistic device reduces the illusion of depth by emphasizing the foreground details. Tiny spider webs are embedded in the grasses, thus the humorous title, standing for World Wide Web. In contrast, a painting made the following year, *Website* (plate 60), named for larger cobwebs in the grass, is a vertical work, much darker in color and mood. Here the vegetation is even more detailed although the sky is ominous. Weymouth visually communicates a sense of foreboding in the darkening sky found in a number of his landscapes. His depiction of storms as natural phenomena uncontrolled by man gives him the opportunity to dramatize the shadows cast on the land by threatening clouds and to highlight elements in the landscape. Unlike Wyeth, Weymouth often employed this artistic device, and even on relatively sunny days, there is a sense that the weather is about to change. Interestingly, toward the end of his career, many of Weymouth's landscapes have dark skies, perhaps expressing the anxiety of the age.

Again Weymouth continued working from the scenery surrounding his house. In *First Cutting*, 2004 (plate 57), he presents the newly mowed hill with neat rectangular haystacks dispersed across the peak, again under a stormy sky. These do not resemble the stacks seen in Martin Johnson Heade's (1819–1904) salt marshes or Claude Monet's (1840–1926) grain stacks in different seasons and times of day. Nor do they resemble typical Dutch landscapes that often depict discernible cumulus cloud formations that compose half or even three-quarters of the picture space. This is clearly a realistic picture of the hill near his house, newly mowed, the same one pictured in *August*. Generally, in late works such as *Before Mowing*, 2009 (plate 53), *Requiem*, and *The Crossing*, his attention to meticulously painted detail in egg tempera and watercolor remained steadfast. For Weymouth, as for Thomas Cole, the sky is the soul of the painting and casts a mood over the landscape. The same sense of nature's cycles is revealed not only in his paintings but also in the chapel he built at The Big Bend [see fig. 14]. Weymouth demonstrated his interest in architecture when he designed this rustic stone structure on his property with large arched glassless windows and a door open to the woods. A slender metal cross draws the visitor into this hallowed space that pays homage to the ephemerality of both nature and man.

EGG TEMPERA PORTRAITS

The Way Back, 1963 (plate 17), is one of Weymouth's most important tempera paintings because it is a symbolic self-portrait of the artist and serves as a link between portraiture and landscape. In the foreground we see the hands of the artist, an award-winning coachman, holding the reins of the horse in front of him. The highlighted hands that stand for the artist are placed prominently, separated from the equally emphasized horse's rear by the cart's front wood panel. Although in this work we see a single-horse driving cart, Weymouth usually drove a four-in-hand, using one hand for the reins and one for the whip. The house in the background is his home, an eighteenth-century stone building that incorporates an earlier, late seventeenth-century Swedish trading post. Weymouth acquired the property in 1961 and painstakingly restored it.

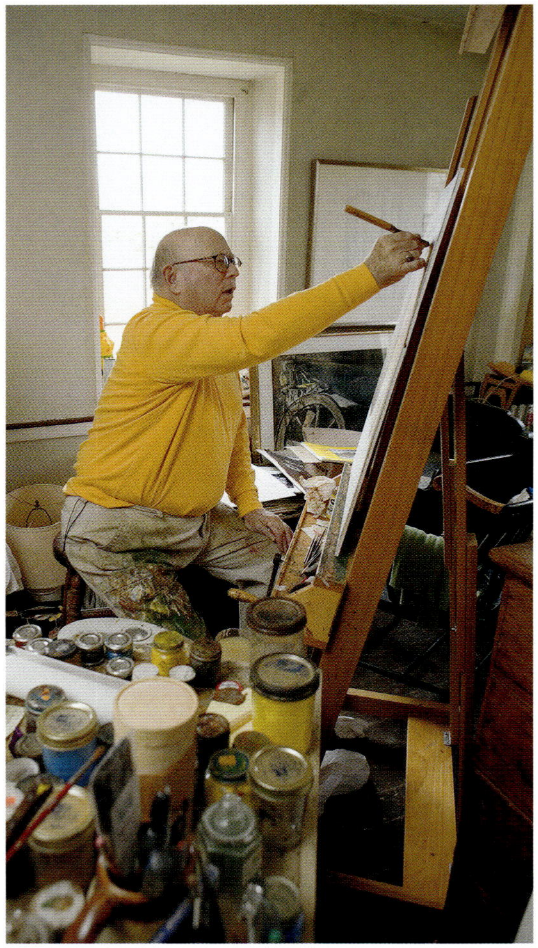

FIG. 15
Weymouth in his studio, 2008
Photograph by Jim Graham
© Jim Graham

When visitors come to The Big Bend, they approach it by a very long driveway that allows them to see the largely unspoiled natural vista. It is in this house that Weymouth's studio was located (fig. 15)—a simple space containing an easel, a chair, a table, and a bench, with windows overlooking the hilly terrain. It does not face north, as many artists require for its pure light. He spent hours, months, even years when working on a painting in this quiet spot where he could labor without disturbance.

Despite his diverse activities, Weymouth considered himself primarily an artist. *The Way Back* reveals the hands that made the paintings and pencil drawings,

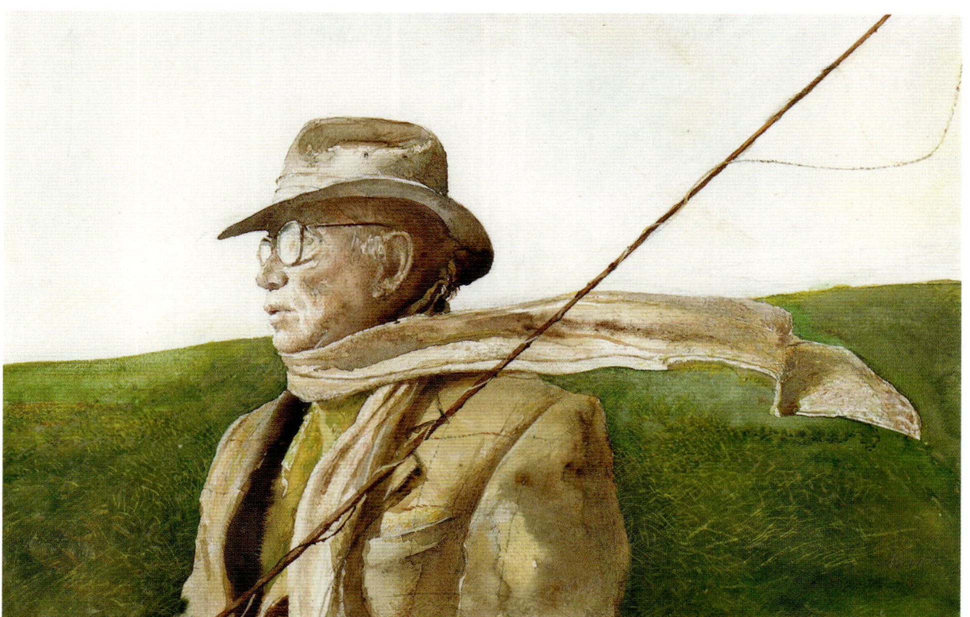

FIG. 16
Andrew Wyeth (1917–2009)
The Whip, 2000
Drybrush watercolor on paper, 12 × 18 inches
Mac Weymouth. © 2018 Andrew Wyeth / Artists' Rights Society (ARS)

the house in which they were created, the land surrounding it that was his frequent subject, and one of his favorite activities, coaching. In his portrait *The Whip*, 2000 (fig. 16), Andrew Wyeth created a candid rendering of Weymouth, suggesting the energy of the man by the fluttering scarf, the whip in hand, and the jaunty hat that was his sartorial signature.

When the artist painted in tempera, he often used an autumnal palette, as in *Gathering Storm*, 1964 (plate 19). In this work he captures the quiet emotion of Ethel Roach who worked in his parents' house as he was growing up and took care of him (fig. 17). In the preparatory sketch for this painting (plate 18), Weymouth lightly traces the whole composition, but the focus is very much on the sitter's face. She is looking out the window, lost in thought—as so many of Weymouth's subjects are—as the weather changes outdoors, thus the title.[15] That Weymouth related how much he cared for this woman is demonstrated in the intimacy of his depiction of her in both the study and in this, one of his tenderest and most emotional tempera paintings.

Weymouth regularly painted people he knew and liked regardless of gender, race, or social status. Among them were many African Americans who worked for Weymouth and his parents, and a genuine reciprocal affection existed between them, from all accounts by family, friends, and former employees. He accepted portrait commissions, but he was highly selective in this regard because of the length of time it took him to complete a portrait in tempera. Harking back to his traditional academic training, he did not like to work from photographs because he said that a photograph is two-dimensional. He also had to like the people and find them interesting to talk with during the multiple sittings he required.

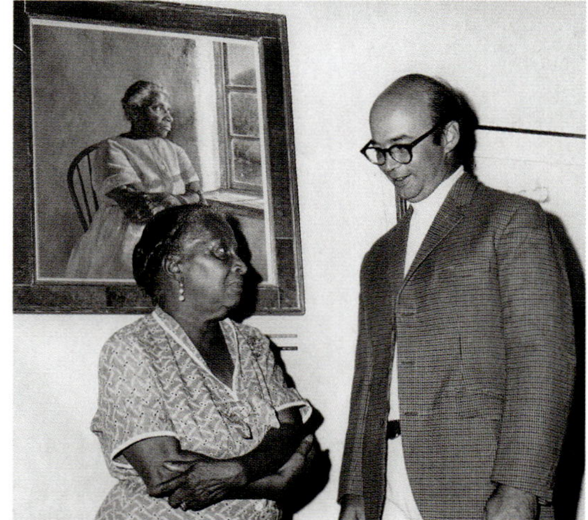

FIG. 17
Weymouth with Ethel Roach, the subject of his painting *Gathering Storm*, on exhibition at "Chadds Ford Days" at the Chadds Ford Historical Society, 1968. Brandywine Conservancy Archives

PORTRAIT HEADS

Like the study for *Gathering Storm*, the detailed head of *Mr. Hilton Taylor*, 1962 (plate 24), is a sensitive portrait painted in watercolor. Mr. Taylor was the butler of Bayard Sharp's family, the artist's cousins. Here Weymouth portrays Taylor's expressive face and quiet demeanor. Similarly, in the portrait *Henry Belin du Pont, Jr.*, 1971 (plate 41), Weymouth captures the personality of the sitter, who was a cousin on his mother's side. In this painting, made shortly before the sitter's death, the artist conveys the signs of age in both the position of du Pont's shoulders and the lines on his face. By leaving so much negative space around the figure, Weymouth focuses on the facial expression of someone deep in thought.

A later portrait head from 2007 is that of Herbert V. Kohler, Jr. (plate 62), a scion of industry and one of Weymouth's longtime friends. It is a beautifully painted, strong portrait of this man, whose graying hair and beard are depicted with the same attention to detail as the artist's grasses and flowers. Weymouth painted Kohler's skin tones as ruddy, his eyes with a twinkle, and his lips with a barely perceptible mischievous smile. The portrait head bounces off the blank white ground, emphasizing the penetrating facial expression. In some respects, portrait heads such as those of Taylor, du Pont, and Kohler resemble the expressive paintings of Thomas Eakins (1844–1918), one of America's greatest realists, who was much revered by Weymouth (fig. 18). I believe that in Weymouth's portraits such as the three examples above, which range from the 1960s to 2007 and beyond, the artist calls attention to the expressions of his sitters to reveal their character, unlike his mentor Andrew Wyeth, whose virtuosic paintings of people appear more clinically direct, yet less accessible.

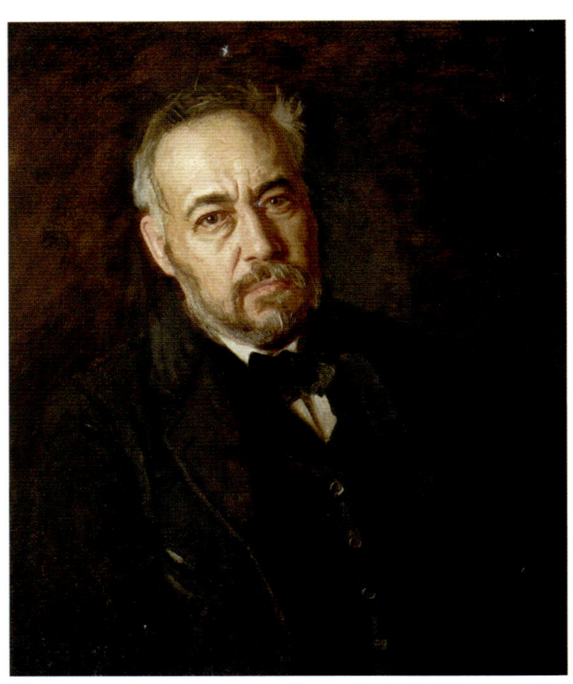

FIG. 18
Thomas Cowperthwaite Eakins
(1844–1916)
Self-Portrait, 1902
Oil on canvas,
30 × 25 inches
National Academy Museum,
New York, USA/Bridgeman Images

FULL-FIGURE PAINTINGS

Most of the genre-like paintings that Weymouth produced were of people he knew who were personal friends or who worked for him. *Eleven O'Clock News*, 1966 (plate 25), is a tempera painting of an African American man who was employed by Weymouth for years and who always listened to the radio while he worked, hence the title. The almost full-length figure is placed close to the picture plane directly in front of the house with some chopped wood between him and the building. The only real depth is on the right, where the trees veer off into the distance. Holding an ax, the man stares out into space as if he has just heard some disturbing news on the transistor radio

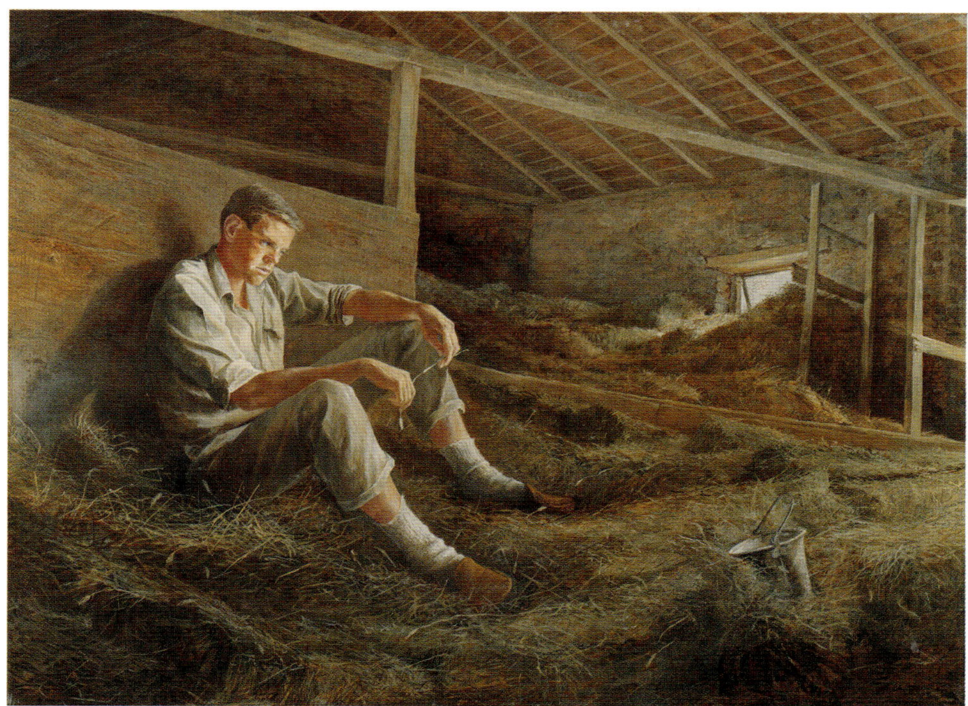

FIG. 19
George A. Weymouth (1936–2016)
Will Farish, 1963
Tempera on panel, 24 × 32⅛ inches
Private collection

on the windowsill. His downward gaze, combined with the wintry palette, creates an ominous, enigmatic narrative for this composition.

Another genre-like portrait is that of *Will Farish*, 1963 (fig. 19), Bayard Sharp's son-in-law, whom Weymouth depicts after Farish had just received news of the death of a cousin. The artist portrays Farish seated in a barn, in a posture that is the visual equivalent of sadness. Weymouth places the figure on the far left, facing across the empty barn interior, leaving a dramatic space in the picture plane that could represent Farish's sense of loss. As in many of Weymouth's paintings, there is little or no direct source of light. Instead, in this tempera painting, only a sliver of light from a background window bathes the subject's face and body in a pallid glow that enhances the pathos of the scene.

Twenty years later, in *Bayard Sharp* (fig. 20), Weymouth would portray another cousin, Farish's father-in-law, an avid sportsman and a horse breeder. The painting depicts Sharp in the open space of what is probably the Delaware Park track. Weymouth painted him to interact visually and compositionally with the park's unassuming setting and the architecture of the pavilion that interrupts the horizon line, as does Sharp's head. The artist seems to have taken particular interest in the contrast of detail between Sharp's plaid jacket and the surrounding dull tan turf. Similarly, Weymouth used this well-honed compositional structure and figural pose in such portraits as *Marshall Haseltine*, 1985; *Edward Cook*, 1988; *The Immigrant*, 1989; and *Prince Michael of Kent*, 1988 (fig. 25). In earlier paintings, he had tended to have sitters situated toward the left of the picture plane facing right, as in *6:59 a.m.*, 1958; *Sidney Scott*, 1962; *Joan Whitney Payson*, 1968; and *Geoffrey Holder*, 1990.

Circa 1965, a couple of years after *Will Farish*, Weymouth painted his then wife, Ann Brelsford McCoy, known as AnnaB (plate 20). At the time, she was working side by side with him

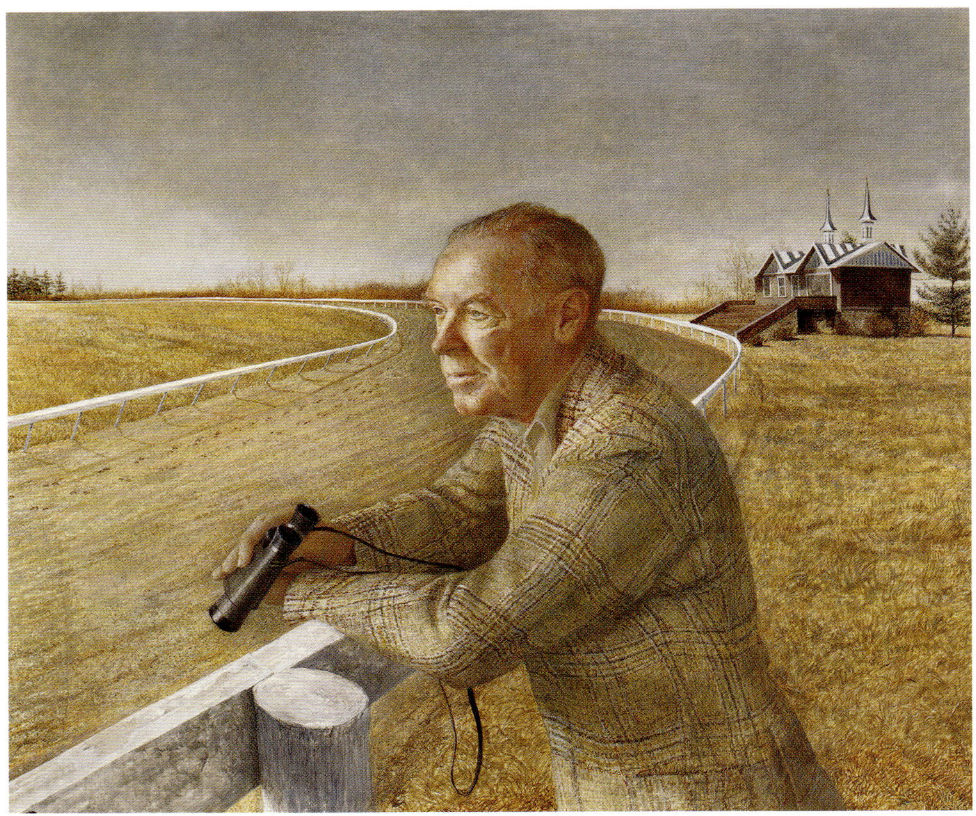

FIG. 20
George A. Weymouth (1936–2016)
Bayard Sharp, 1963
Tempera on panel, 37⅞ × 42¾ inches
Private collection

in restoring The Big Bend and in acquiring the antique furnishings for the house. Weymouth depicts her as a pensive, beautiful figure in a white jacket embroidered in black, the tones of which provide contrast to the dimly lit scene. With her head bent in thought and her downward gaze, the figure here recalls Thomas Eakins's *Young Girl Meditating* (fig. 21). As often in Weymouth's paintings, symbolism presents itself in the candle, emblematic of life, love, and the human soul, that most certainly represents his feelings for his wife.

Pennsylvania Indian (fig. 22) painted the same year, is different from many of his other portraits in two respects: the figure is placed at the center of the composition and the room in which he stands seems too small to contain him. This genre-like image depicts Jack Campbell, who worked for several years on the restoration of Weymouth's eighteenth-century home. The artist placed Campbell between a window and open door, his pervasive presence filling the picture plane. Weymouth created a mysterious snapshot of the man by obscuring his face but revealing a glimpse of his eye and ear. The artist's attention to the detail on Campbell's tan leather, sheepskin-lined jacket is in deliberate contrast

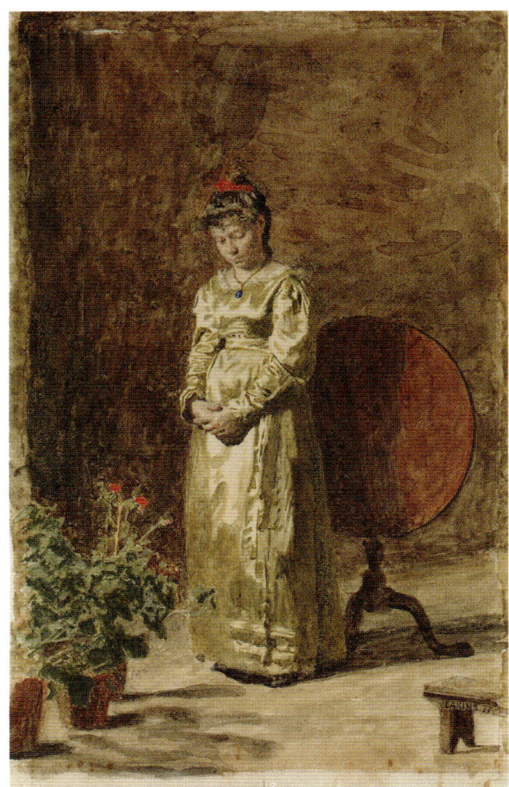

FIG. 21
Thomas Cowperthwaite Eakins (1844–1916)
Young Girl Meditating, 1877
Watercolor and gouache on off-white wove paper, 9⁹⁄₁₆ × 6⅛ inches
The Metropolitan Museum of Art, New York, NY
Fletcher Fund, 25.97.2
Image copyright © The Metropolitan Museum of Art. Image source: Art Resource, NY

to his treatment of the subject's visage. A self-portrait tempera painting, *The Revenant*, 1949 (fig. 23), by his mentor Andrew Wyeth, almost certainly served as an example for Weymouth. There is a compositional similarity in setting large looming figures into a constricted, heavily backlit space. But whereas Wyeth used a symphony of white tones to bathe the entire scene in a gauzy, otherworldly scrim of diffusing atmosphere, Weymouth, in *Pennsylvania Indian*, selectively chose to render parts of the composition in sharp focus so that the jacket and hat serve to describe the man.

Portrait of William W. Scranton, 1969 (plate 40), is another full-figure tempera portrait, this one of Scranton, governor of Pennsylvania from 1963 to 1967. This painting differs from many of Weymouth's portraits, as the seated figure is shown in full except for his feet. He is posed with an august air appropriate for a statehouse portrait. As so often in his work, Weymouth depicts his sitter gazing out the window, the light creating shadows of the panes on him and the wall.[16] In this view at Marworth, the former Scranton family estate in northeastern Pennsylvania, Weymouth carefully observed how the wall moldings echo the geometric windowpanes. He similarly draws a parallel between the rounded forms of Scranton's body and the chair in which he is seated and the right angles of the pale colored walls. Scranton, as conveyed by Weymouth, is a contemplative figure, appearing lost in thought, hand raised to his chin. Wyeth's *Up in the Studio*, 1965 (fig. 24), provides an illustrative antecedent. Although Weymouth's painting differs from Wyeth's in color, style, and purpose, both artists are drawing on the tradition of earlier precedents, most notably in the celebrated portrait by James Abbott McNeill Whistler (1834–1903) of his mother seated and

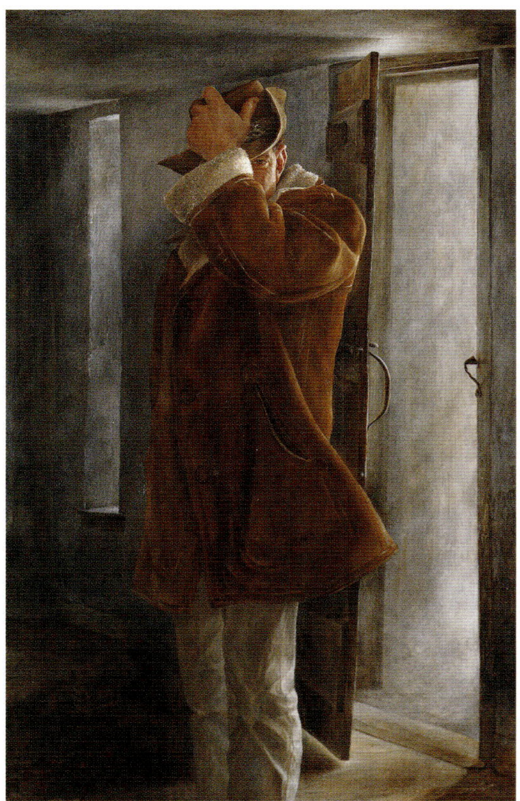

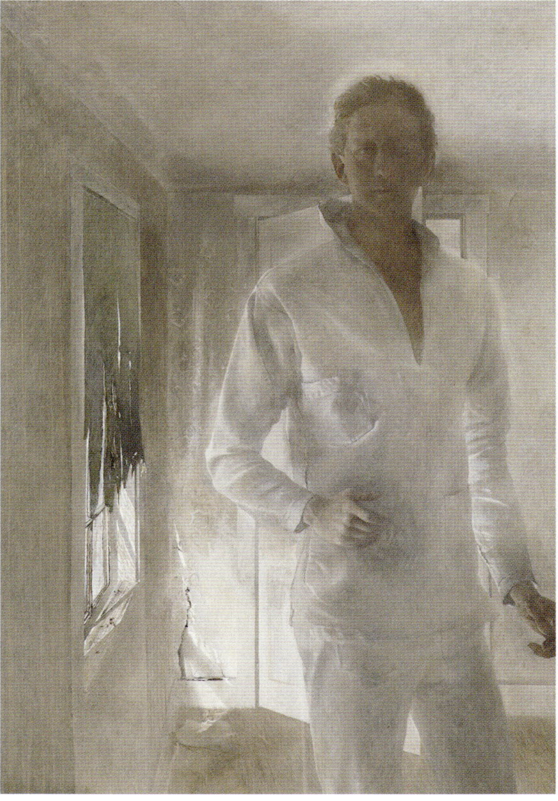

FIG. 22
George A. Weymouth (1936–2016)
Pennsylvania Indian, 1963
Tempera on panel, 42 × 30 inches
Private collection

FIG. 23
Andrew Wyeth (1917–2009)
The Revenant, 1949
Tempera on panel, 30 × 20 inches
New Britain Museum of American Art, the Harriet Russell Fund © 2018 Andrew Wyeth / Artists' Rights Society (ARS)

in profile (*Arrangement in Grey and Black No. 1*, 1871, Musée d'Orsay, Paris). As noted art historian Avis Berman said in a recent lecture, affinities in art are easy to identify, but when the emulation is transformed into something distinctive the connections become more interesting.

Weymouth knew many interesting people and painted a number of them including Luciano Pavarotti, Edgar Bronfman, and English nobility such as the Earl of Westmorland, Master of the Horse. Weymouth had played polo in England in his early years and became friends with David Thomas Fane, Lord Westmorland, whom he painted in tempera in 1980. Lord Westmorland held several royal positions, including that of Master of the Horse from 1978 to 1991, an important ceremonial place in the Queen's household, and one in which he shared Weymouth's passion for

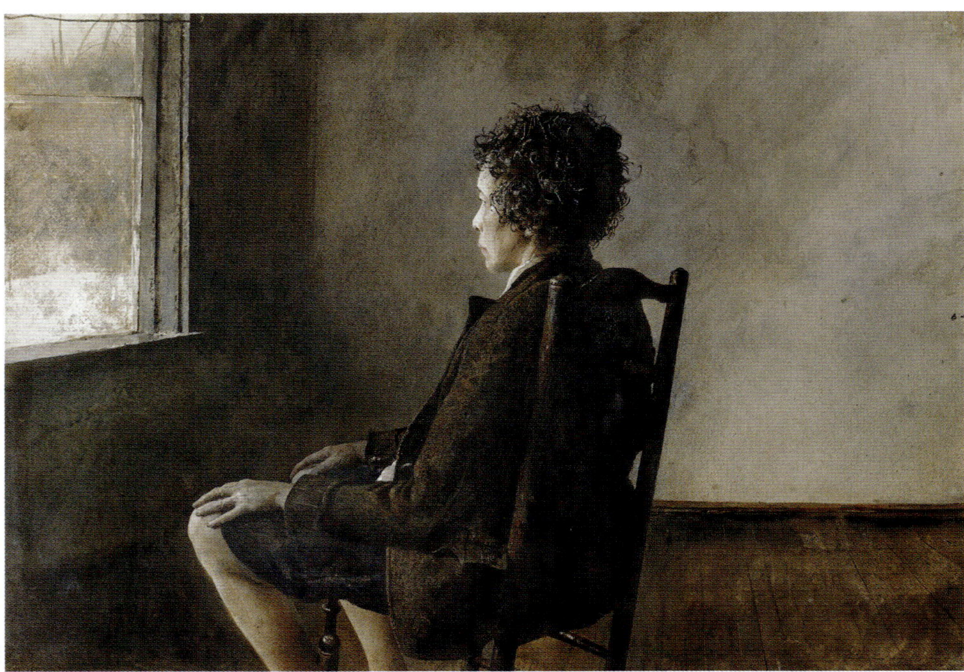

FIG. 24
Andrew Wyeth (1917–2009)
Up in the Studio, 1965
Watercolor and tempera on paper, 17 × 23⅞ inches
The Metropolitan Museum of Art, New York, NY, Gift of Amanda K. Berls, 1966 (66.216) Image copyright © the Metropolitan Museum of Art. © 2018 Andrew Wyeth / Artists' Rights Society (ARS)

equestrian pursuits. It was probably he who introduced Weymouth to other nobility and the royal family—some of whom sought out Weymouth for portraits. In *The Earl of Westmorland, Master of the Horse* (plate 61), which now hangs in Buckingham Palace, Weymouth focused on Fane's head and merely suggested the rest of the figure seated on a horse, thereby emphasizing the ceremonial pomp associated with the royal family. He worked in a studio at the Royal Academy without his sitter present most of the time, instead painting directly from his dress uniform and helmet. It was almost certainly Fane who introduced Weymouth to Prince Michael of Kent, whom he painted in 1988 (fig. 25). Prince Michael actually asked Weymouth to come to London to paint him; instead, Weymouth persuaded him to sit for him in Chadds Ford, where the artist happily entertained the prince daily at The Big Bend, with its gardens, horses, carriages, and lively company.

Weymouth's English portraiture culminated in the most prestigious of his subjects, H.R.H Prince Philip, the Duke of Edinburgh (fig. 1), whom the artist had met through polo in the 1960s.

In 1995, Weymouth indicated his interest in painting the prince's portrait, and a volley of letters ensued between Weymouth and the prince's staff. Prince Philip himself wrote: "Dear Frolic, It would be silly to pretend that I would not be delighted to have such a picture . . . I notice that you expect sittings of two hours . . . I have discovered that one hour is as long as I can do . . . without losing complete interest."[17] A schedule of sittings was arranged for Weymouth to work in a room at Buckingham Palace.[18] Instead of mimicking formal English "Grand Manner" portraits, Weymouth stayed true to his own visual compass. He suggested that he paint the portrait with Prince Philip dressed in casual attire at Windsor Castle, against the backdrop of one of the rooms damaged by fire in 1992. The prince was deputy director of the Restoration Committee, and quite fittingly for Weymouth, who had undertaken his own fervent restoration of The Big Bend, the artist chose to depict Prince Philip with reconstruction plans in hand. The stone wall against which he leans and the view of parts of the castle in the background reveal Weymouth's continuing attention to architecture. Multiple pencil sketches were executed for this painting, which now hangs in Windsor Castle. As in earlier portraits, Weymouth situated the prince on the periphery of the picture plane and depicts him gazing out the window. As captured by Weymouth, the prince's thoughtful gaze likely signifies the daunting task of restoring the castle.

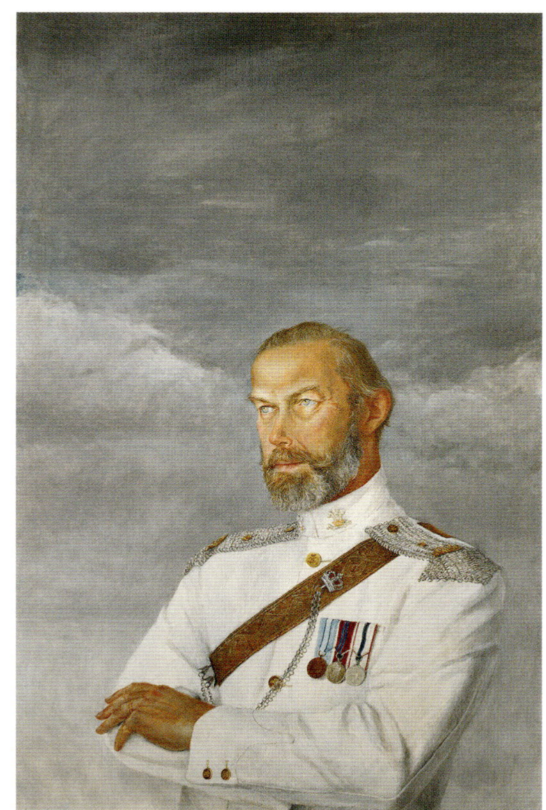

FIG. 25
George A. Weymouth
Prince Michael of Kent, 1988
Tempera on panel, 40 × 25½ inches
Private collection

Weymouth was personally acquainted with many powerful and wealthy men and women, but in his portraits, he secluded them in the quiet of his studio or in rooms of their choice. Except in the portraits of Bayard Sharp, Lord Westmorland, and Prince Philip, Weymouth seldom used a sitter's attire or surroundings to denote his occupation or status. In omitting references to his subjects' social standing, Weymouth conveyed figures alone yet connected to a greater humanity. This focus on the identity of the individual amid isolated surroundings is akin to the approach of Edward Hopper (1882–1967), an artist whom Weymouth admired, in iconic works such as *Automat*, 1927 (fig. 26).

RECOGNITION

Beginning in 1962, Weymouth's work was exhibited regularly in museums and galleries across the country, enumerated in the Chronology of this book. In 1991, for example, the Brandywine River Museum of Art organized an exhibition that then traveled to the Jacksonville Art Museum

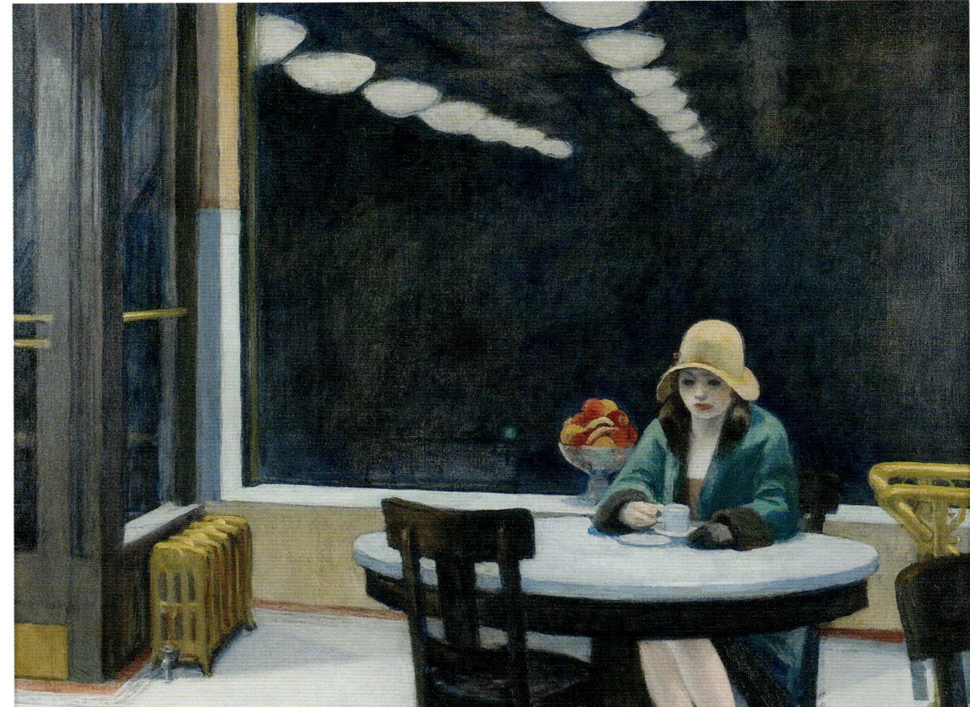

FIG. 26
Edward Hopper (1882–1967)
Automat, 1927
Oil on canvas, 28⅛ × 36 inches
Des Moines Art Center,
Permanent Collections,
purchased with funds from
the Edmundson Art
Foundation, Inc., 1958.2

in Florida. The exhibition was accompanied by a catalogue with an essay written by the renowned art historian Richard J. Boyle. Walter Annenberg, the distinguished collector, wrote to Weymouth on the occasion of the exhibition, complimenting him "on the impressive work assembled."[19] Another exhibition of Weymouth's paintings was organized in 2001 by the Haggerty Museum of Art at Marquette University in Milwaukee. Weymouth was humble about his talent and did not seek publicity nor foster commercial success, yet it came nonetheless in portrait commissions and numerous articles in magazines and newspapers that detailed his various activities. Almost every article pointed out that despite all the pursuits at which he was so adept, Weymouth was first and foremost an artist. And that he was!

From the mid-twentieth century on, the term *art* has encompassed works in a huge variety of mediums—from detritus to electronics—yet some artists have persevered in painting on canvas, paper, or board. George A. Weymouth was one of them. His elegant, distinctive, intuitive paintings not only resonate with his personal history, his cultural milieu, and his sense of place, but they also preserve and maintain the realist legacy of the Brandywine Valley artists for the twenty-first century and beyond.

1. George A. Weymouth was known as "Frolic" to family, friends, and employees, and even signed some of his paintings "F. Weymouth."

2. It has been my great privilege to work with Director Thomas Padon, Virginia O'Hara, Manager of the Walter and Leonore Annenberg Research Center; and the Brandywine staff. I am also grateful to James H. Duff, former director of the Museum, who imparted much inside information in our many emails and chats. A special thanks goes to editor Lucie Teegarden, who was a great sounding board.

3. Richard E. Noble, *The Echo of Their Voices: 150 Years of St. Mark's School* (Hollis, NH: Hollis Publishing, 2015). Noble speedily sent pages from his book to meet my short deadline.

4. Art Carey, "Frolic in Winter: Weymouth Still Active," *The Philadelphia Inquirer,* May 22, 2007, A7.

5. Interview April 7, 1993, with Richard Boyle, Hilton Brown, and James H. Duff; transcript, Walter and Leonore Annenberg Research Center, Brandywine River Museum of Art; also mentioned in Winterthur article, "A Man for All Seasons," by Susan Weissman, *Winterthur Magazine,* 2007; and other published interviews.

6. Deane Keller's papers, including teaching notes and materials, are in the collections of the Yale University Library Archives and can be viewed through the library's finding aid at: http://drs.library.yale.edu/HLTransformer/HLTransServlet?stylename=yul.ead2002.xhtml.xsl&pid=mssa:ms.1685&clear-stylesheet-cache=yes%20

7. *George A. Weymouth: A Retrospective* (Chadds Ford, PA: Brandywine River Museum of Art, 1991), 12.

8. Interview April 7, 1993, with Richard Boyle, Hilton Brown, and James H. Duff for Brandywine River Museum of Art exhibition "Milk and Eggs," in 2002.

9. Richard Boyle, "Connection with a Place: the Collection of the Brandywine River Museum," in *Brandywine River Museum: Catalogue of the Collection* (Chadds Ford, PA: Brandywine Conservancy, 1991), 20.

10. "Indian Hanna/h" was reported to have been the last surviving member of the Lenni Lenape, but that was not the case. Many individuals of Lenape descent still live in the region. Further historical and contemporary information about the Lenape is available at Lenape Lifeways, lenapelifeways.org. Additional information about Hannah Freeman is available through the blog of the Pennsylvania Historic Preservation Office at https://pahistoricpreservation.com/remembering-indian-hannah/. Accessed April 8, 2017.

11. Stephen Doherty, "George A. Weymouth," *American Artist,* January 1987, 93.

12. Author's conversation with James H. Duff, April 2017.

13. Susan Weissman, "A Man for All Seasons," *Winterthur Magazine,* Spring 2007, 13.

14. Weissman, "A Man for All Seasons," 28.

15. Weymouth's title for the portrait of Ethel Roach reflects the tensions and unrest that accompanied passage of the Civil Rights Act in 1964.

16. As revealed in the recent Wyeth catalogue and exhibition at the National Gallery of Art, windows were a frequent and powerful compositional metaphor in Wyeth's work, as they became for Weymouth himself. Nancy Anderson and Charles Brock, *Andrew Wyeth: Looking Out, Looking In* (Washington, DC: National Gallery of Art, 2014).

17. H.R.H Prince Philip to George A. Weymouth, letter dated August 12, 1994; Walter and Leonore Annenberg Research Center, Brandywine River Museum of Art.

18. Weymouth asked for ten sittings at two hours each. The schedule set by Major Charles Richards of the Welsh Guards in a letter to Weymouth dated December 30, 1994, was for ten one-hour sessions except for two hours at the first sitting. Walter and Leonore Annenberg Research Center, Brandywine River Museum of Art.

19. Walter Annenberg to George A. Weymouth, letter dated June 13, 1991; Walter and Leonore Annenberg Research Center, Brandywine River Museum of Art.

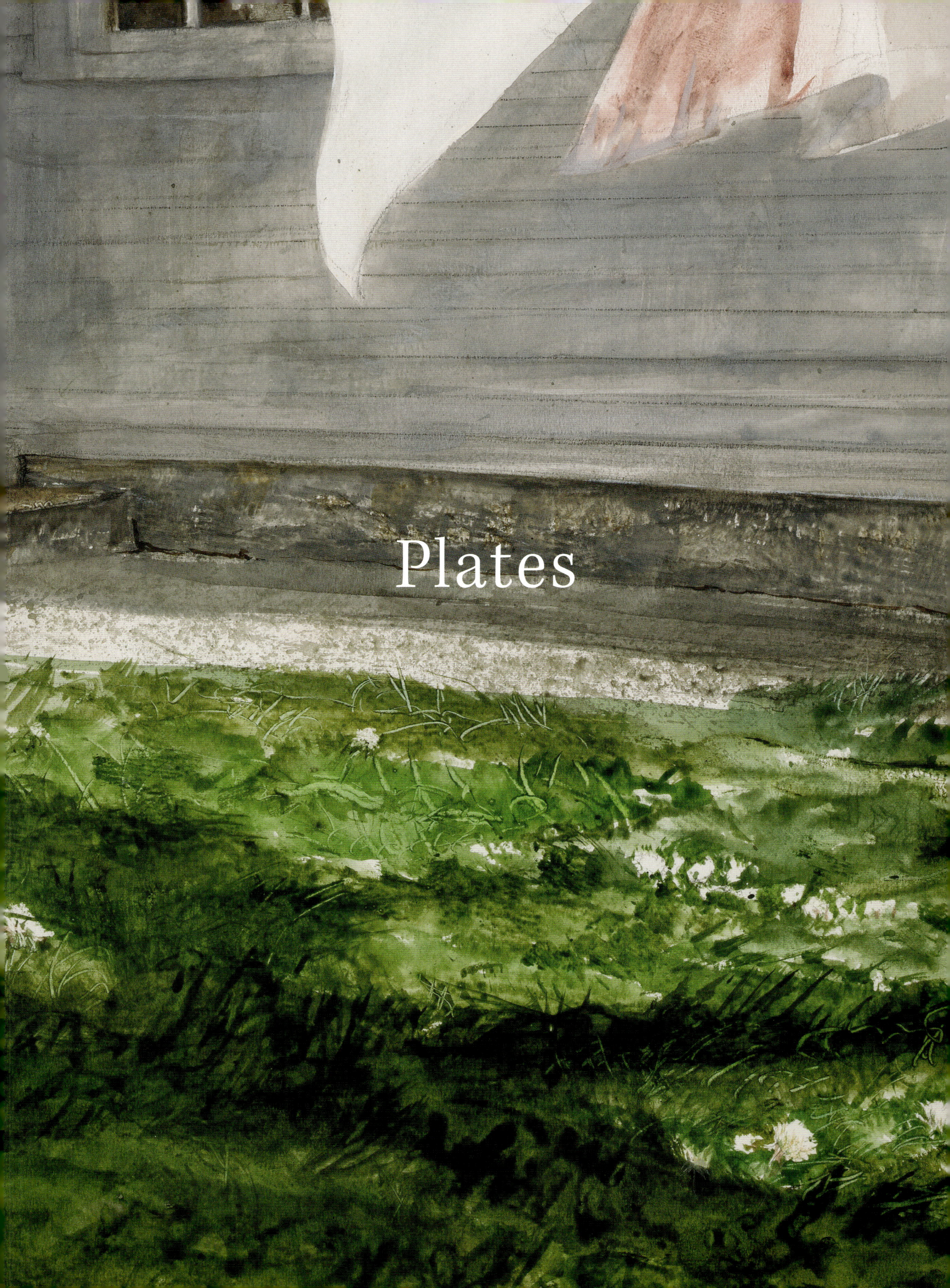

Plates

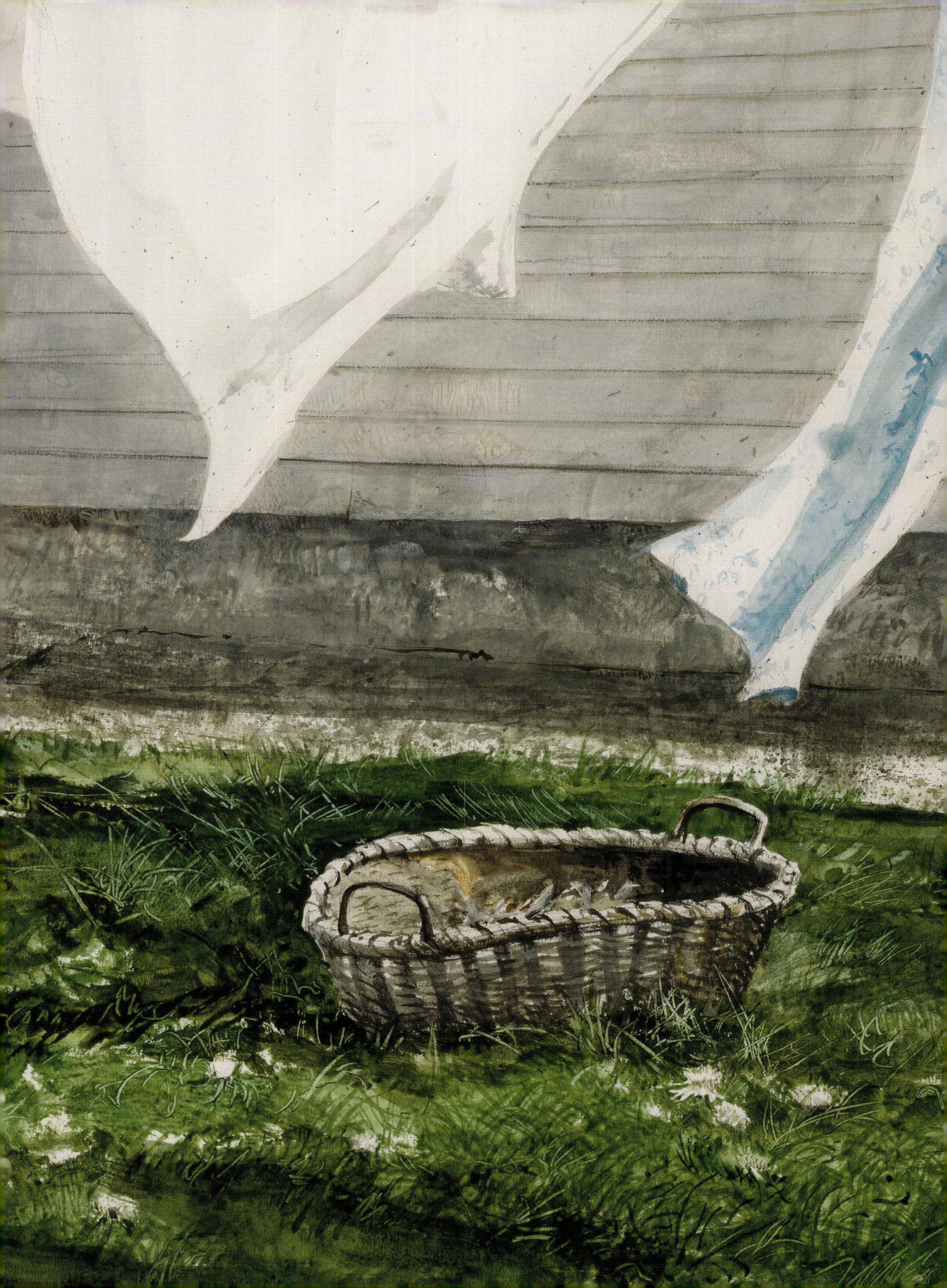

1

***CHICKEN FIGHT*, CA. 1948**

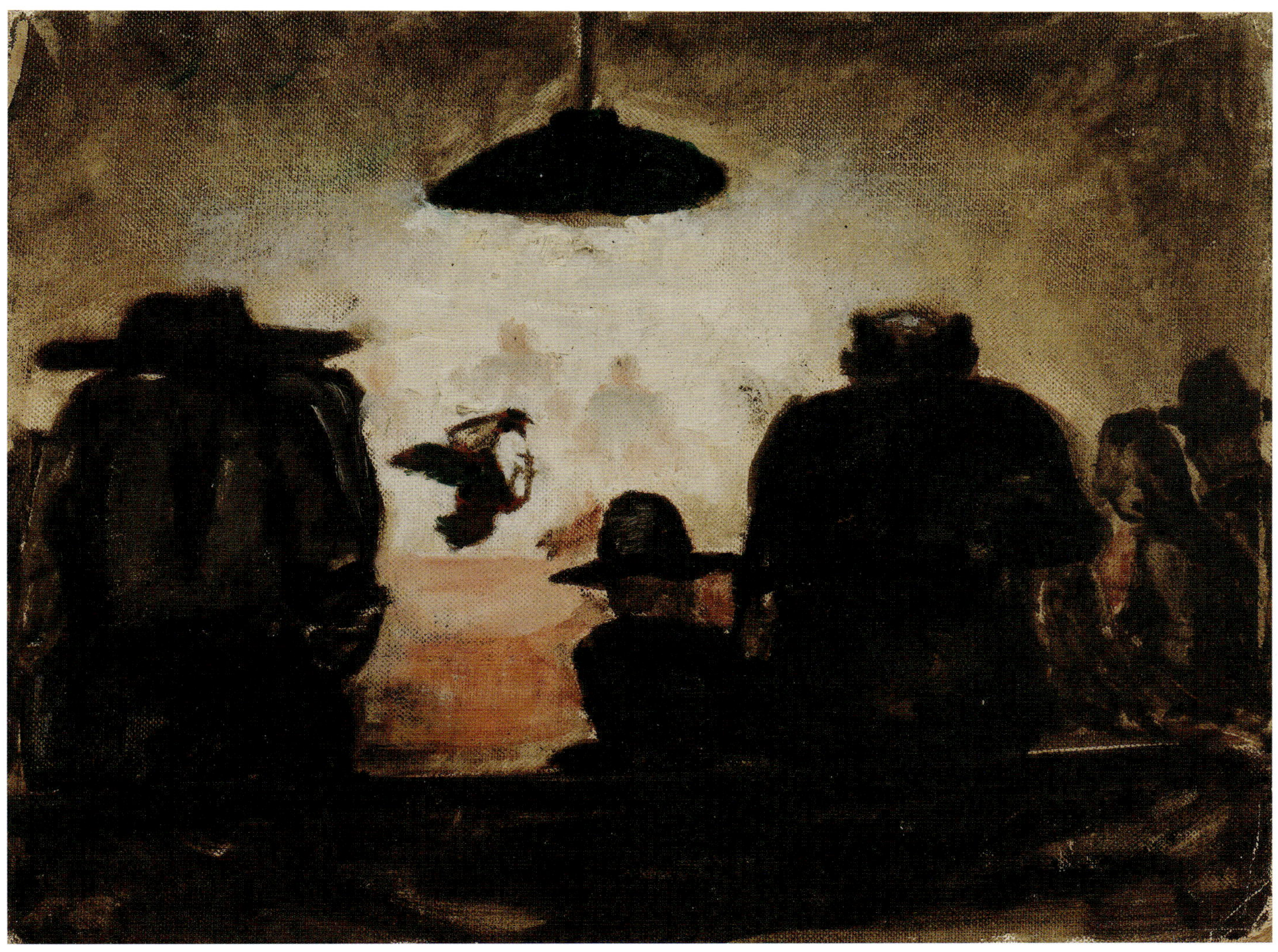

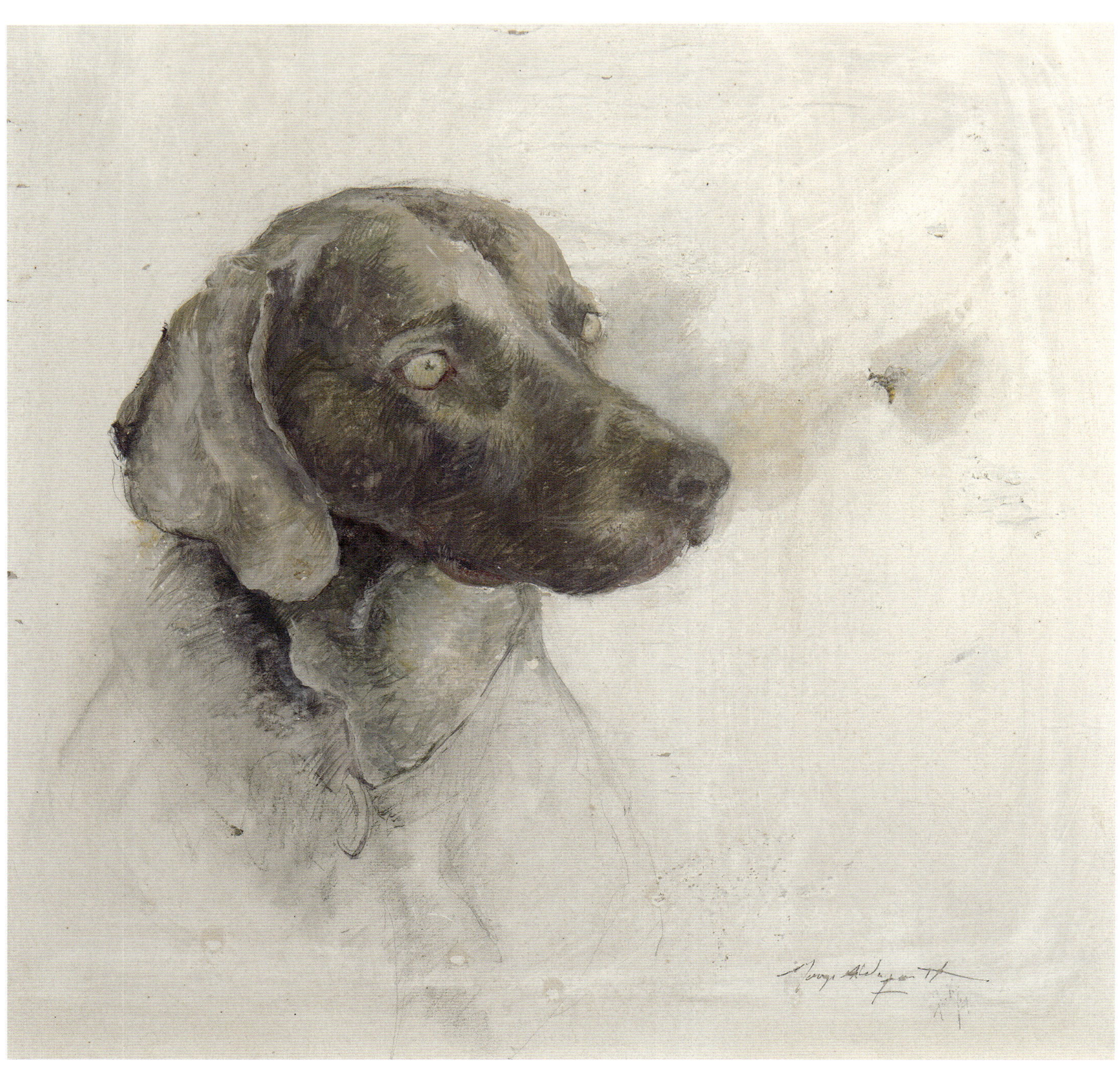

2
***CHUCKER*, 1957**

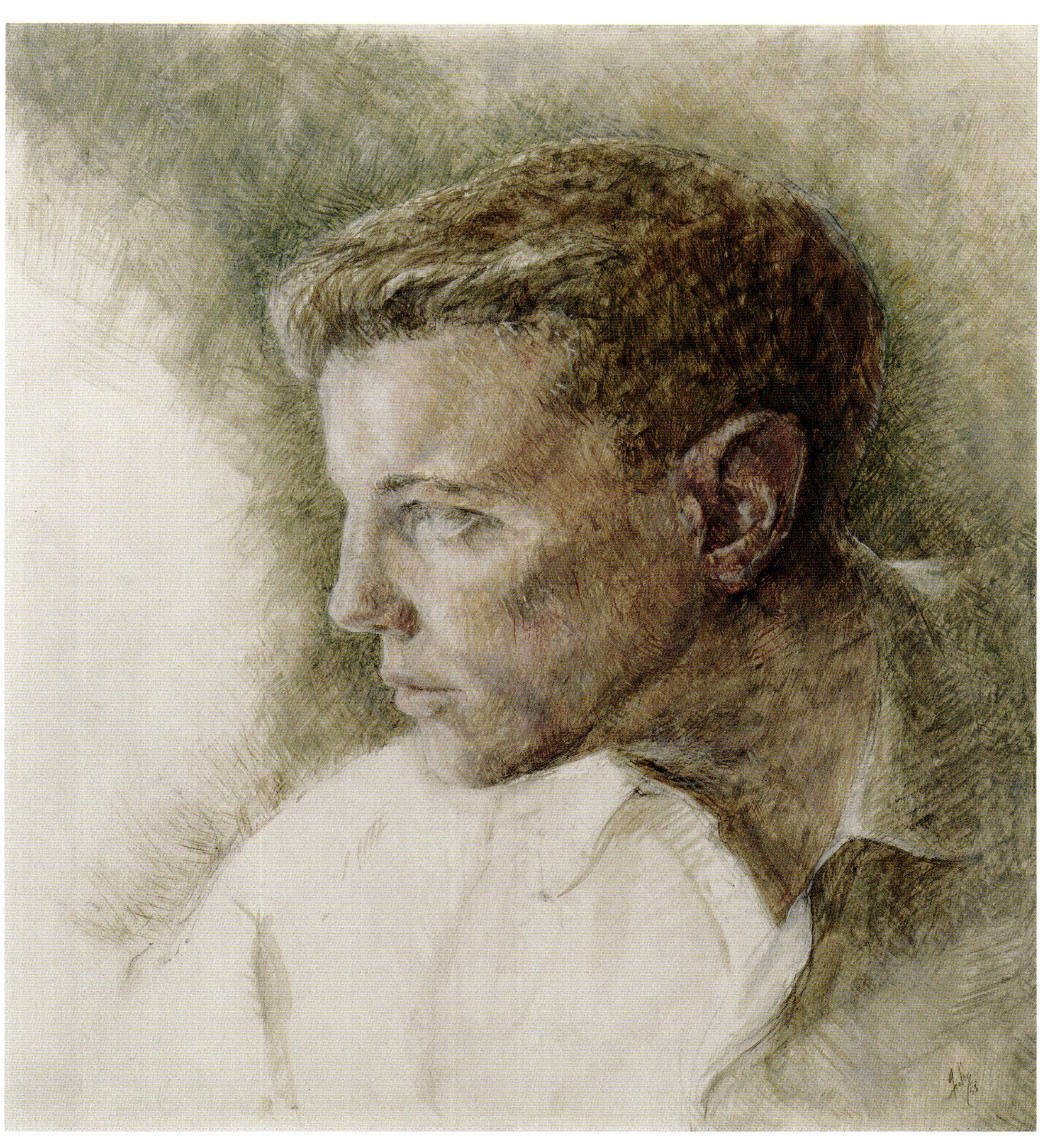

3
***ANSON*, 1956**

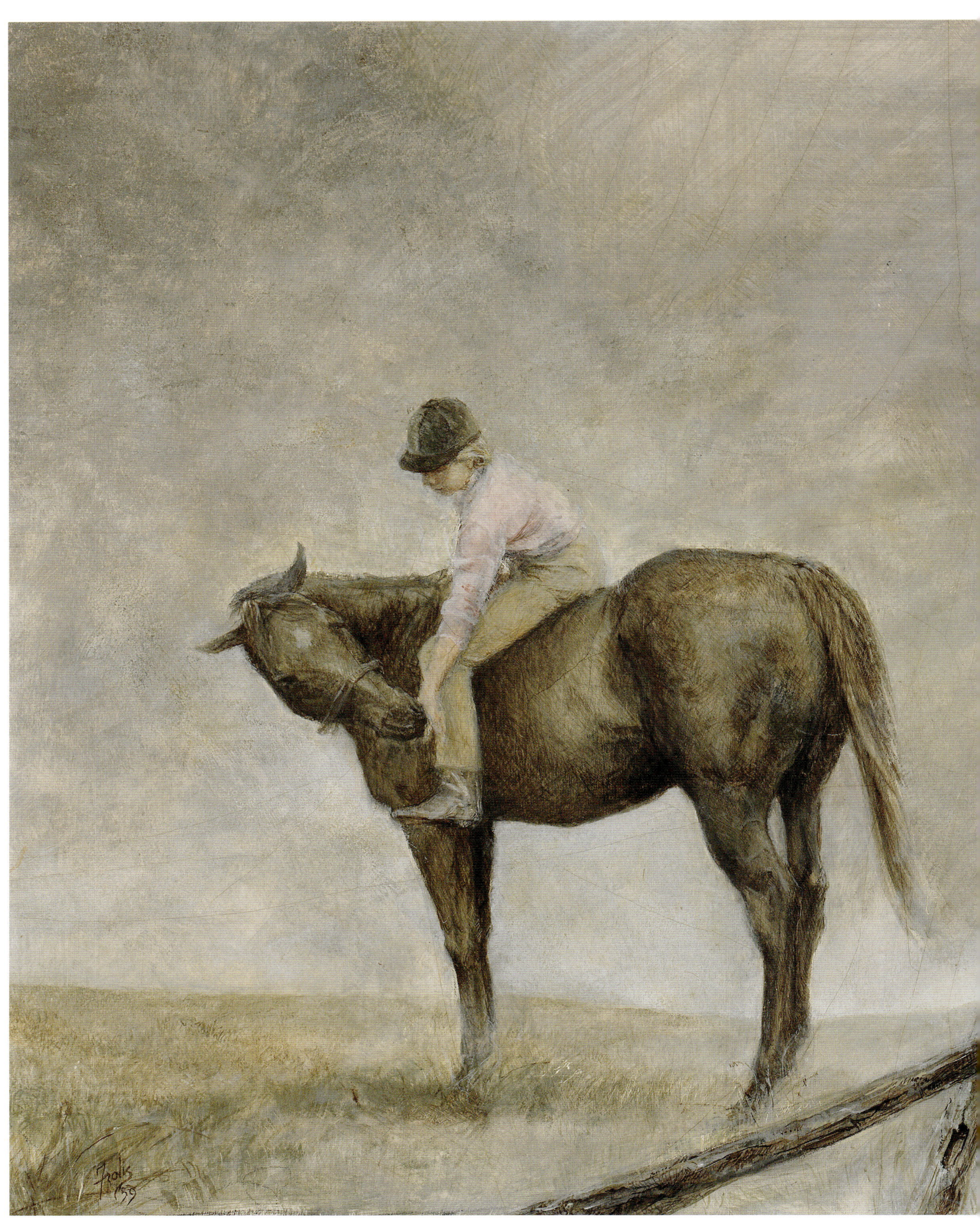

4
***CHARFOOT*, 1959**

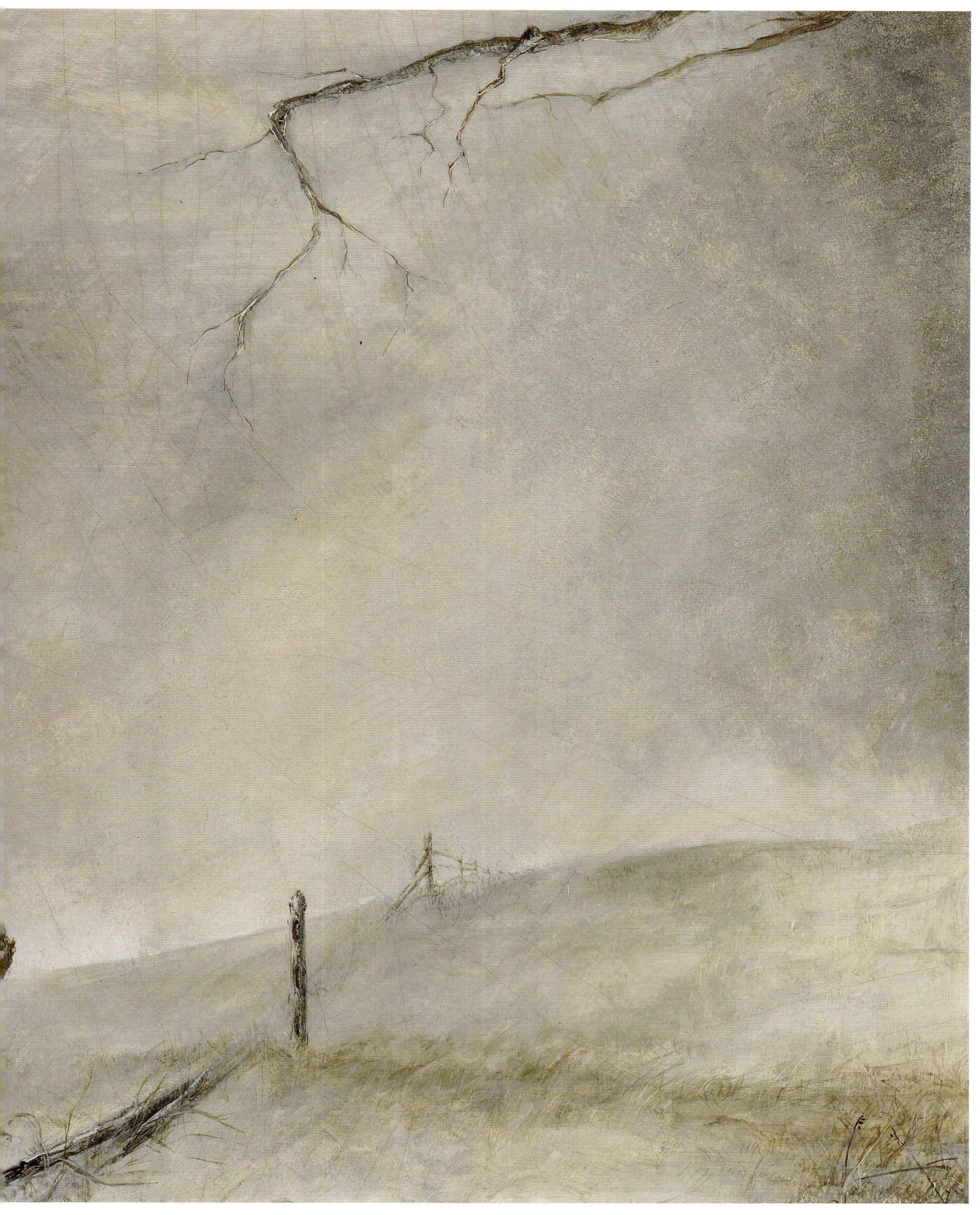

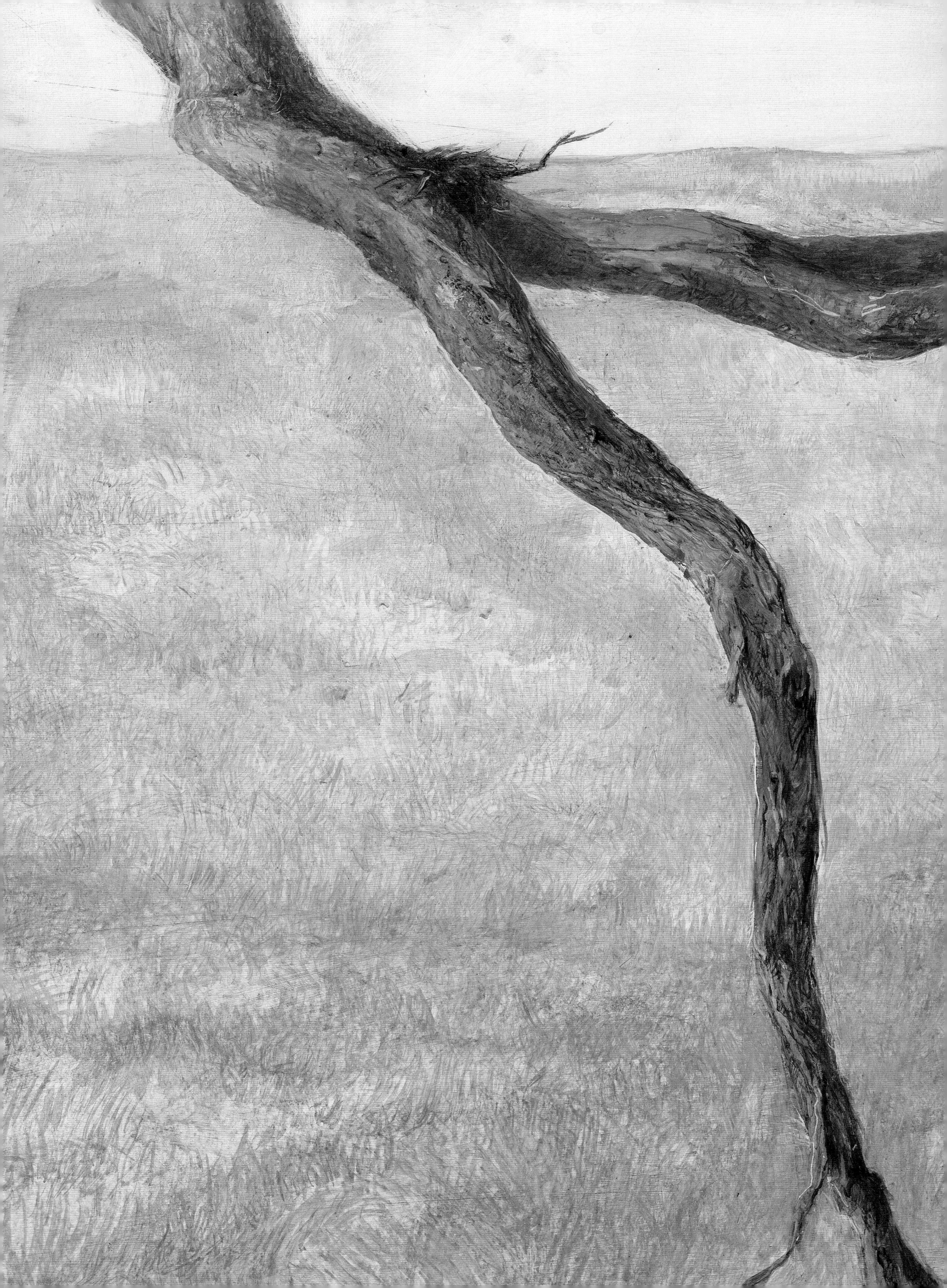

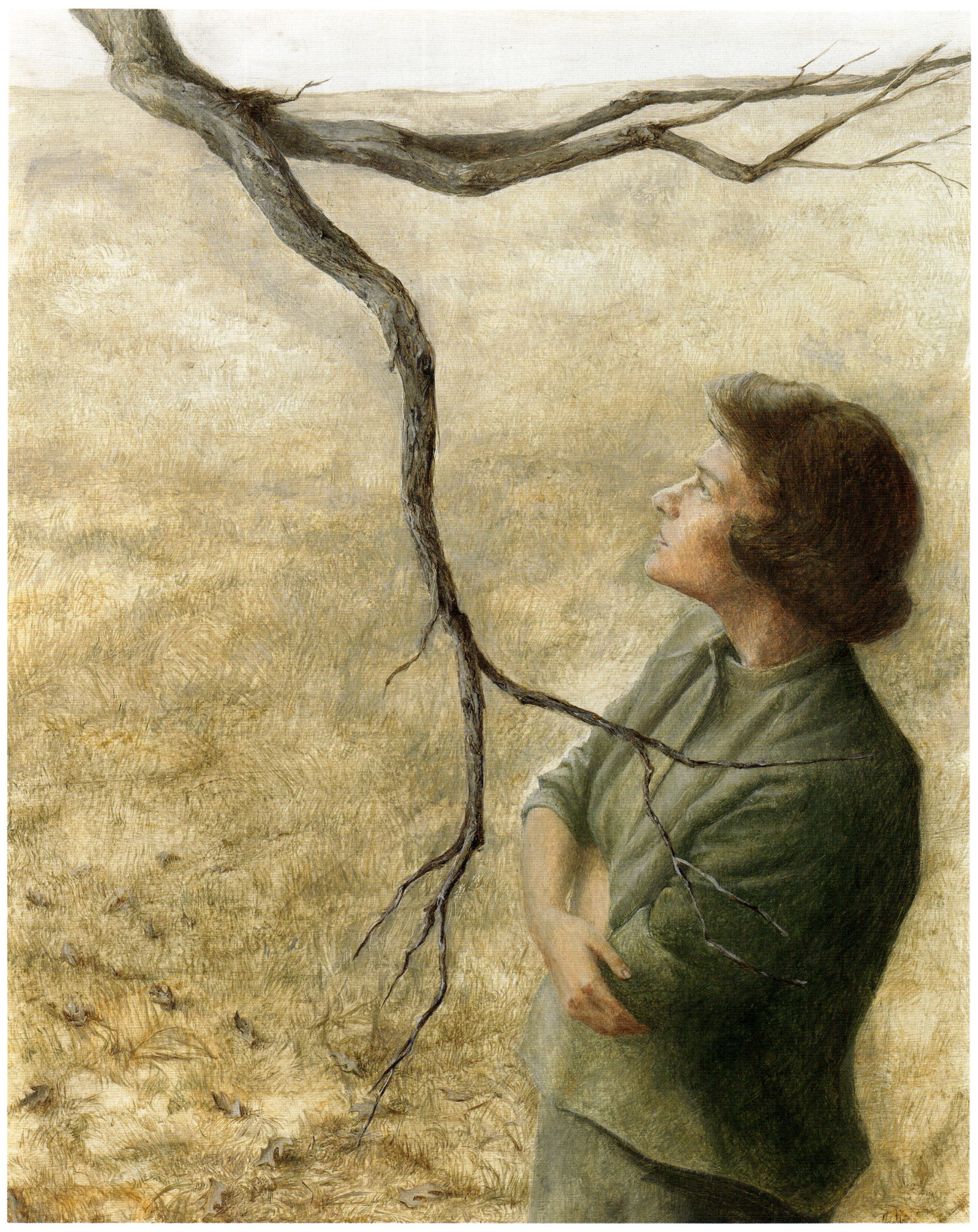

5

***FIELD SPARROW*, 1959**

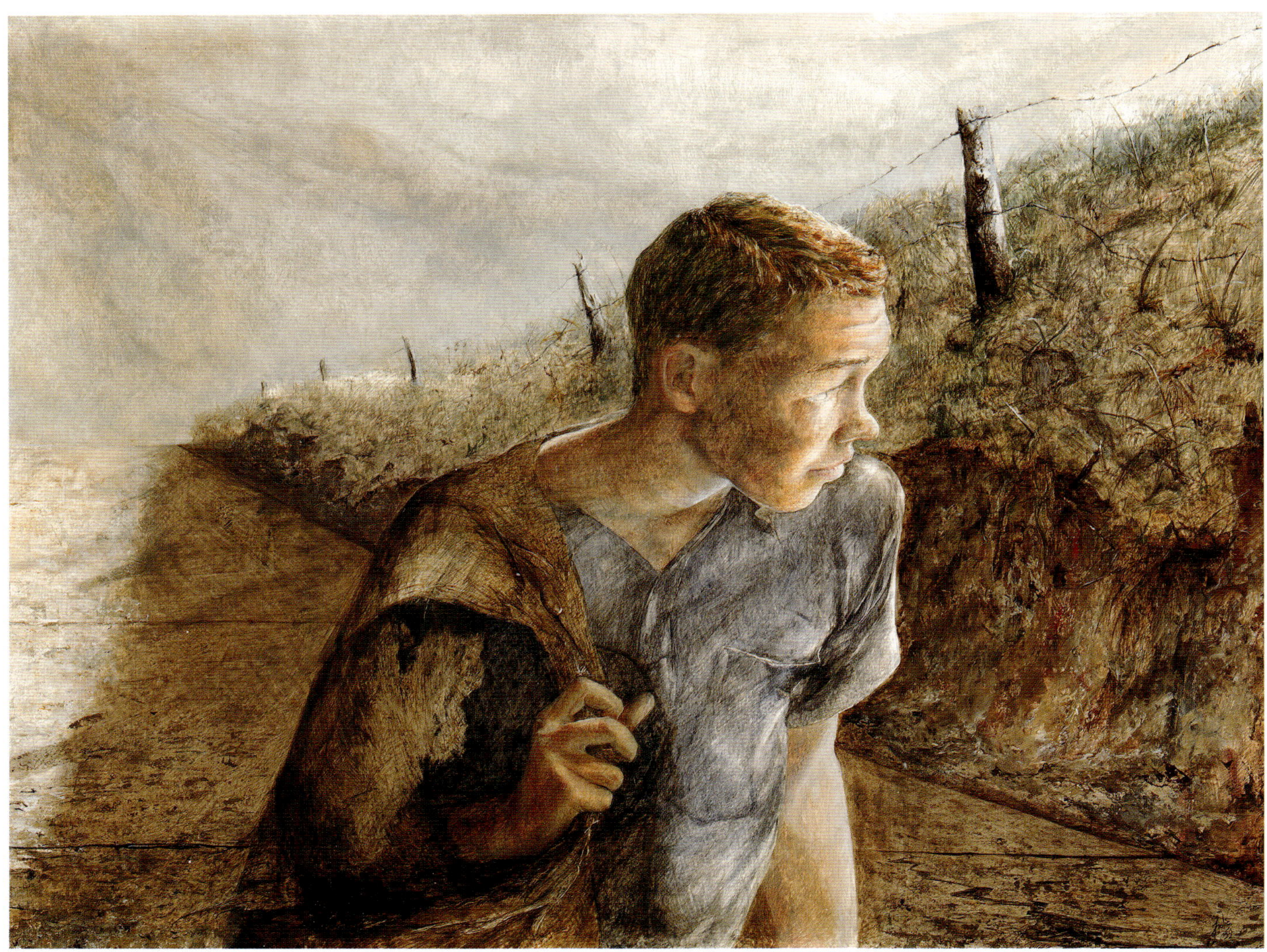

6
***PETE*, 1959**

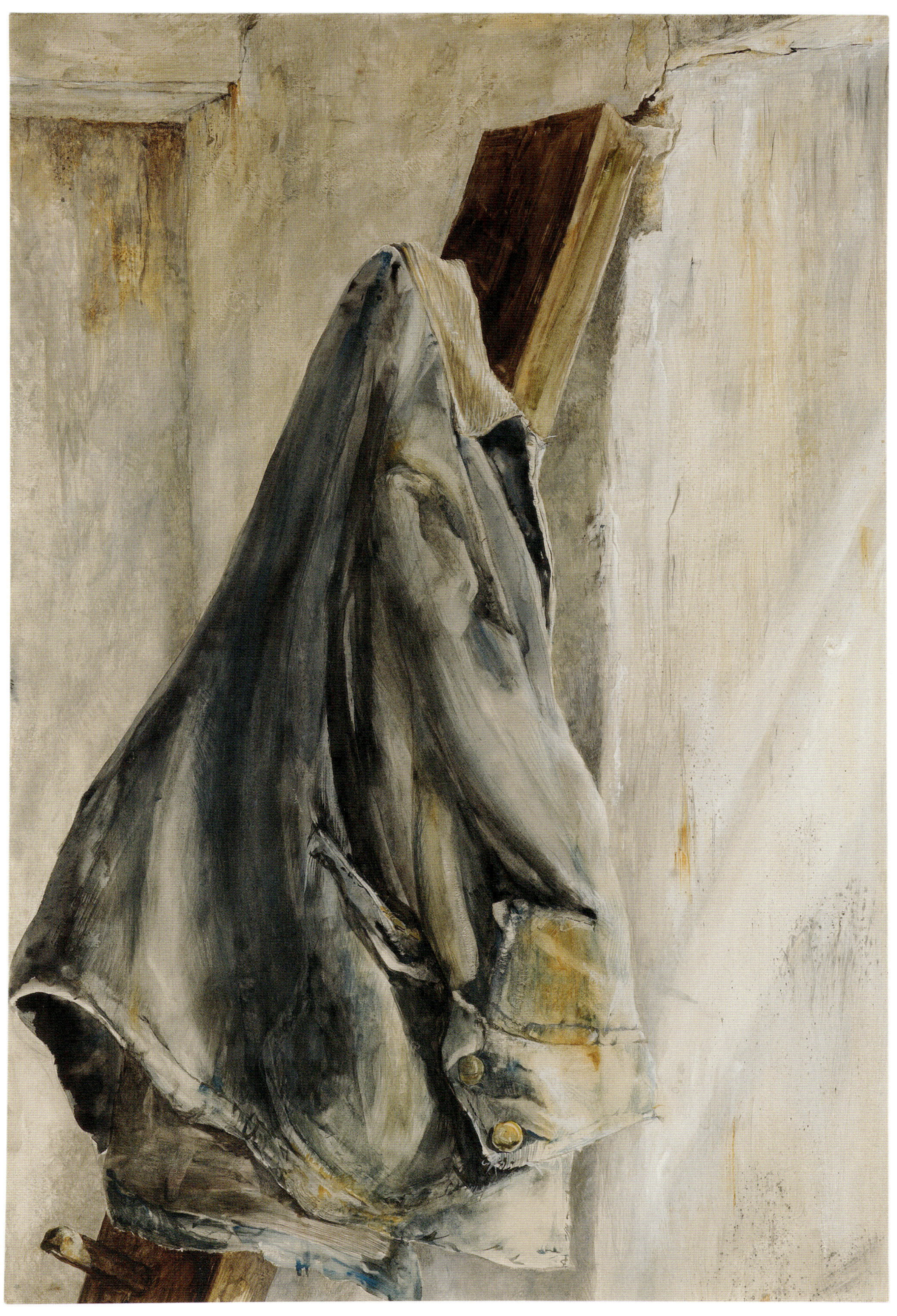

7
***JACK CAMPBELL'S COAT*, 1961**

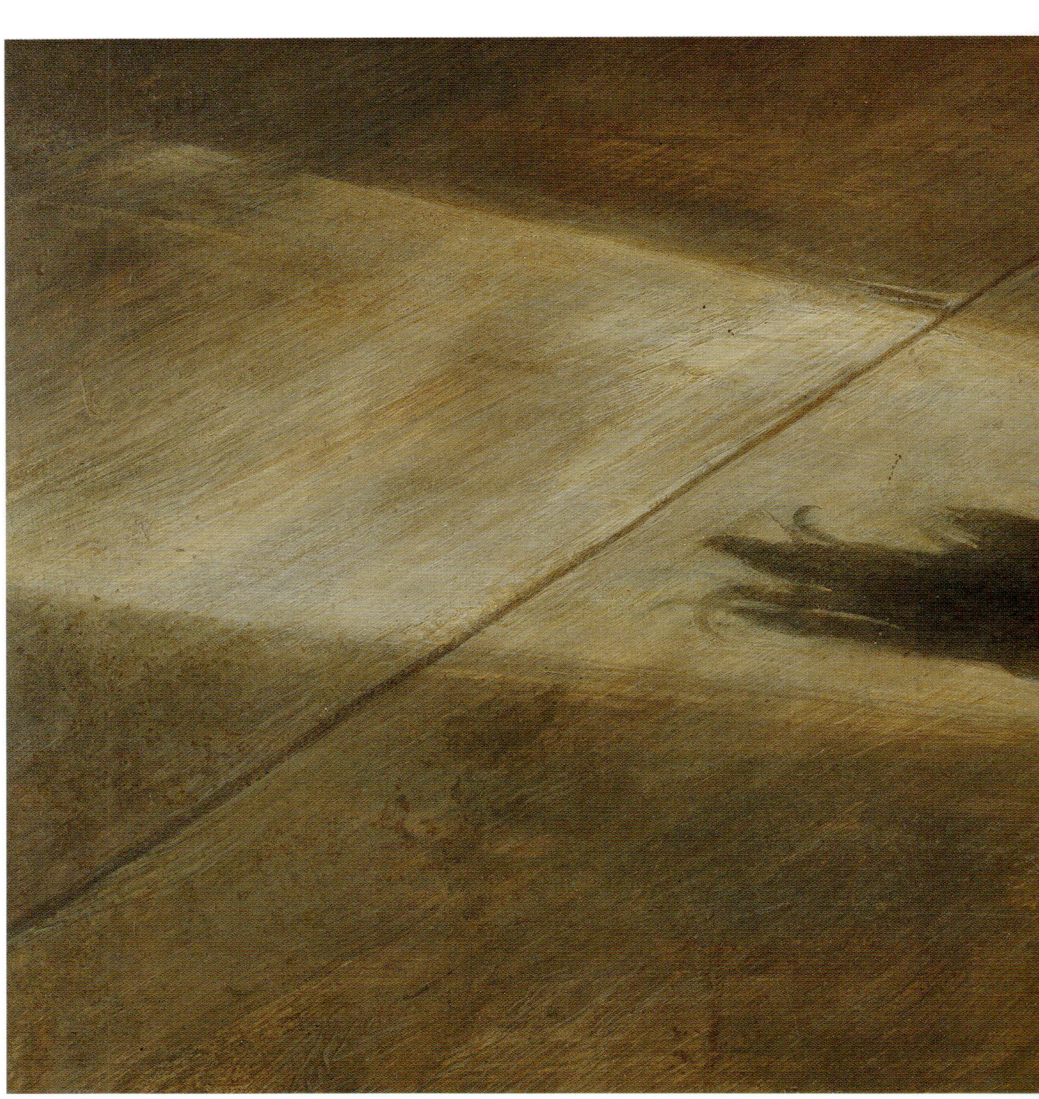

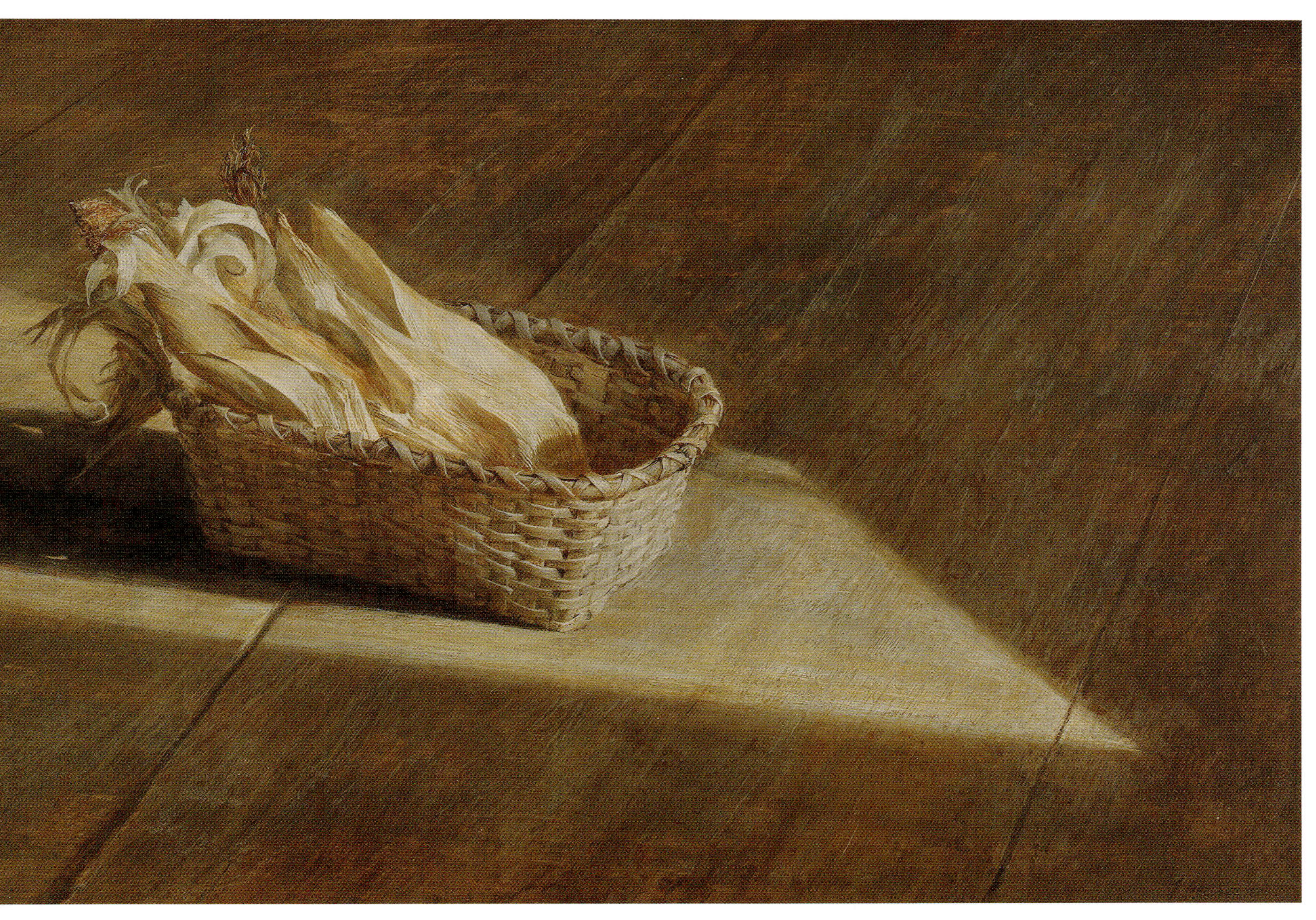

8
***CORN BASKET*, 1965**

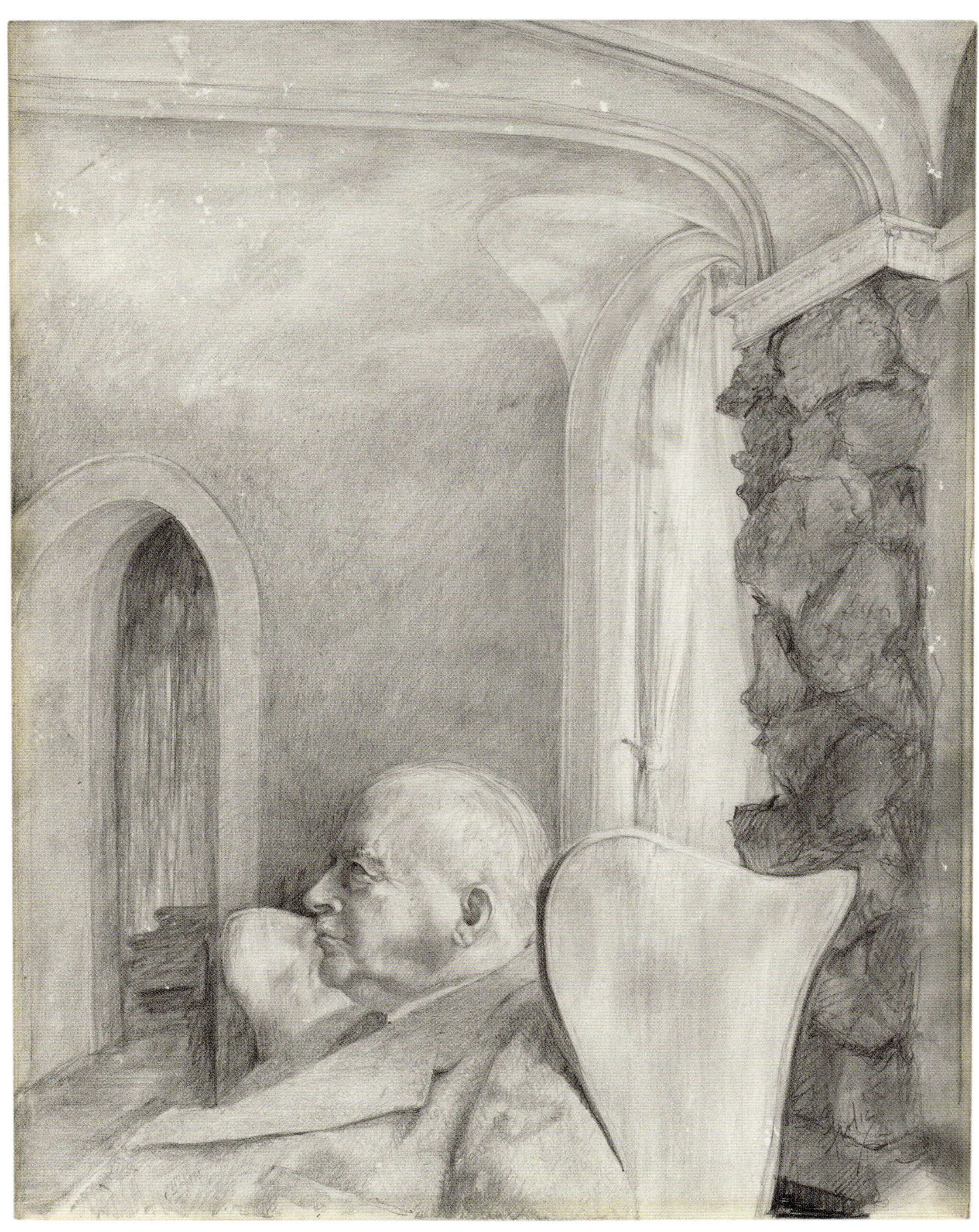

9

STUDY FOR *EUGENE ELEUTHÈRE DU PONT*, 1958

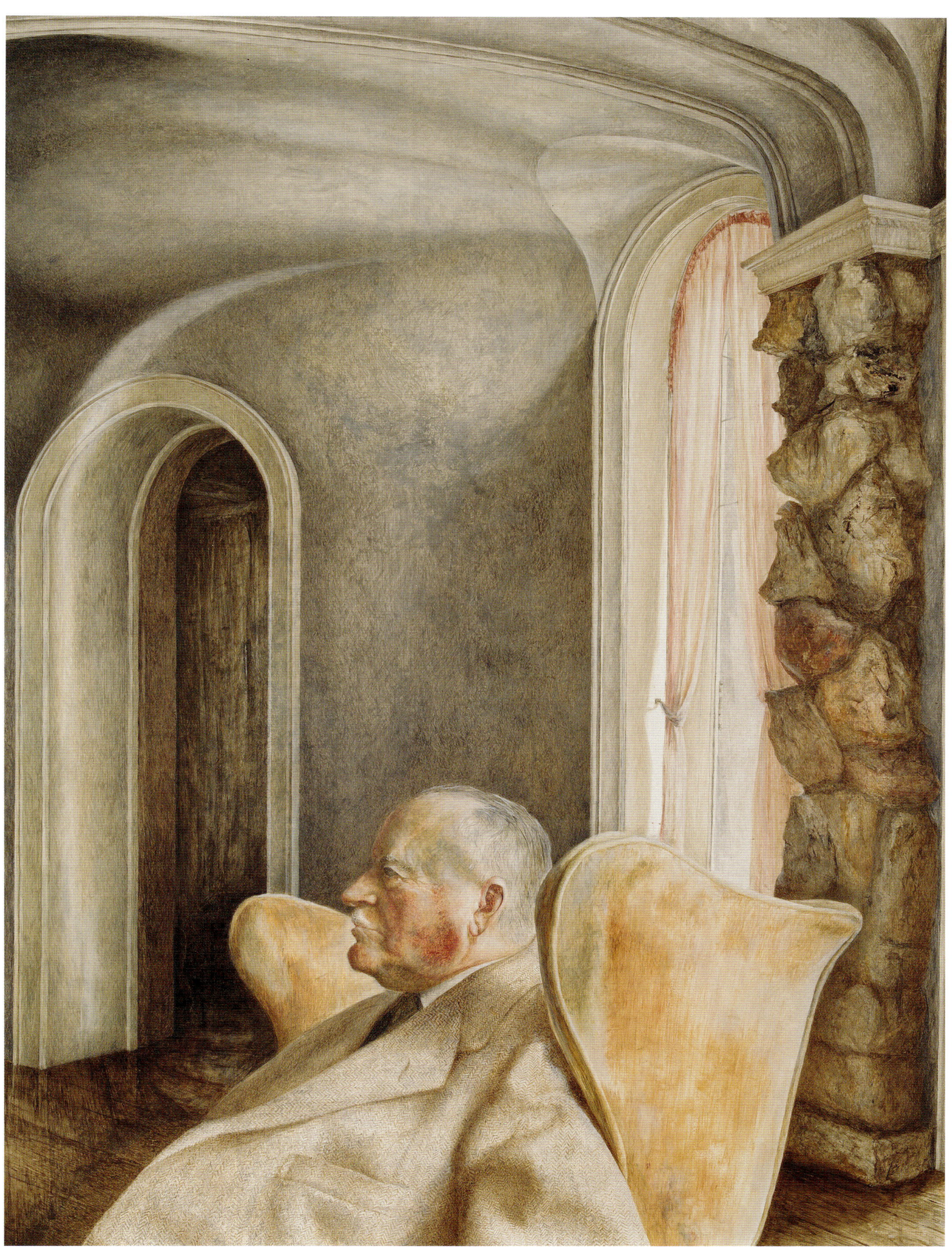

10

***EUGENE ELEUTHÈRE DU PONT*, 1958**

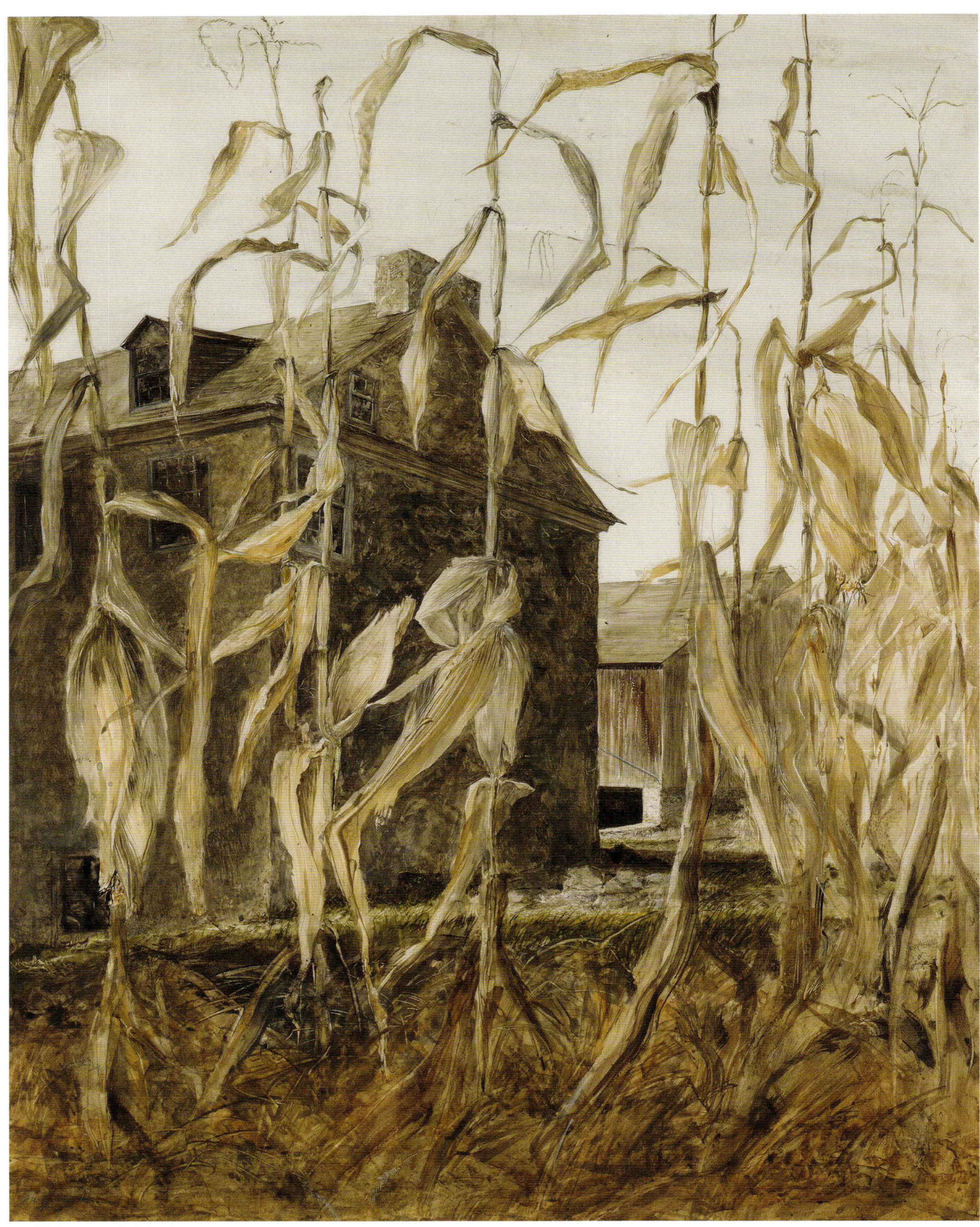

11
CORNFIELDS, 1962

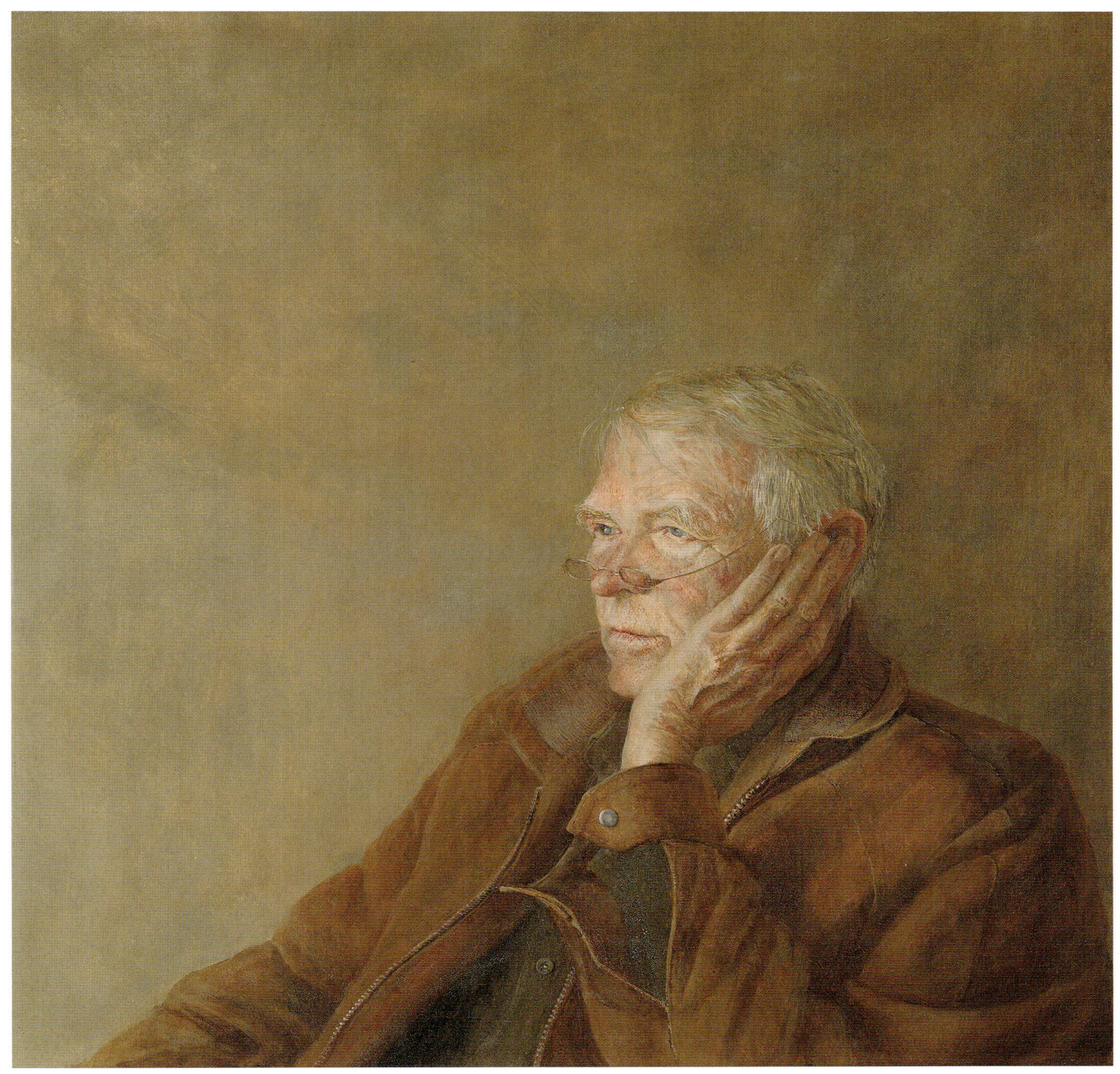

12
***MICHAEL WALL*, 1997**

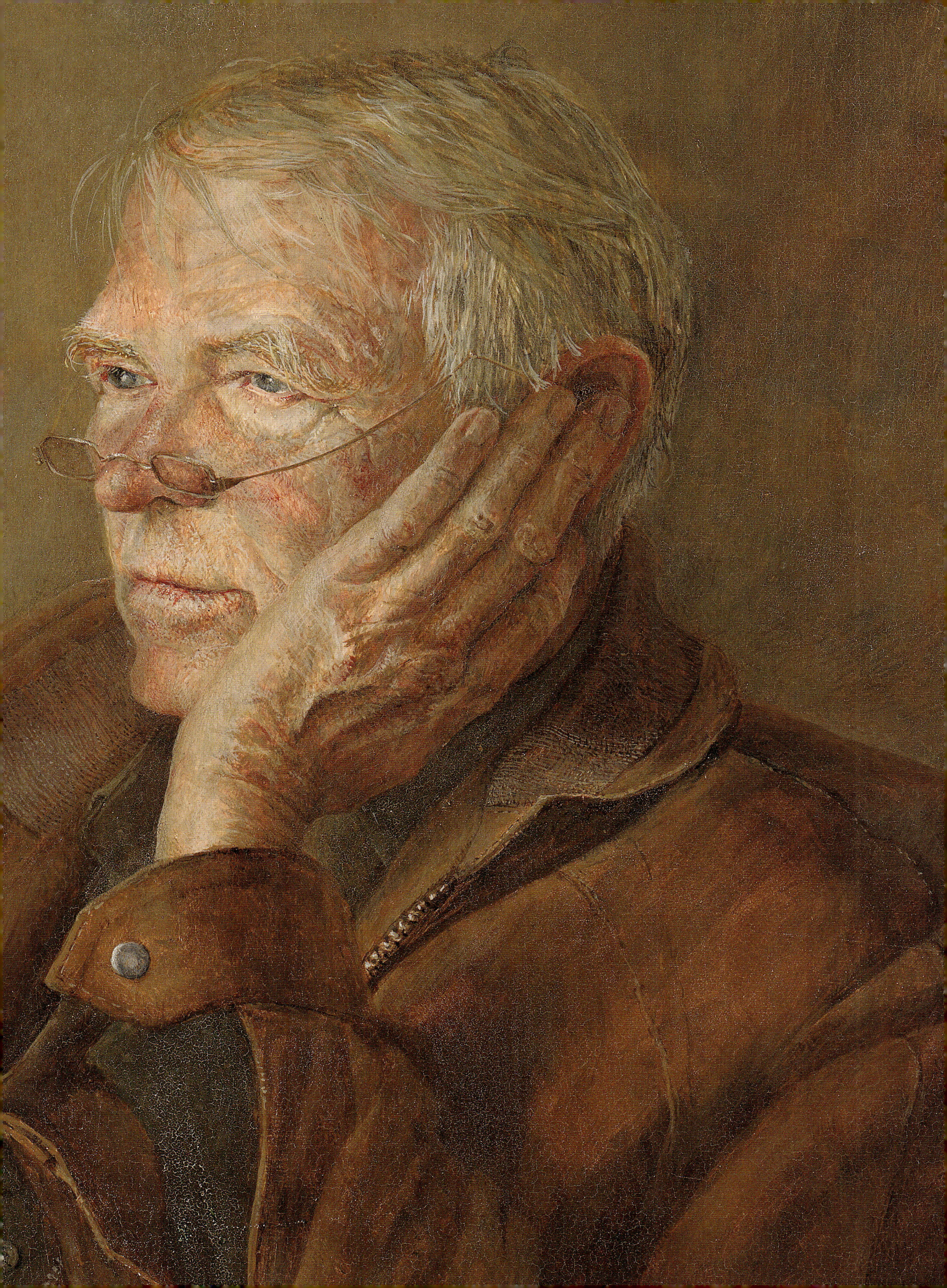

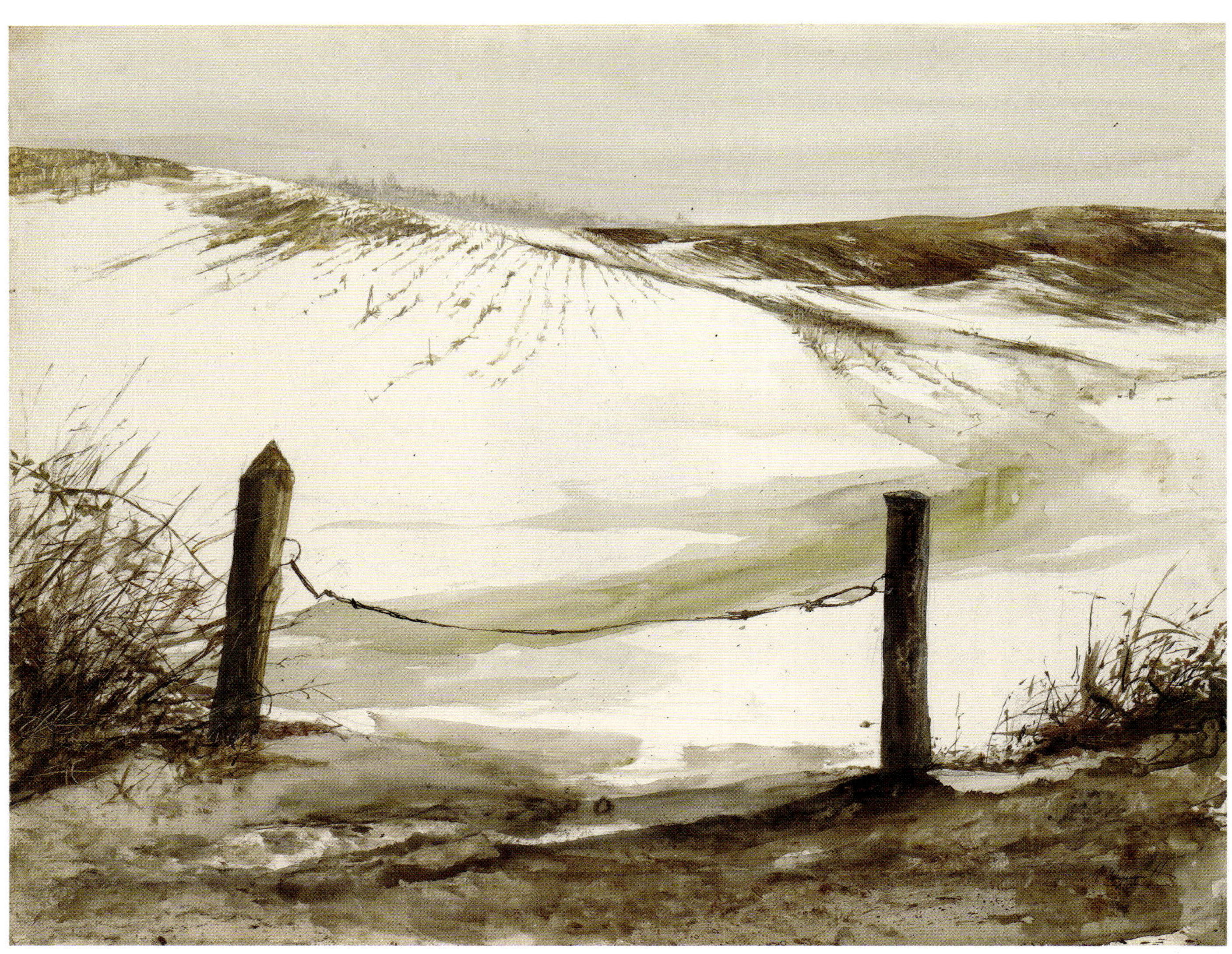

13
UNTITLED (STUDY FOR *MRS. E. MILES VALENTINE*), CA. 1966

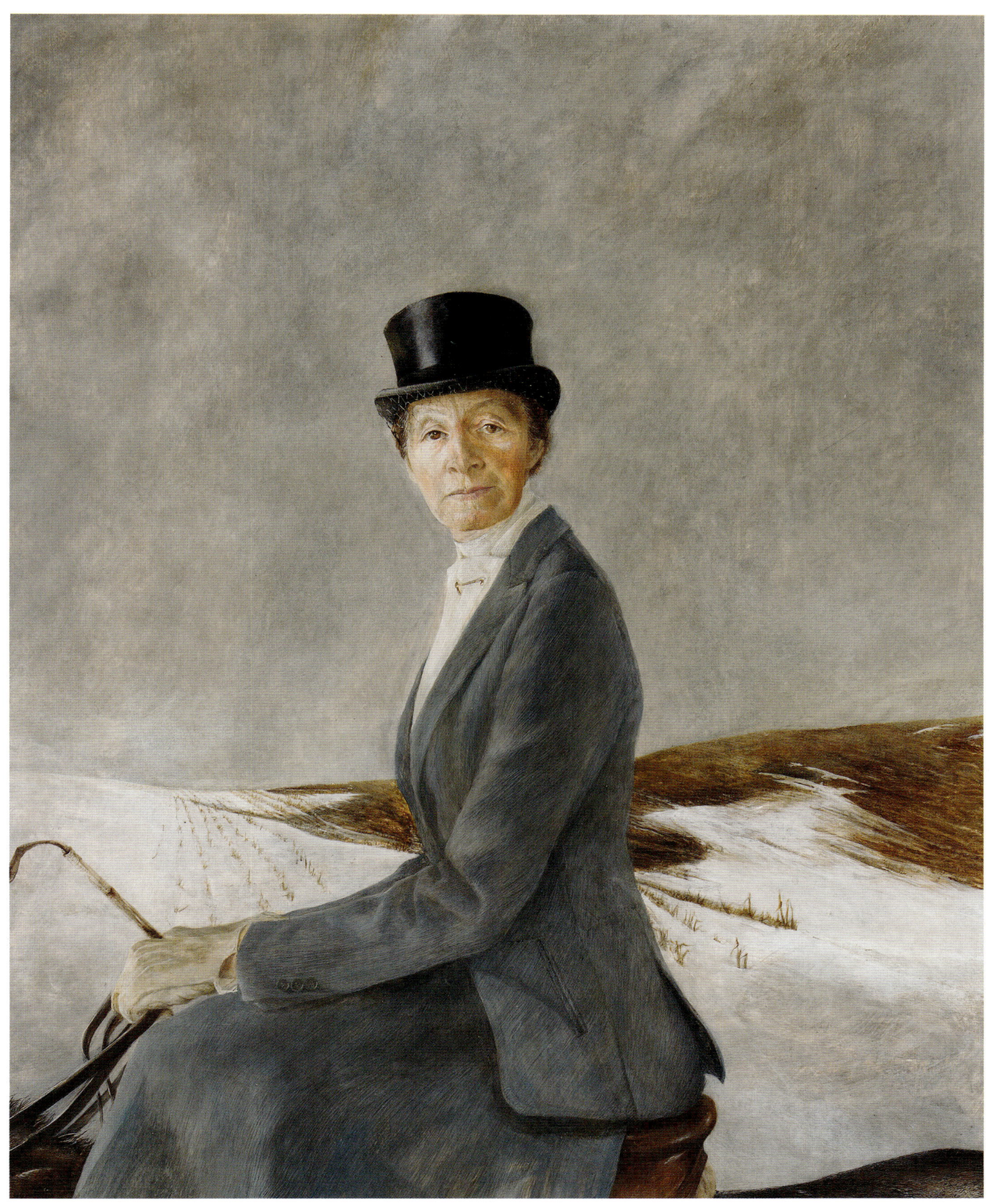

14
***MRS. E. MILES VALENTINE*, 1966**

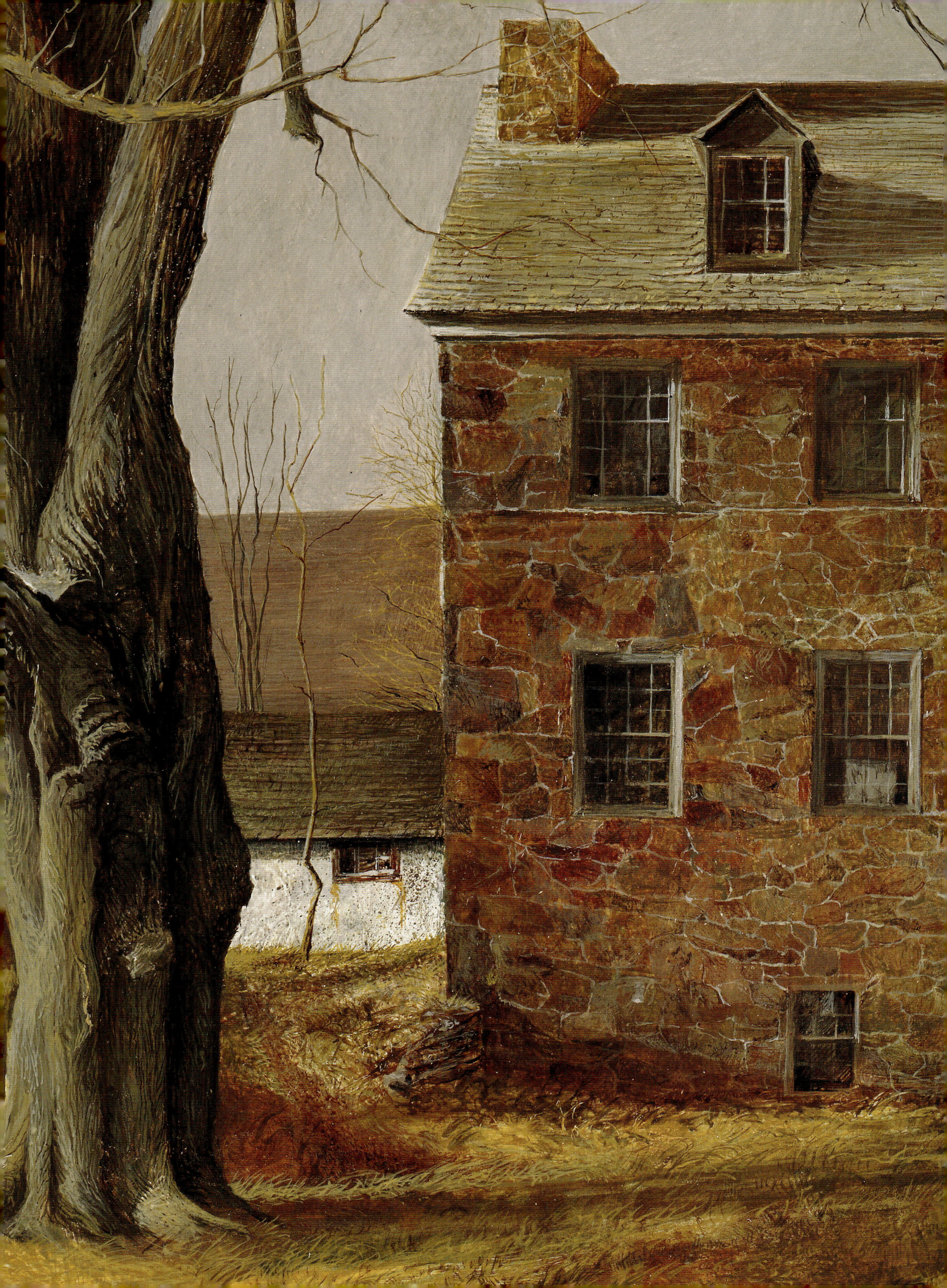

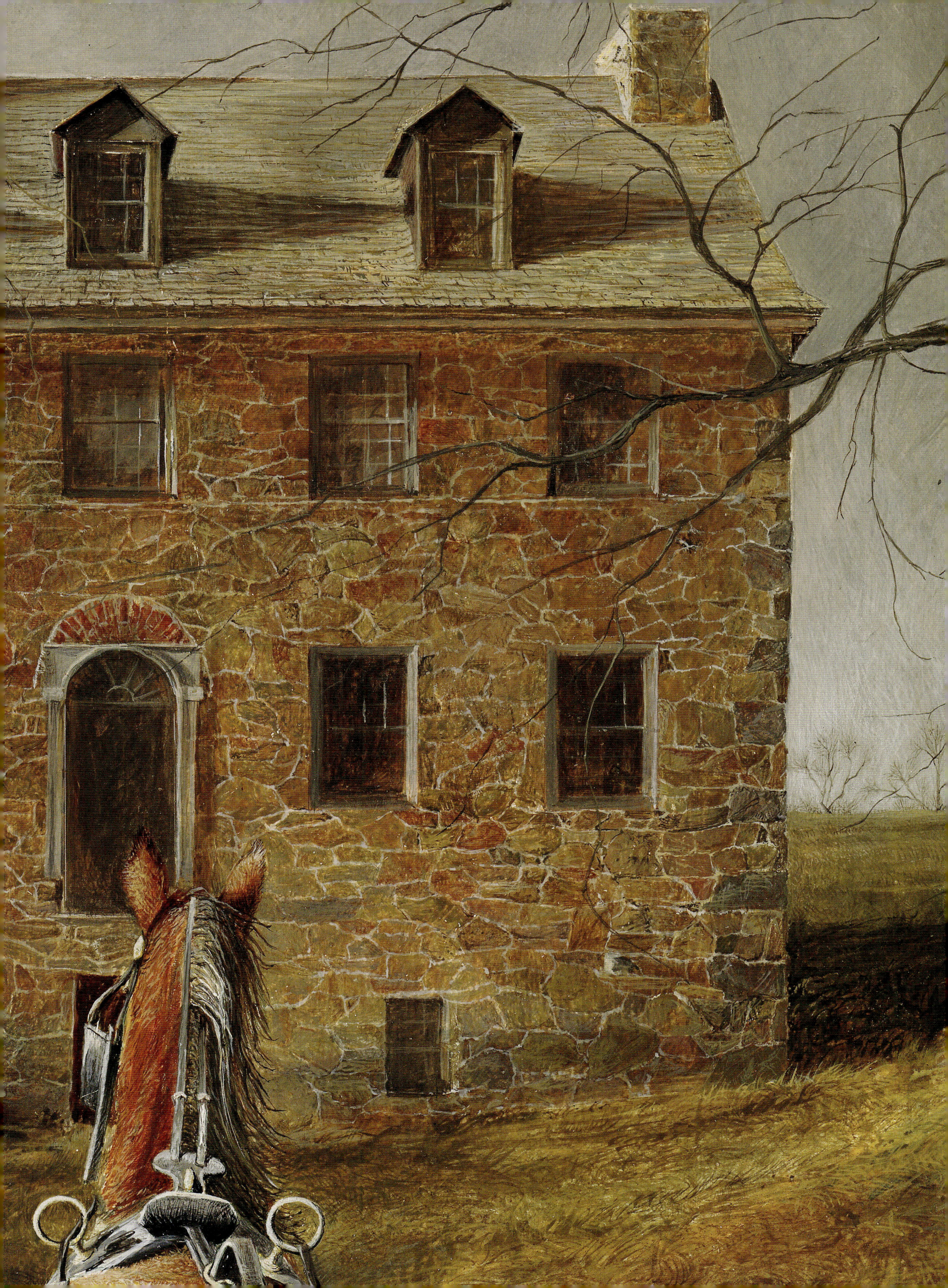

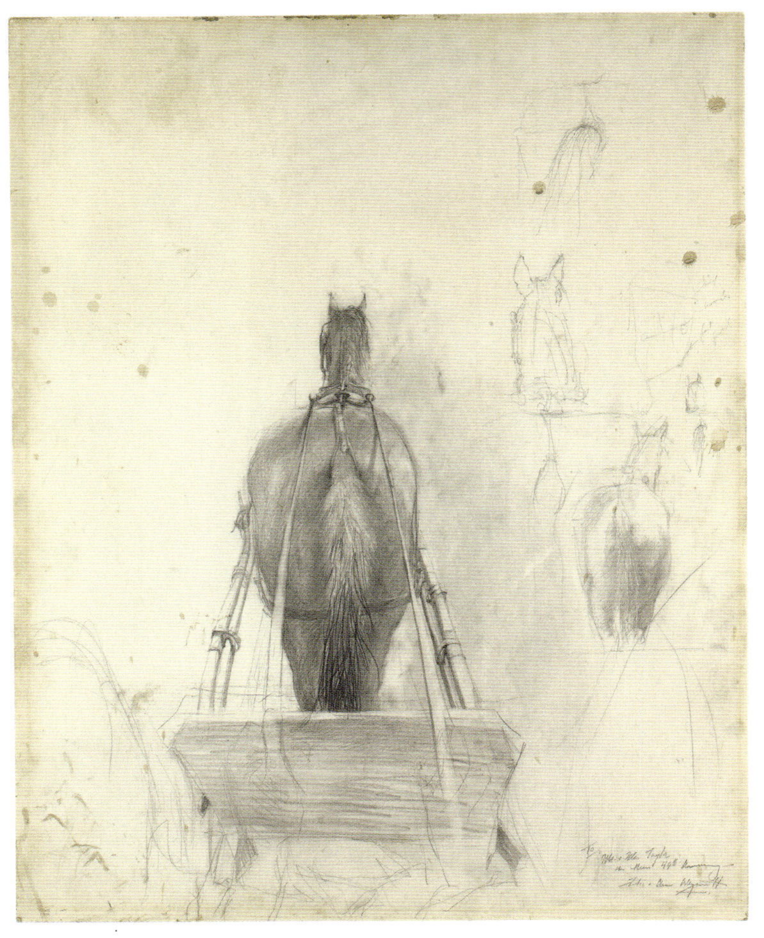

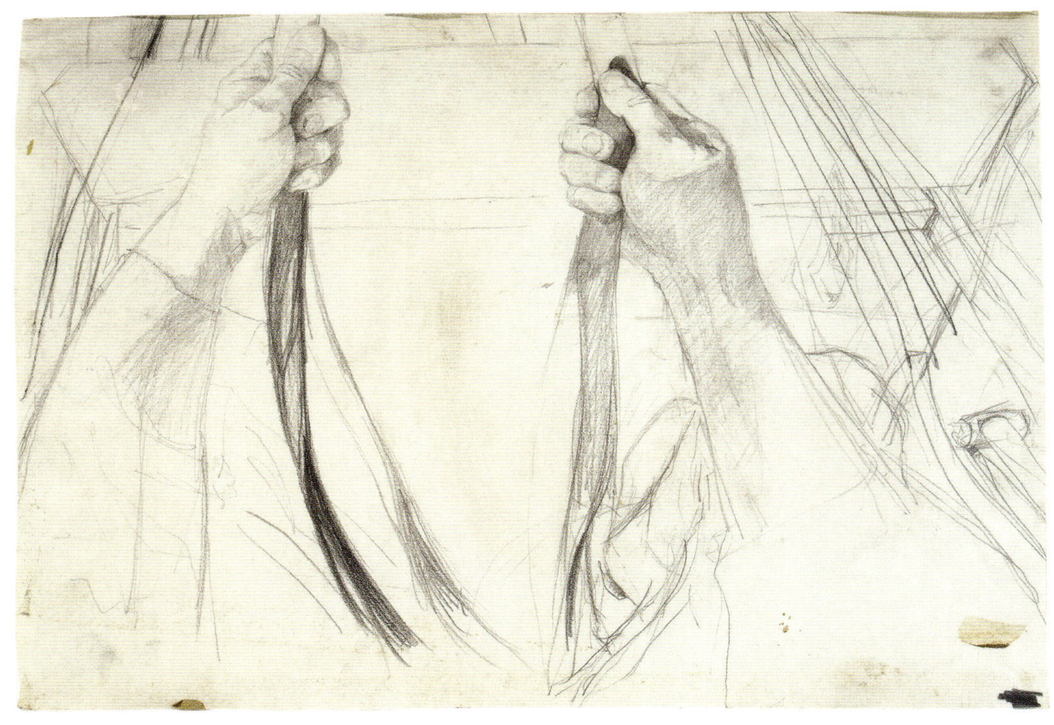

15

STUDY FOR *THE WAY BACK*, 1963

16

STUDY FOR *THE WAY BACK*, 1963

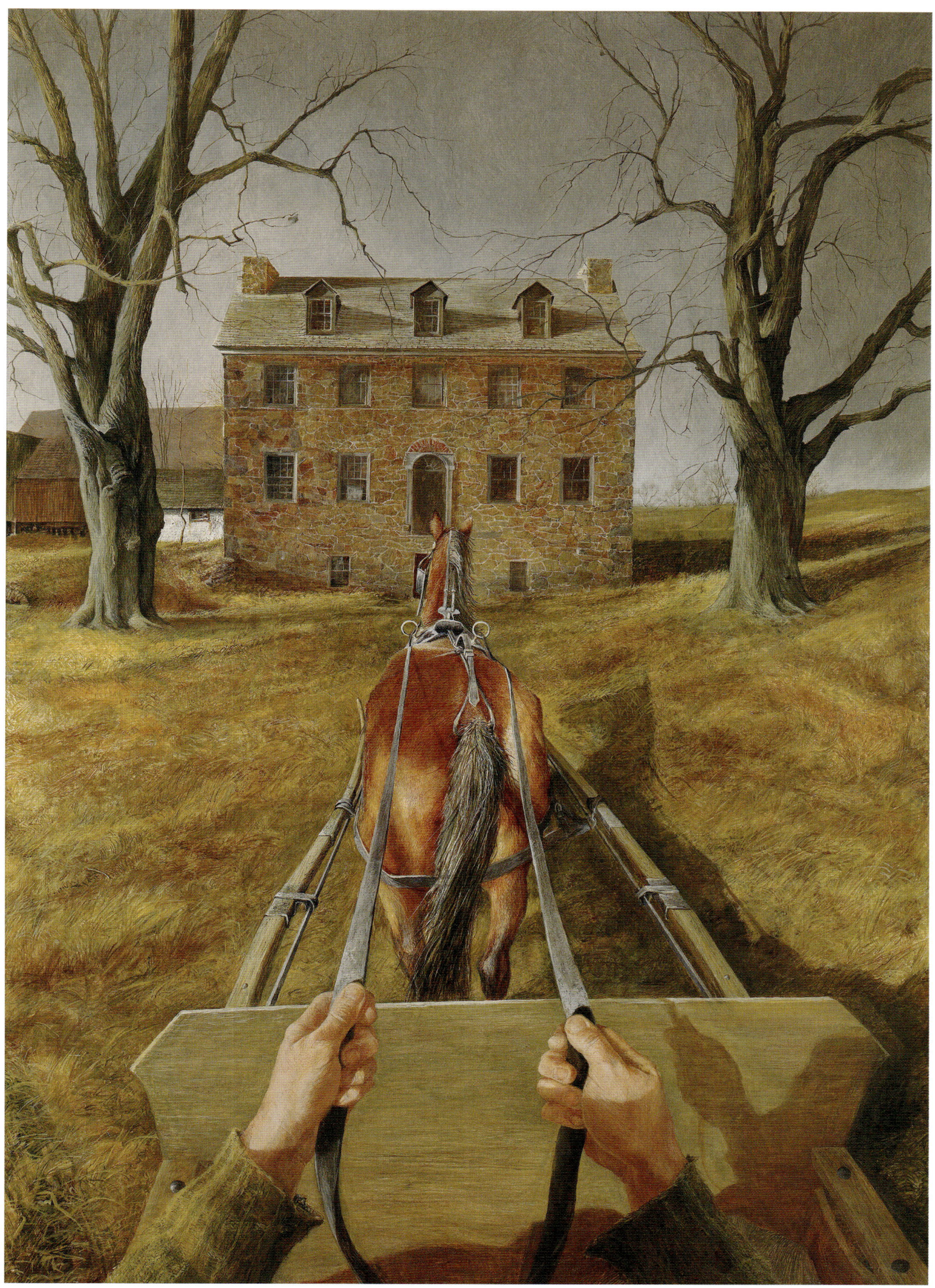

17
***THE WAY BACK*, 1963**

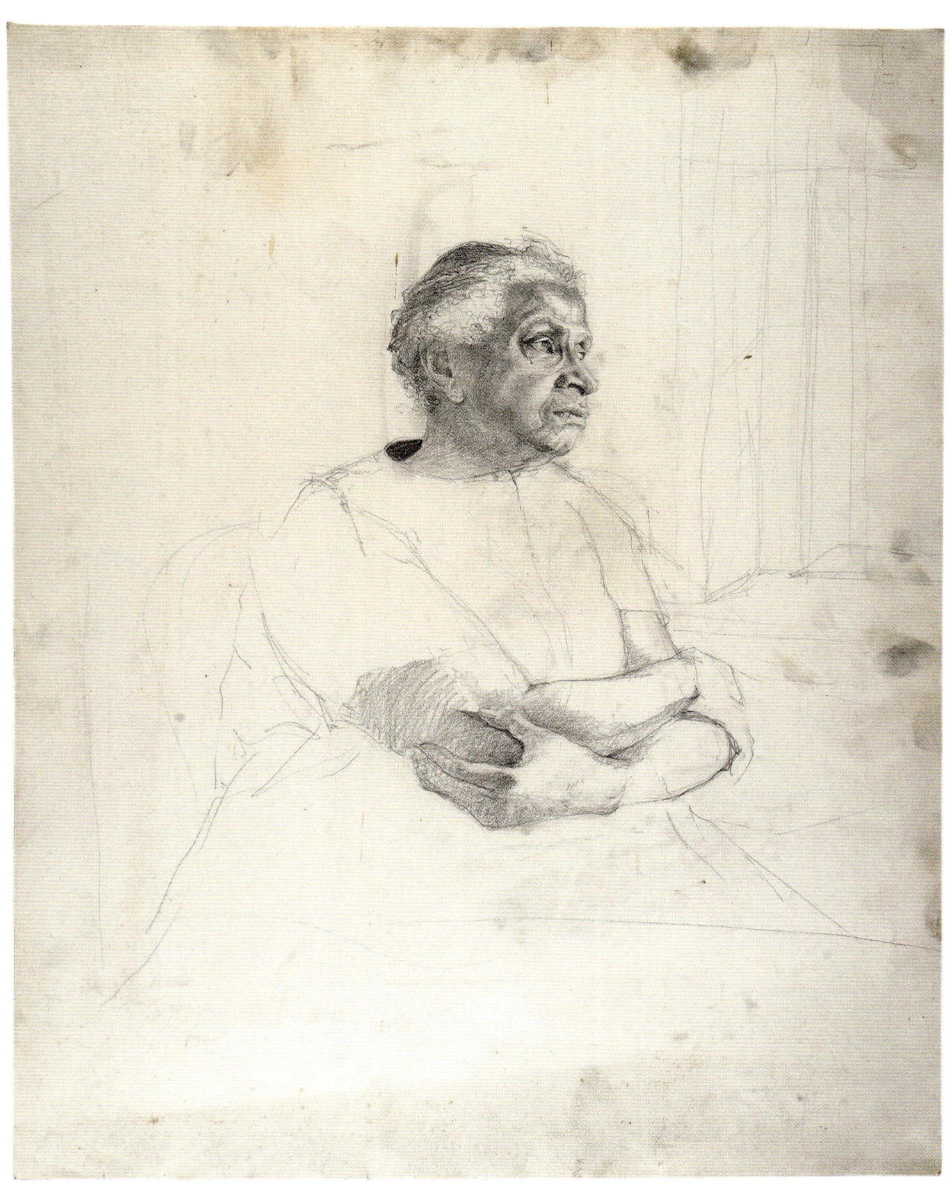

18
STUDY FOR *GATHERING STORM*, 1964

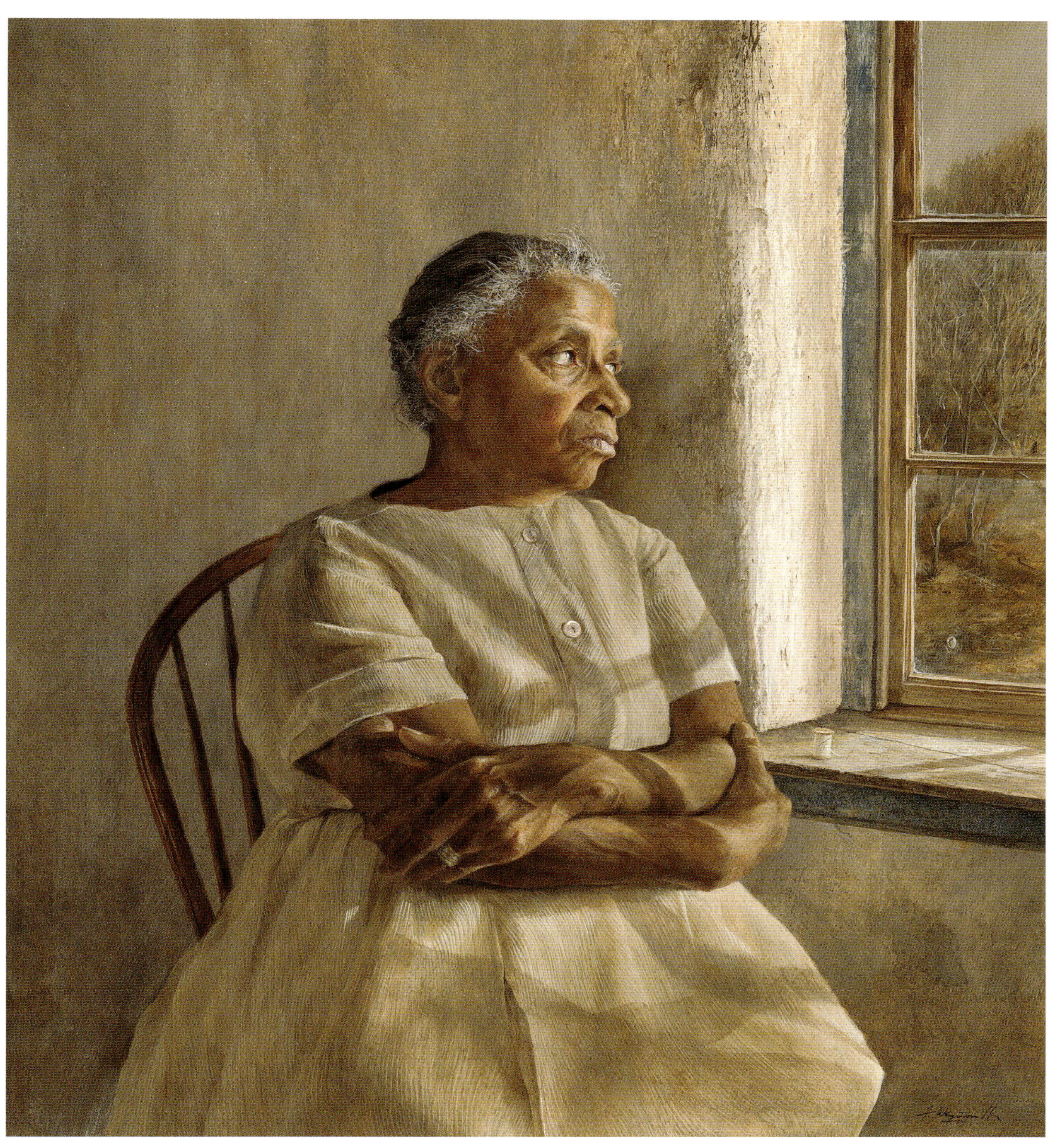

19
GATHERING STORM, 1964

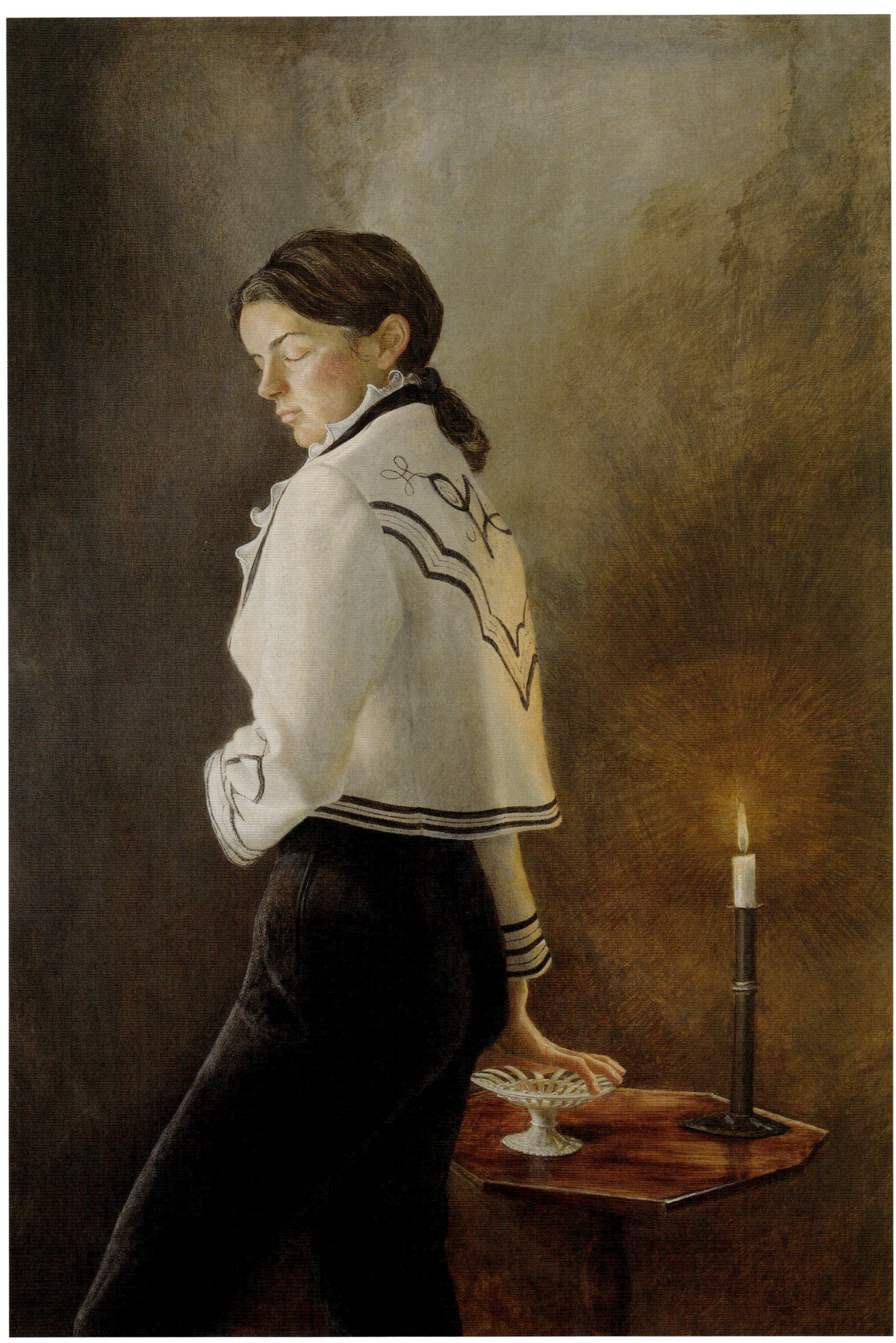

20

***PORTRAIT OF ANNAB*, CA. 1965**

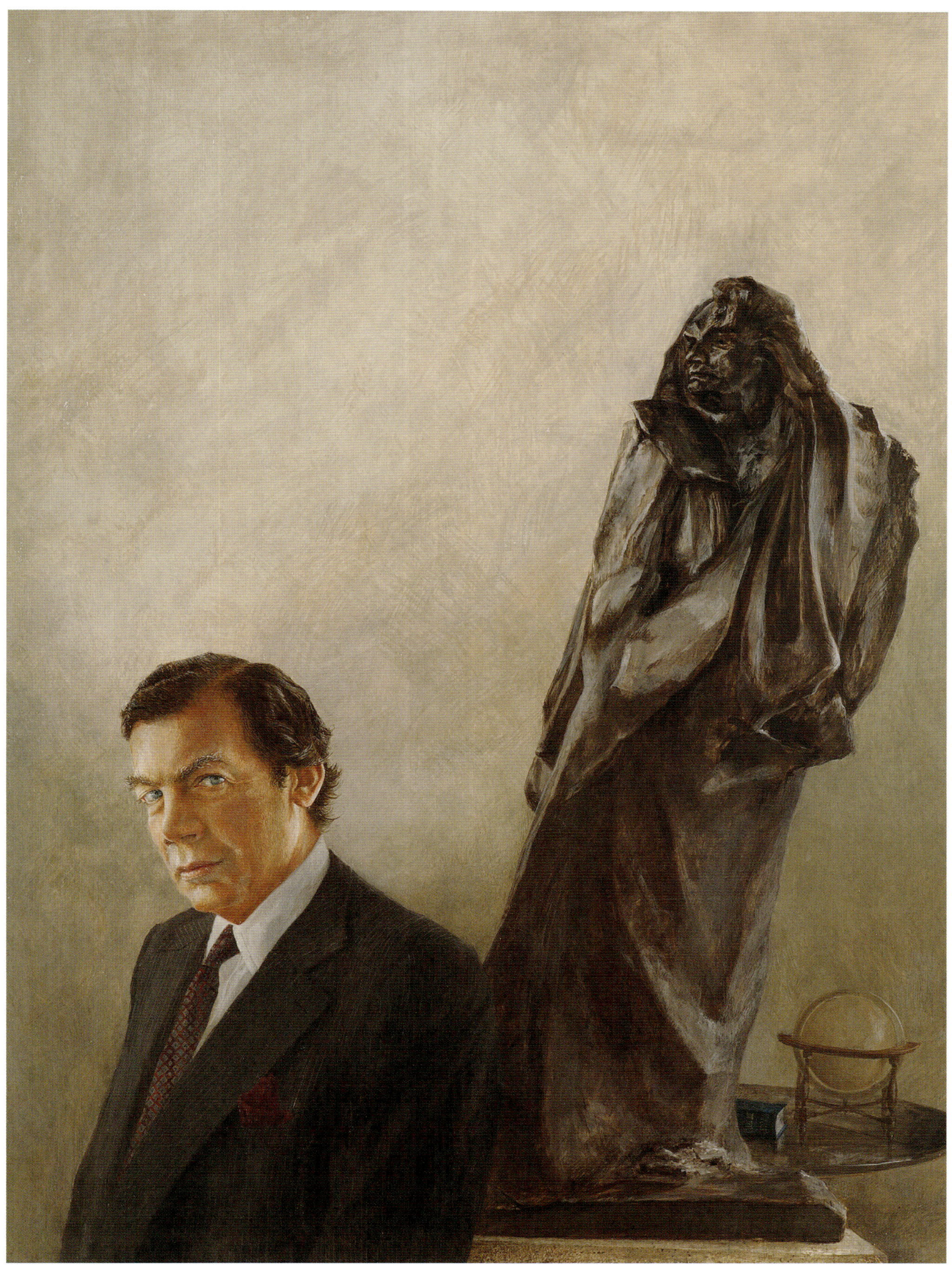

21
EDGAR BRONFMAN, 1980-81

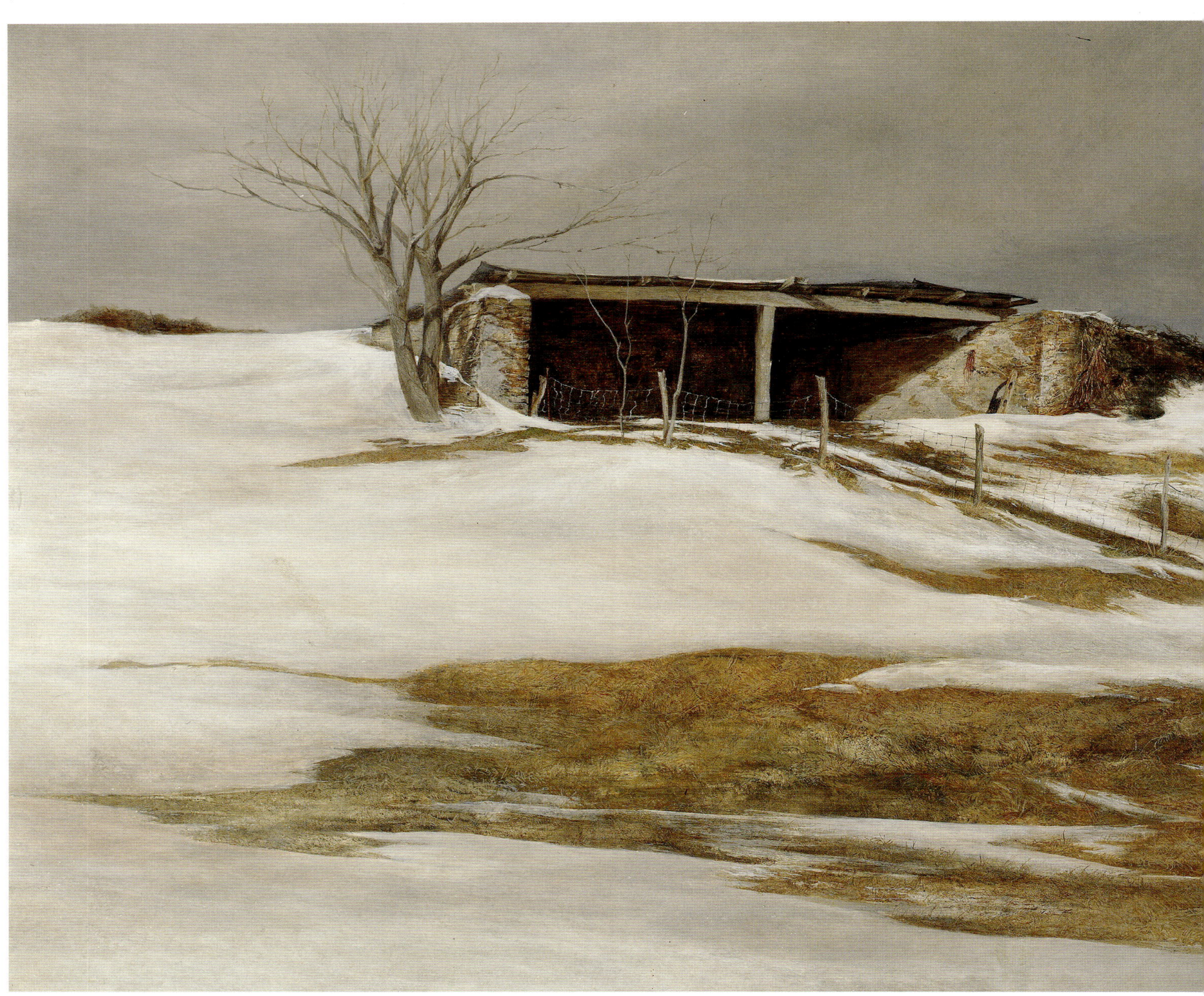

22
***THE SHELTER*, 1964**

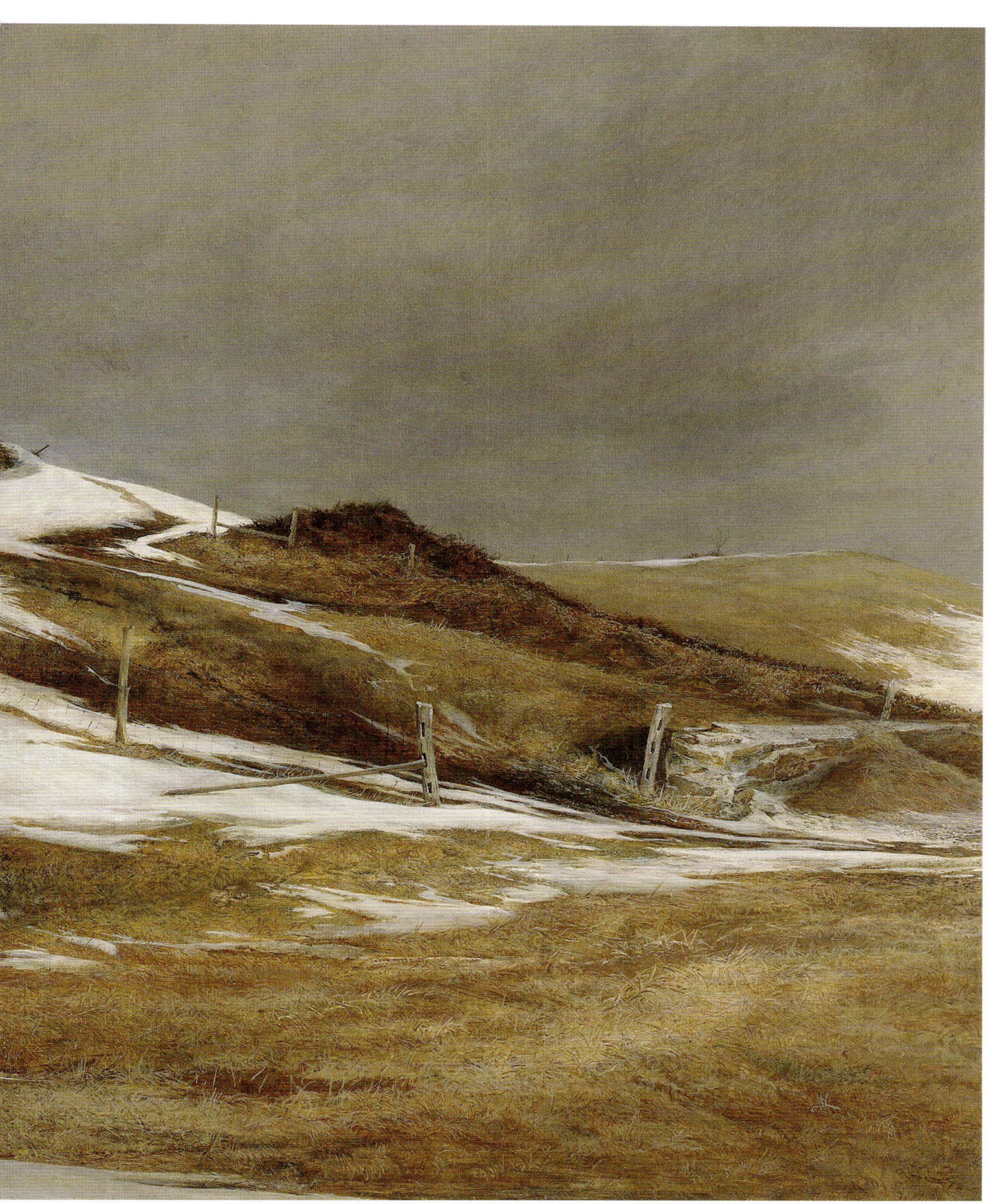

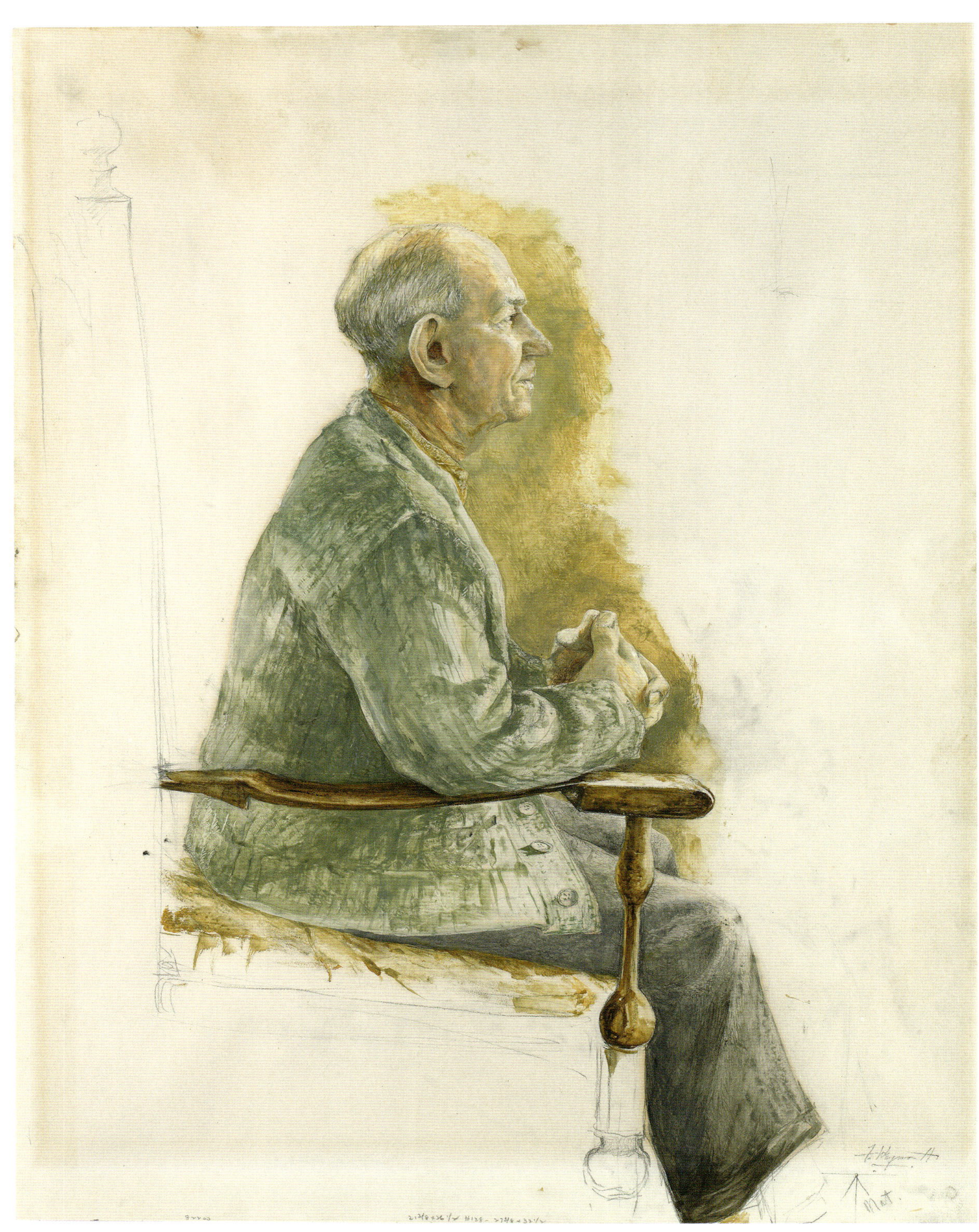

23
***BUCKLEY*, 1964**

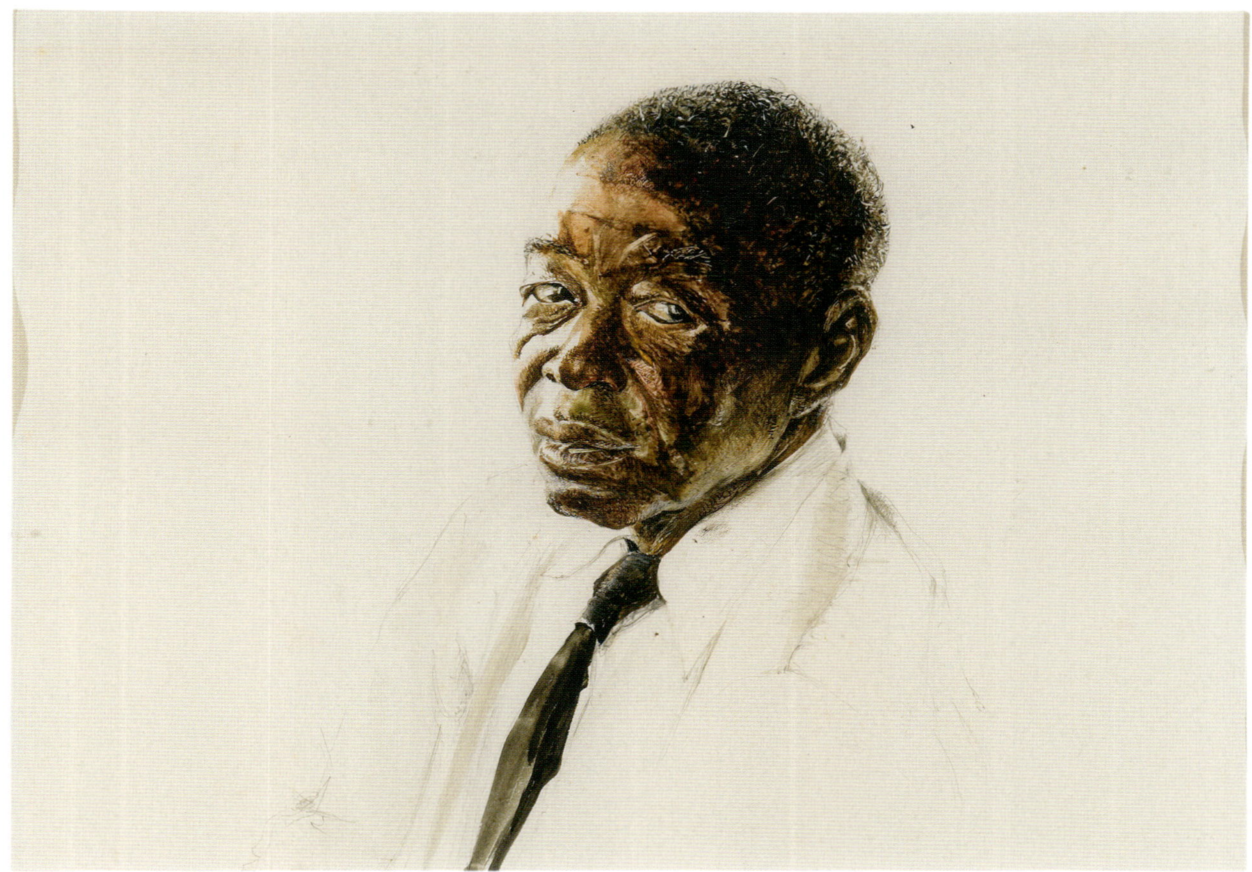

24
***MR. HILTON TAYLOR*, 1962**

25

***ELEVEN O'CLOCK NEWS*, 1966**

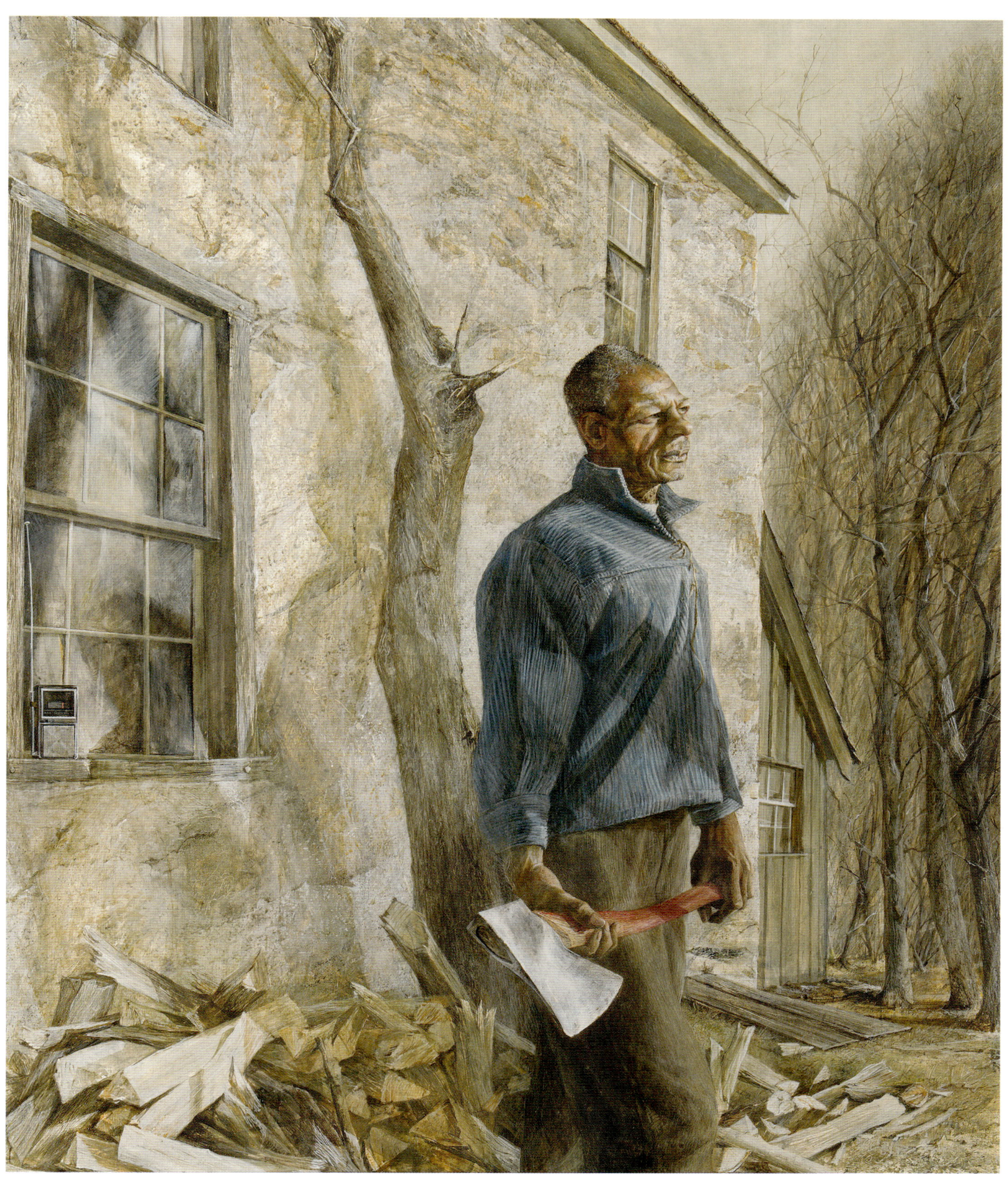

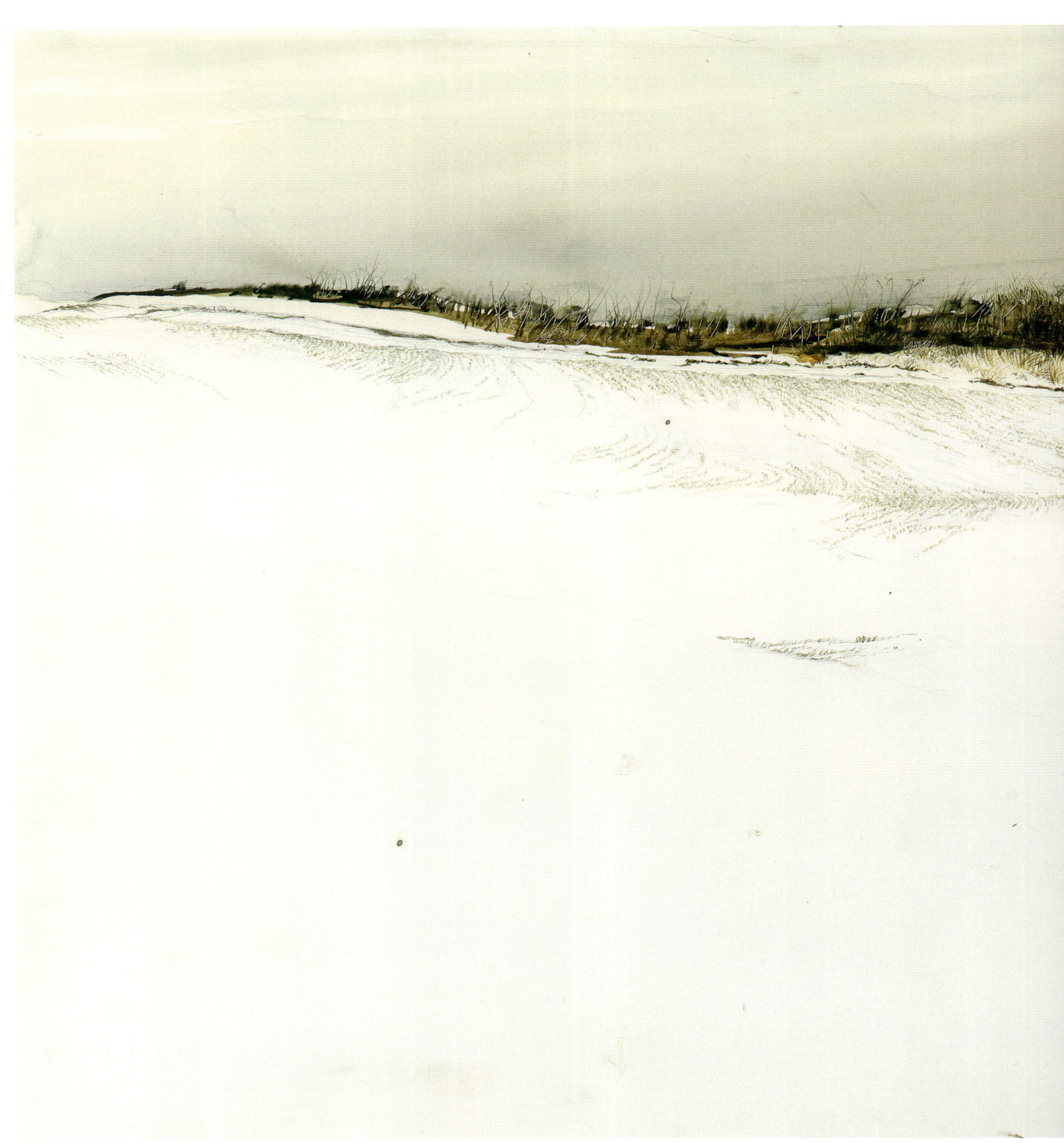

26
***ROBIN'S HOUSE*, 1972**

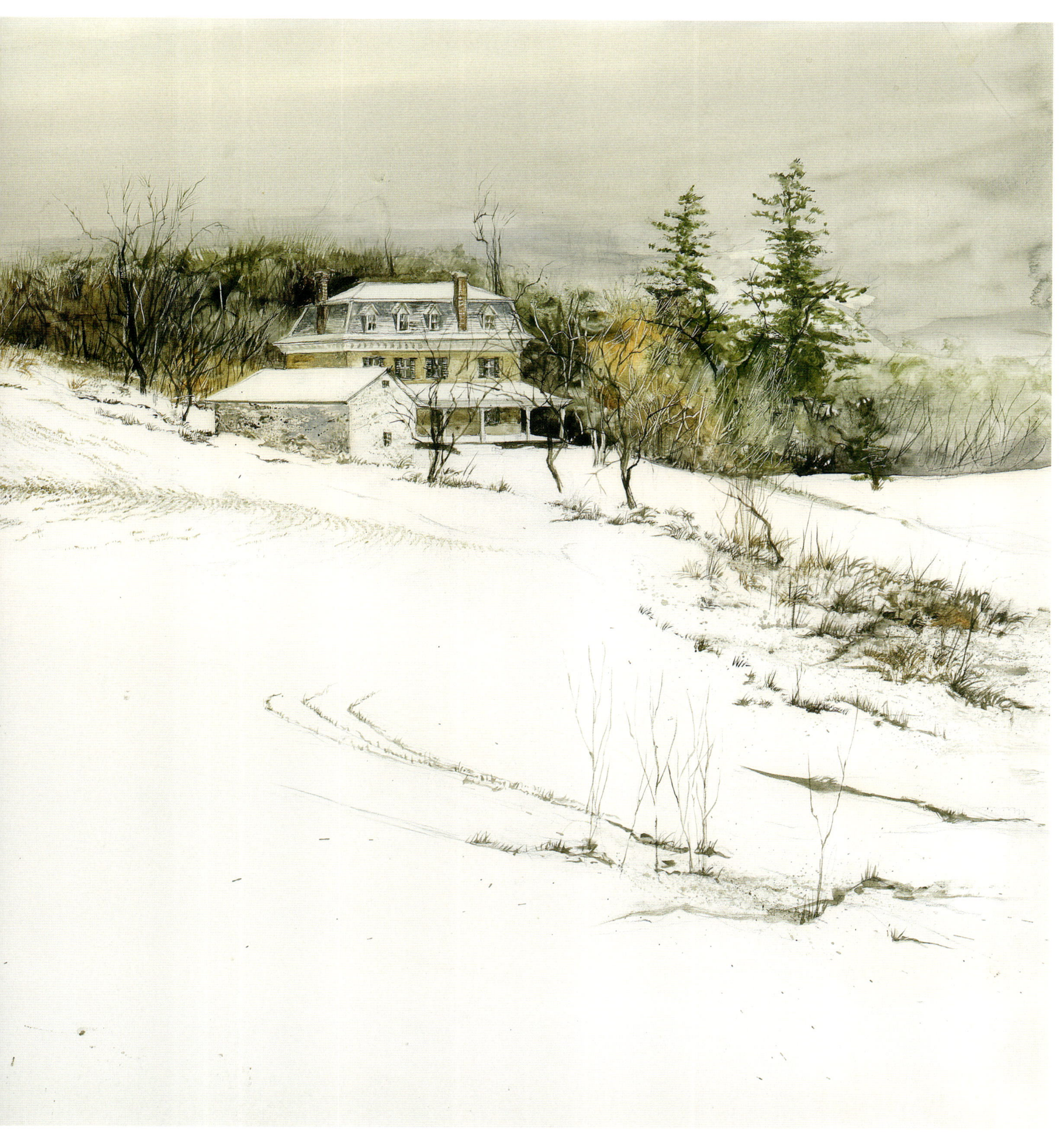

27

COUNTESS WESTMORLAND, 1985

28

MAC WEYMOUTH, 1990

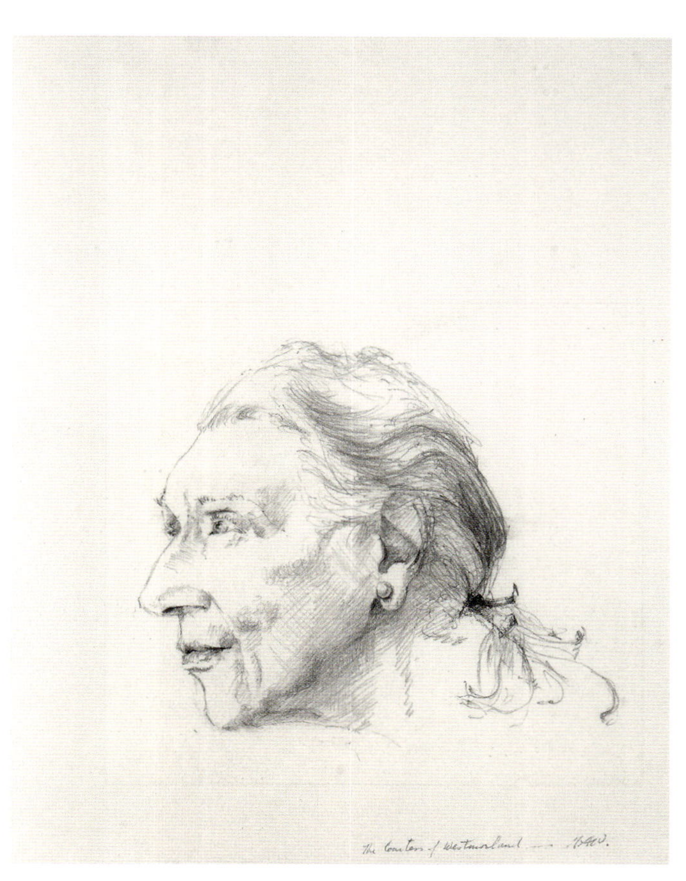

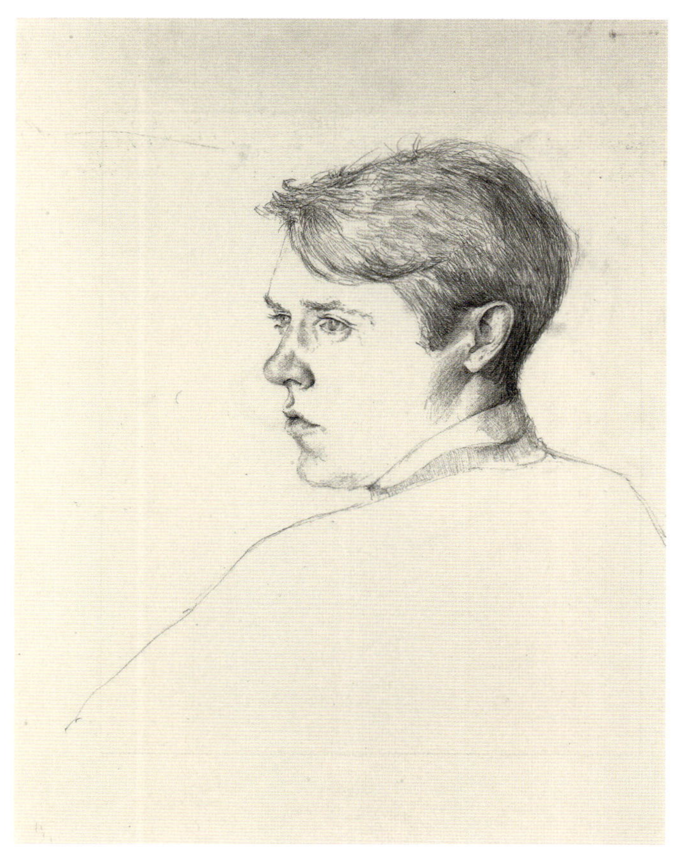

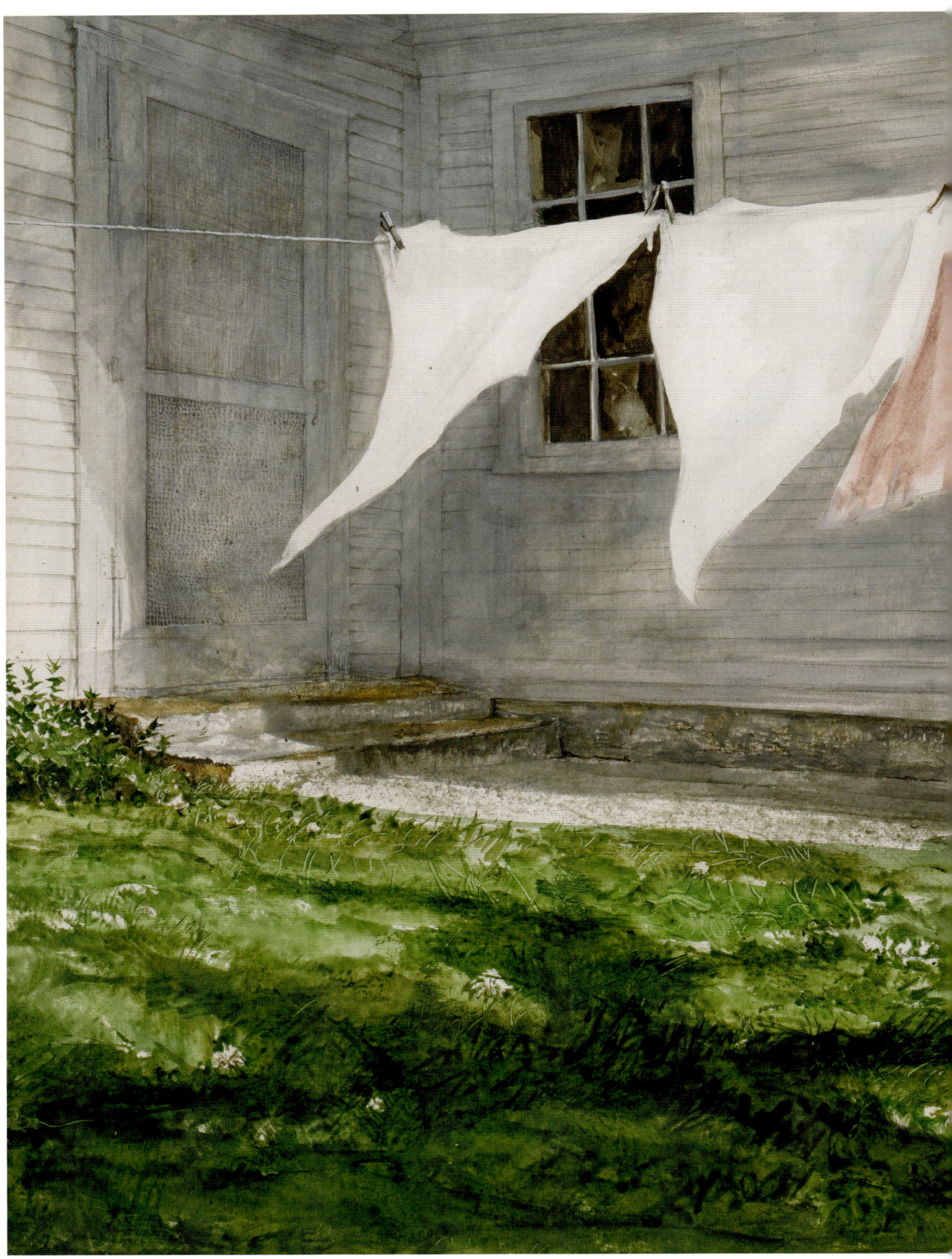

29
CLOTHESLINE, 1971

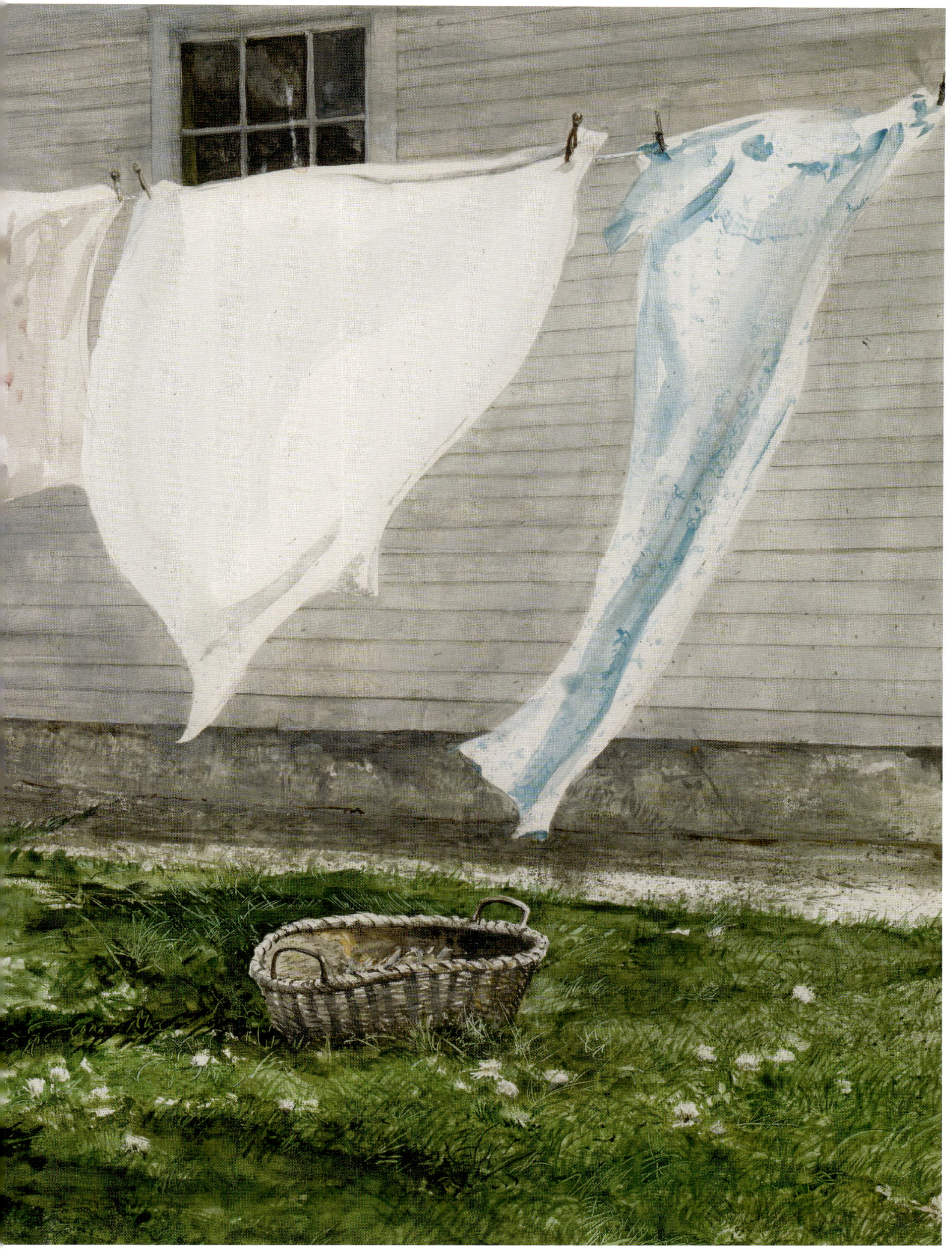

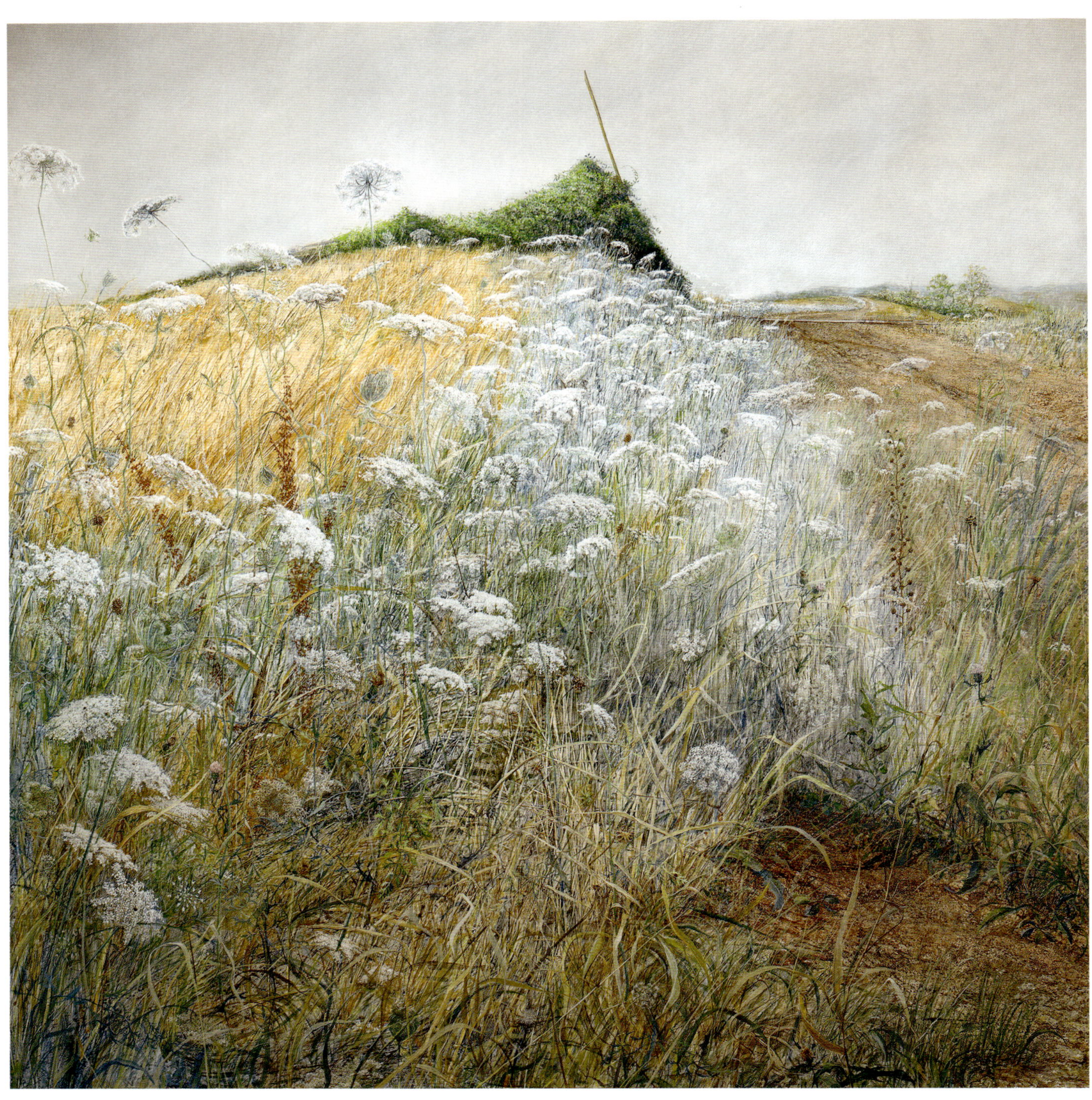

30

***AUGUST*, 1974**

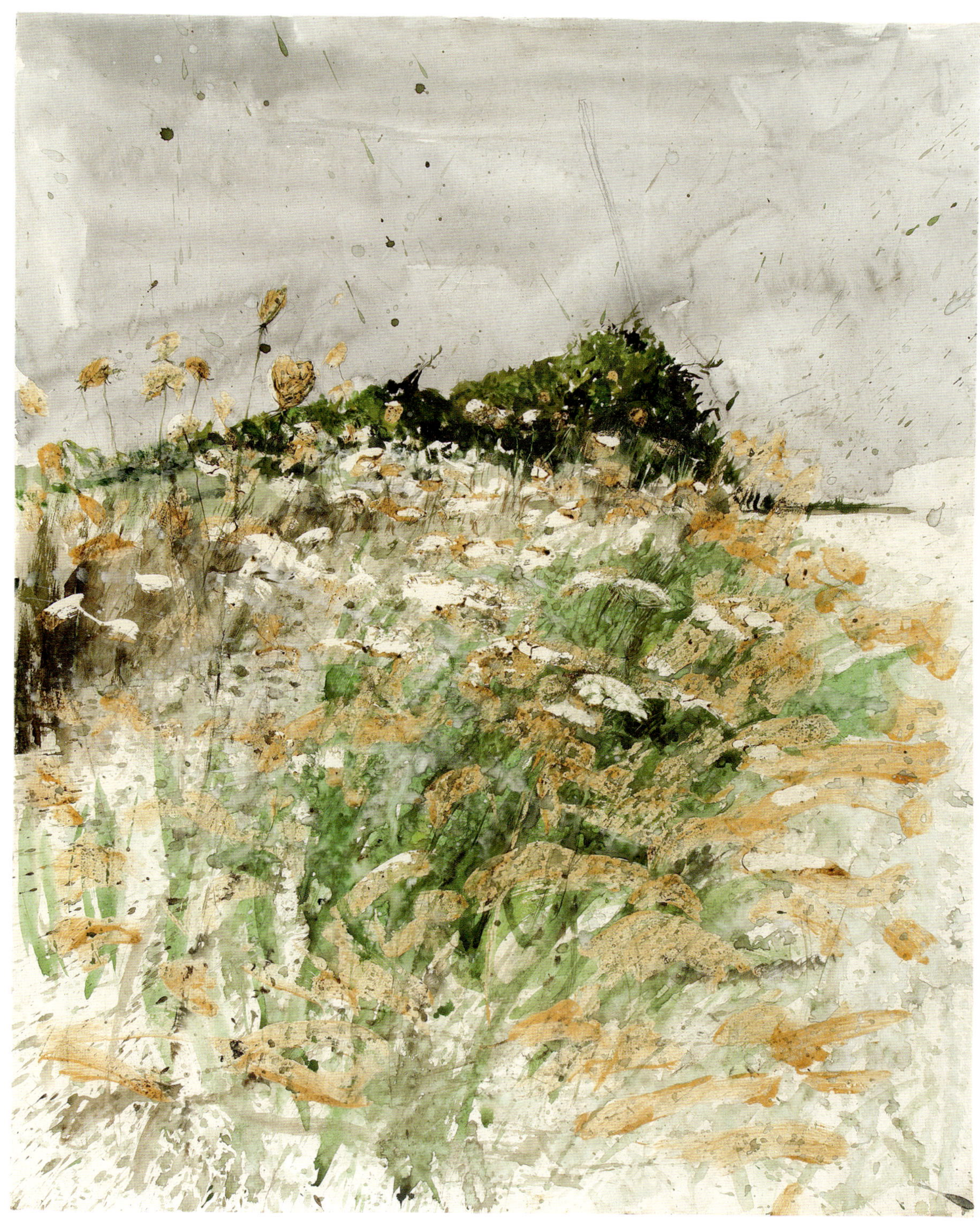

31

STUDY FOR *AUGUST*, 1974

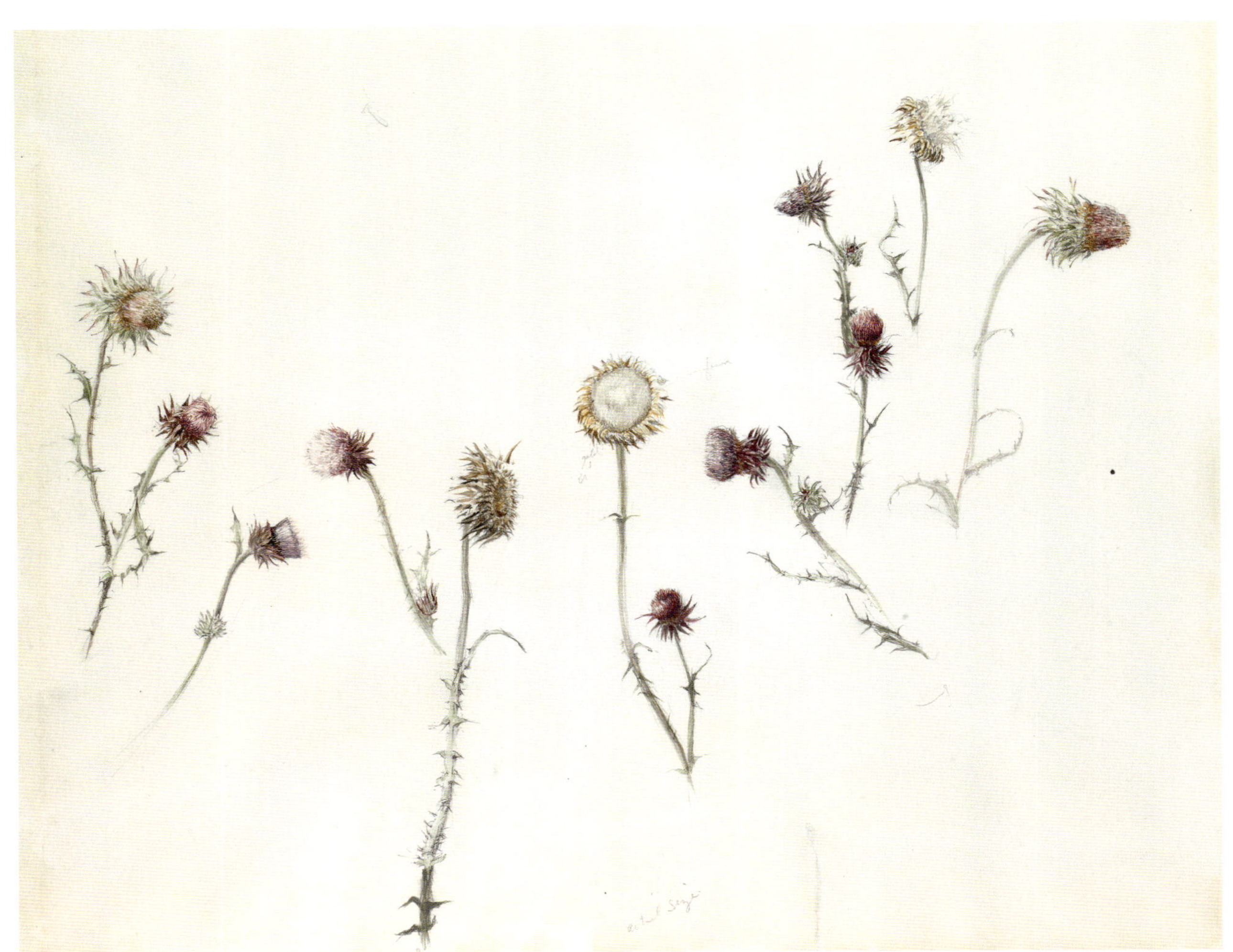

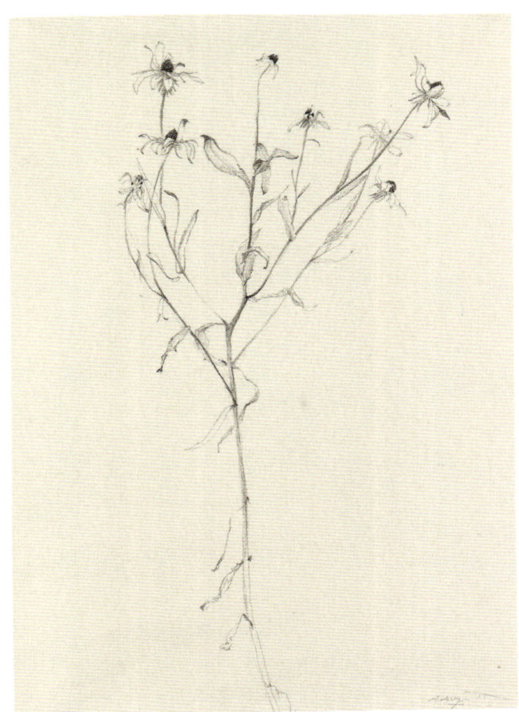

32
STUDY FOR *AUGUST*, #1, 1974

33
STUDY FOR *AUGUST*, #2, 1974

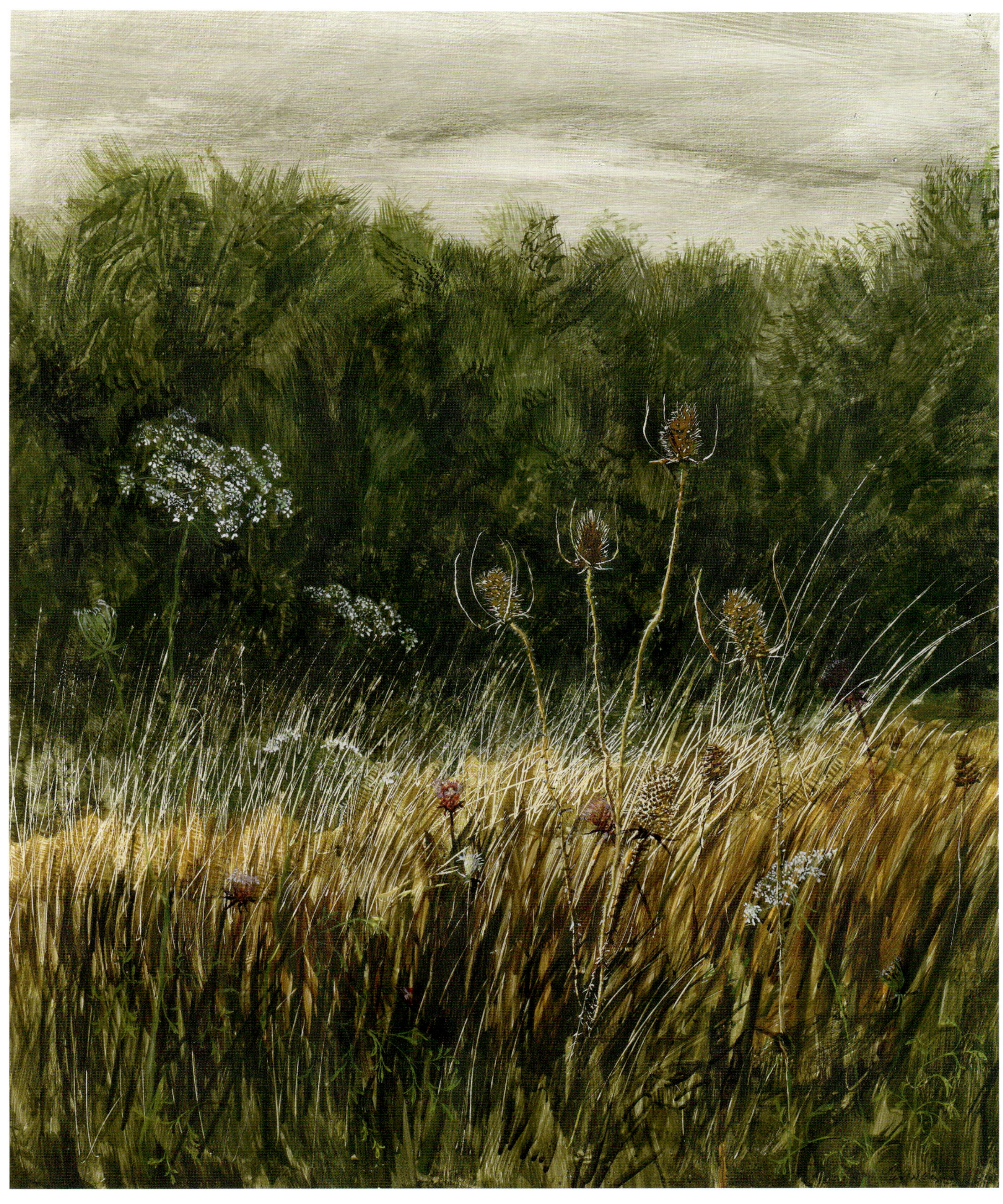

34
***TEASEL*, 2000**

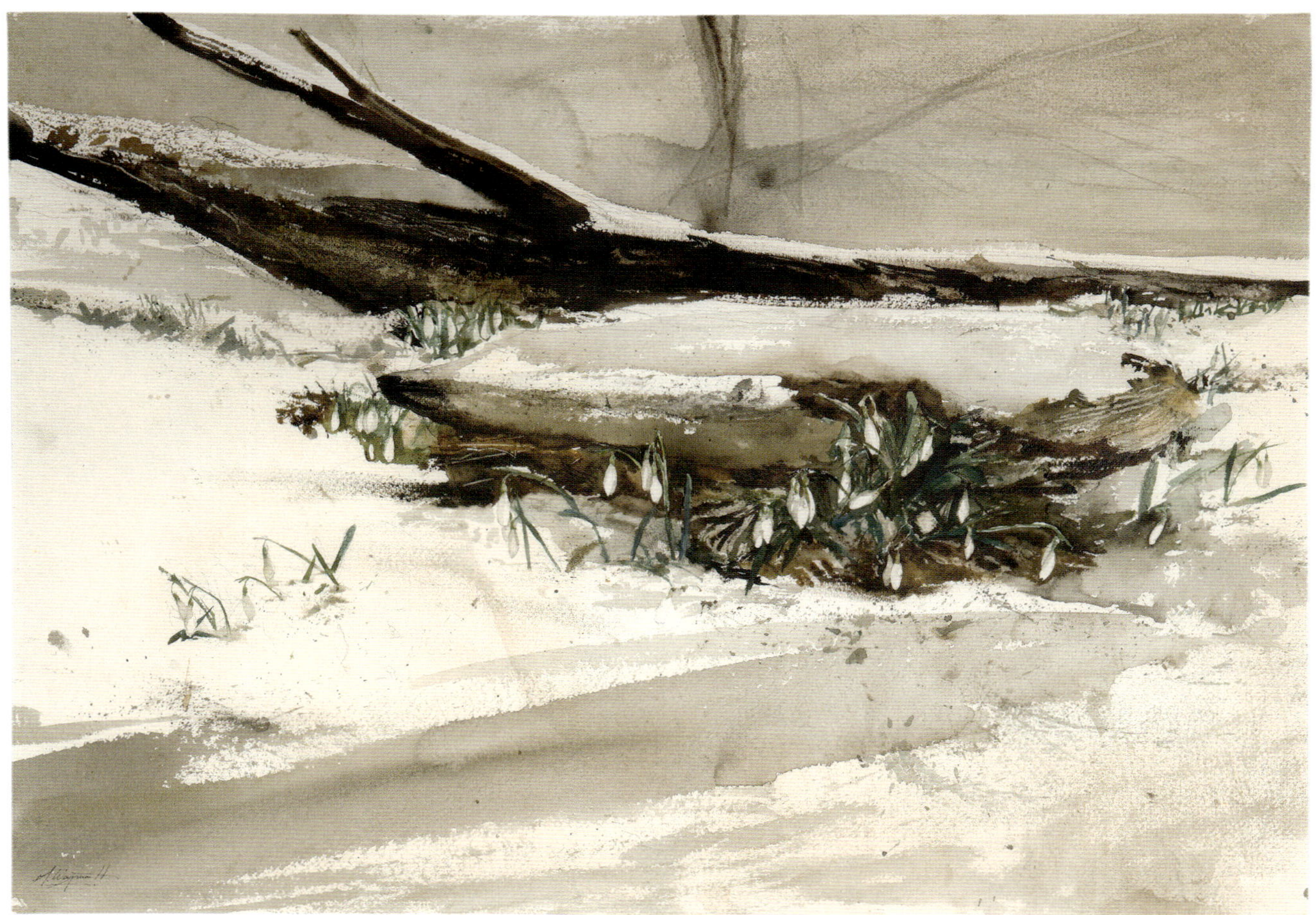

35
SNOW DRIFTS, 1966

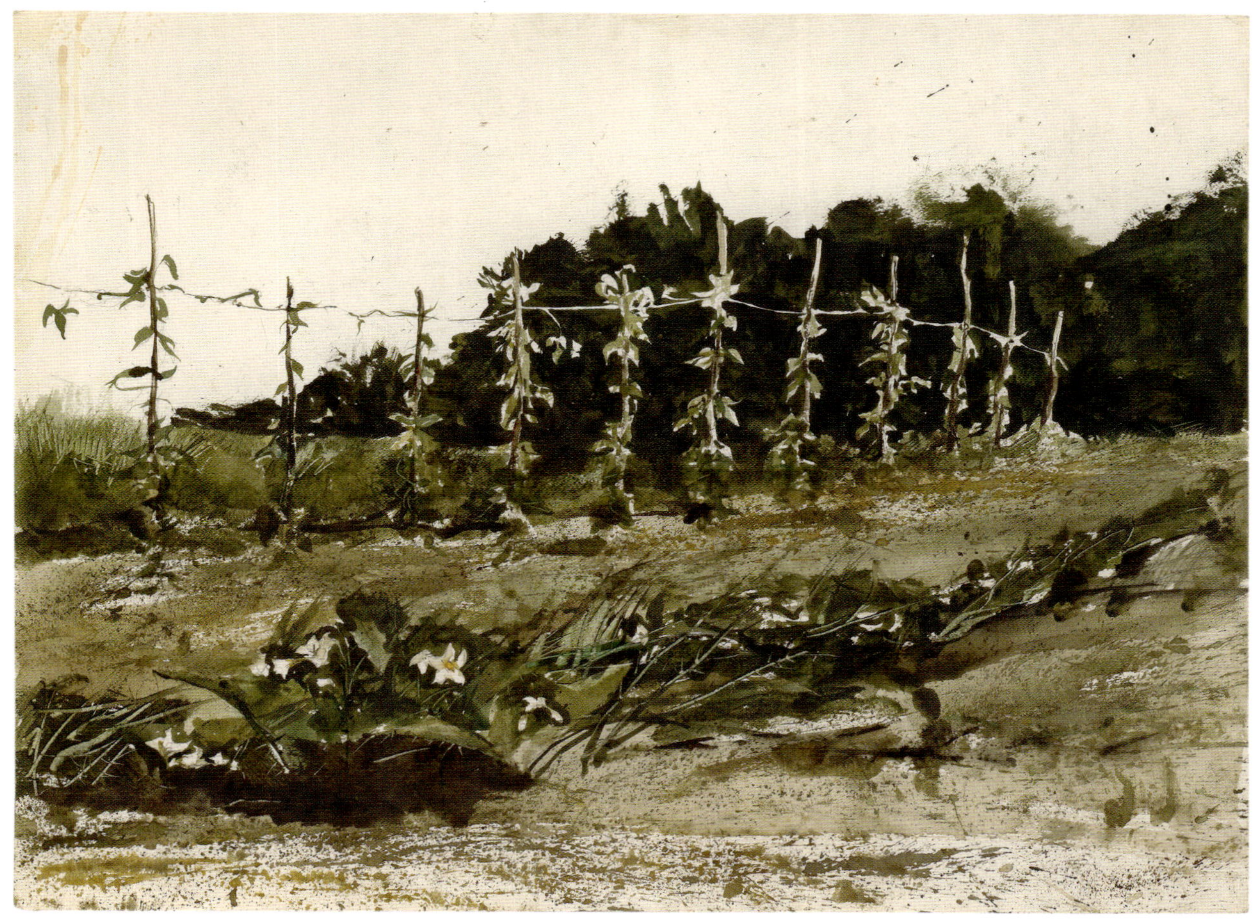

36
UNTITLED (*POLE BEANS*), CA. 1990

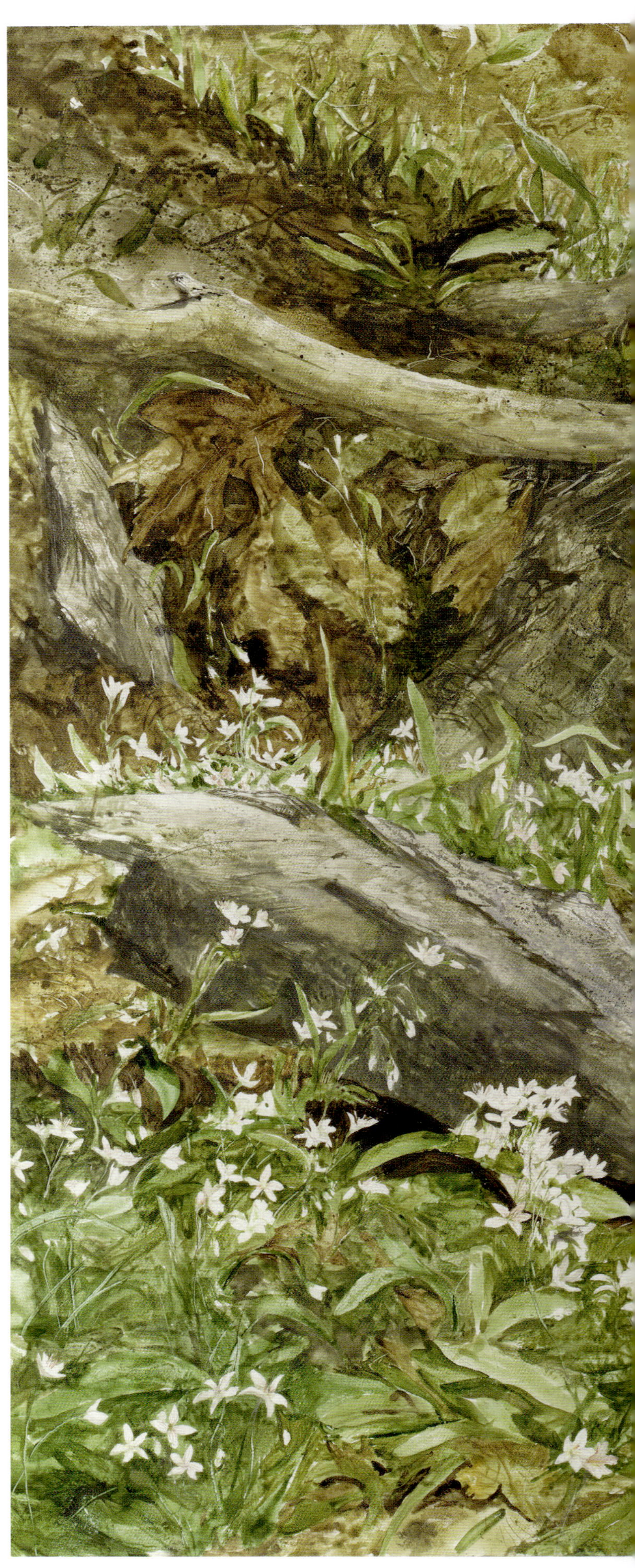

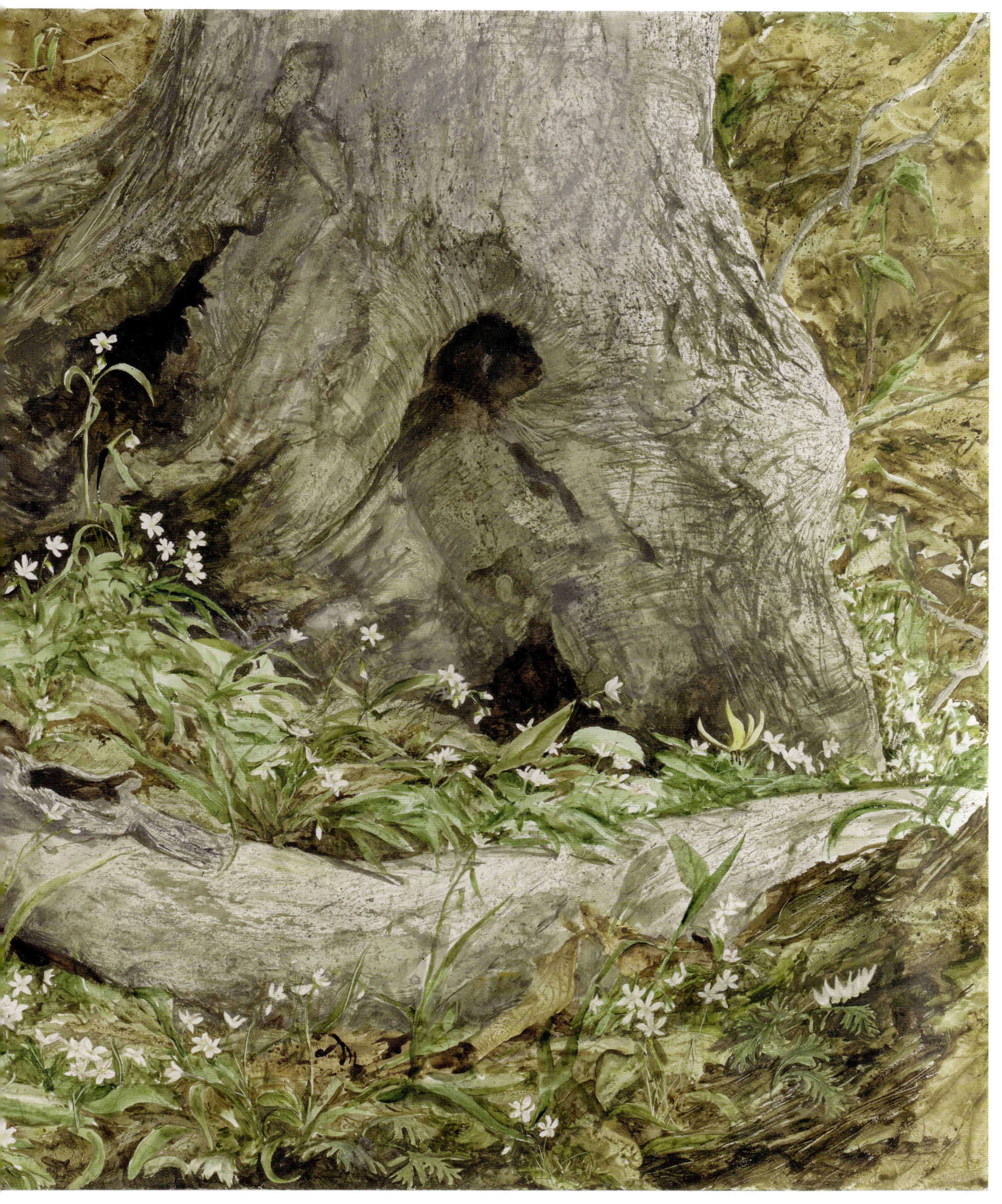

37
TREE TRUNKS, 1968

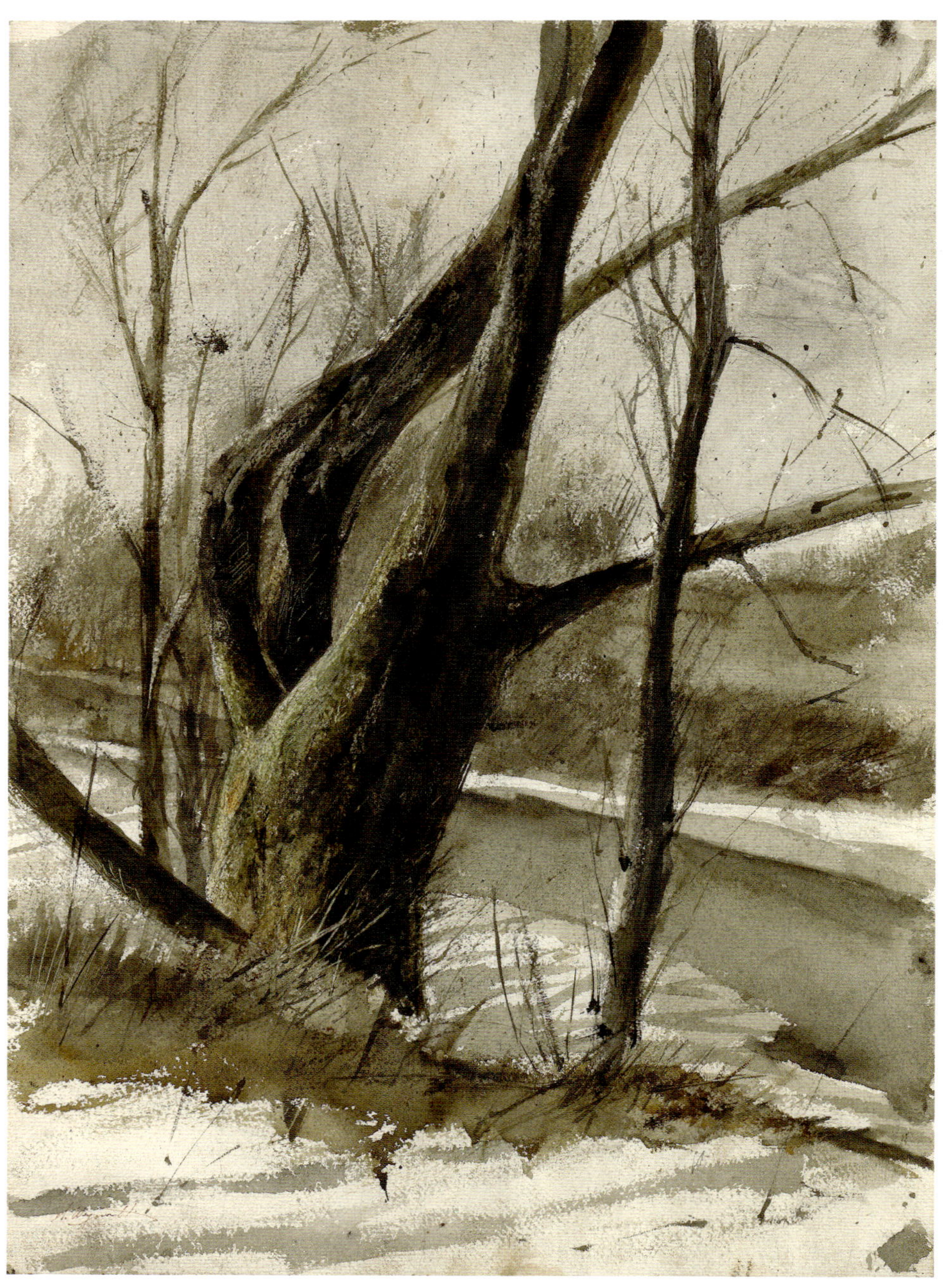

38
***THAW*, 1962**

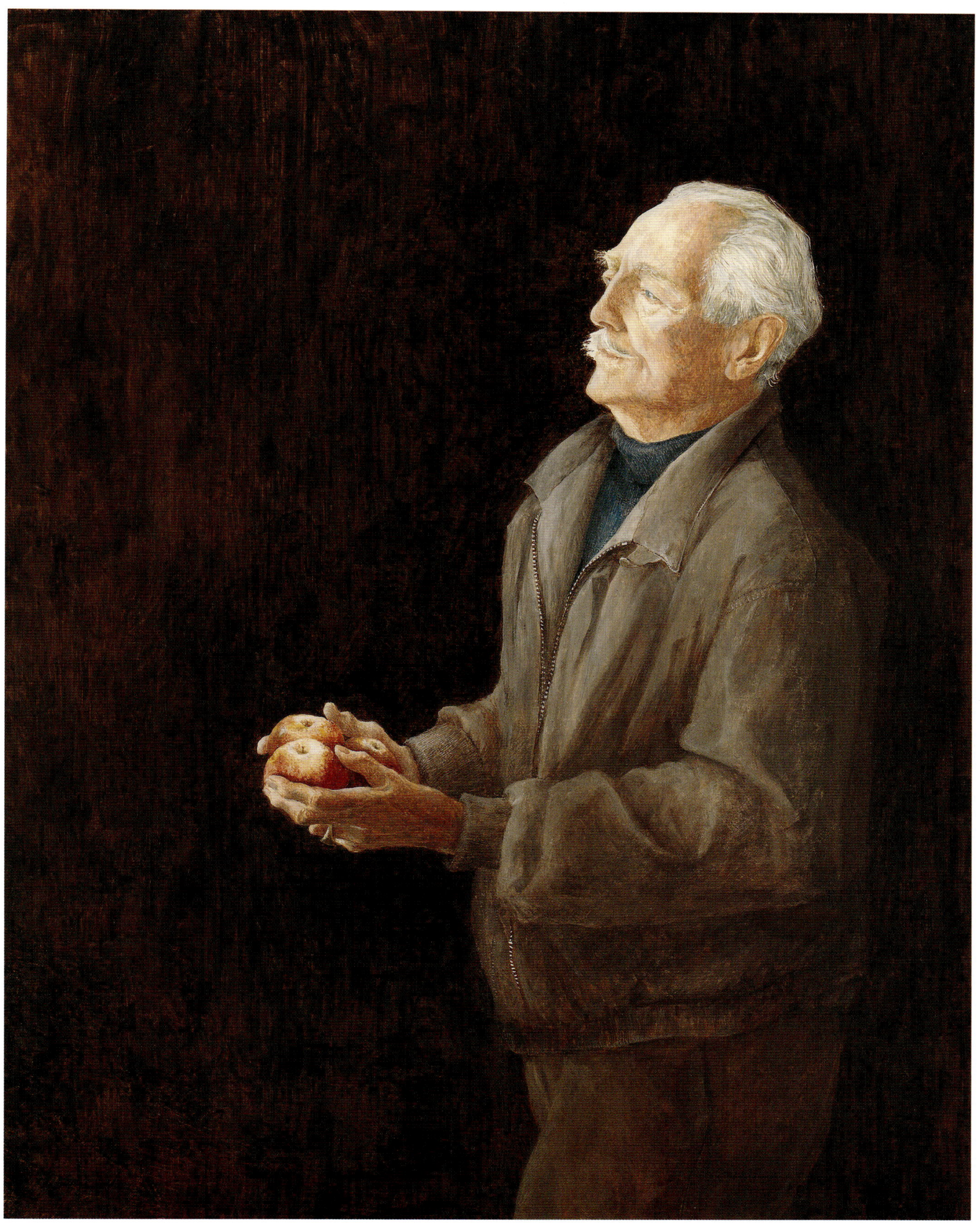

39
***THE OFFERING*, 2001**

40

PORTRAIT OF WILLIAM W. SCRANTON, 1969

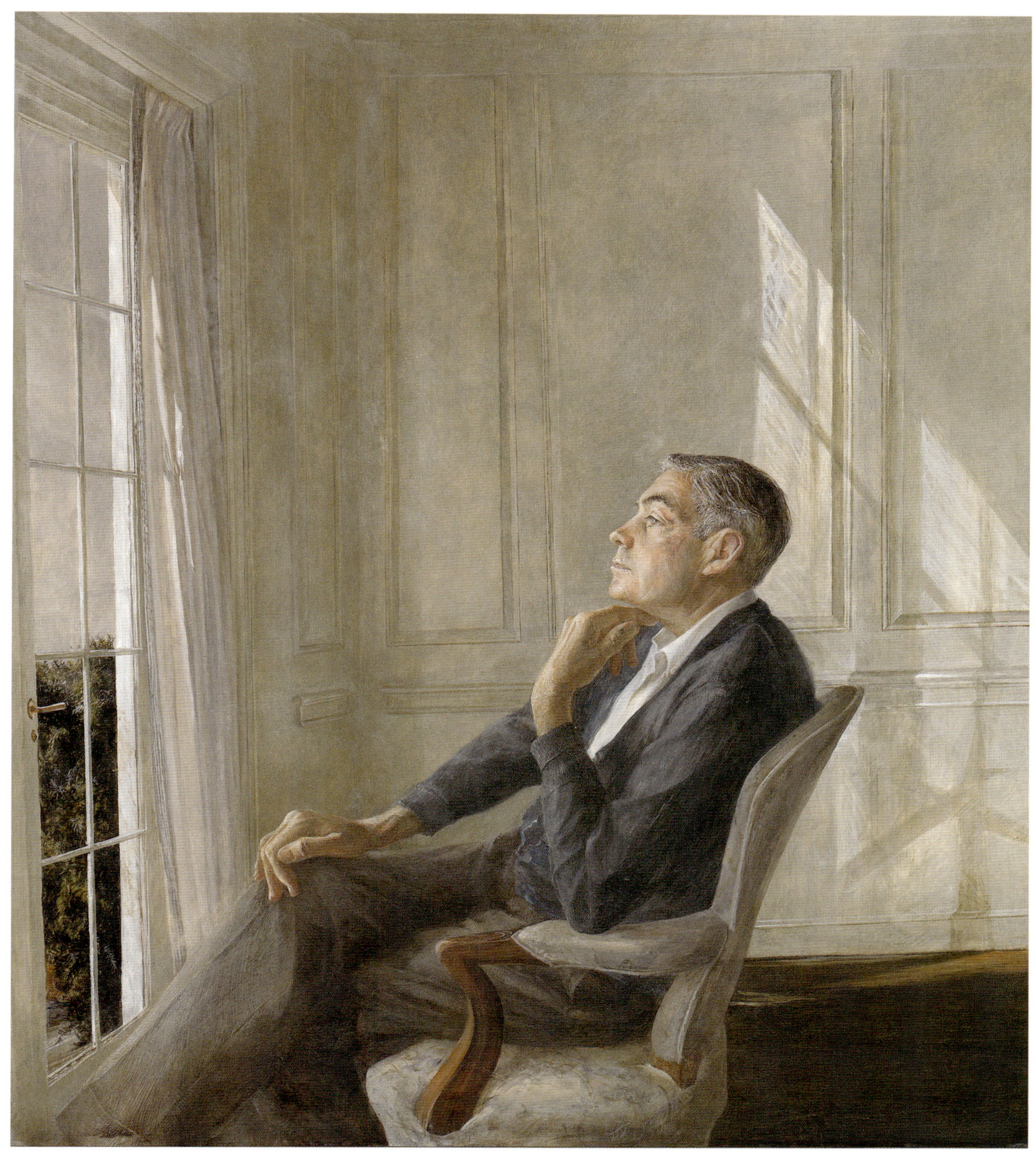

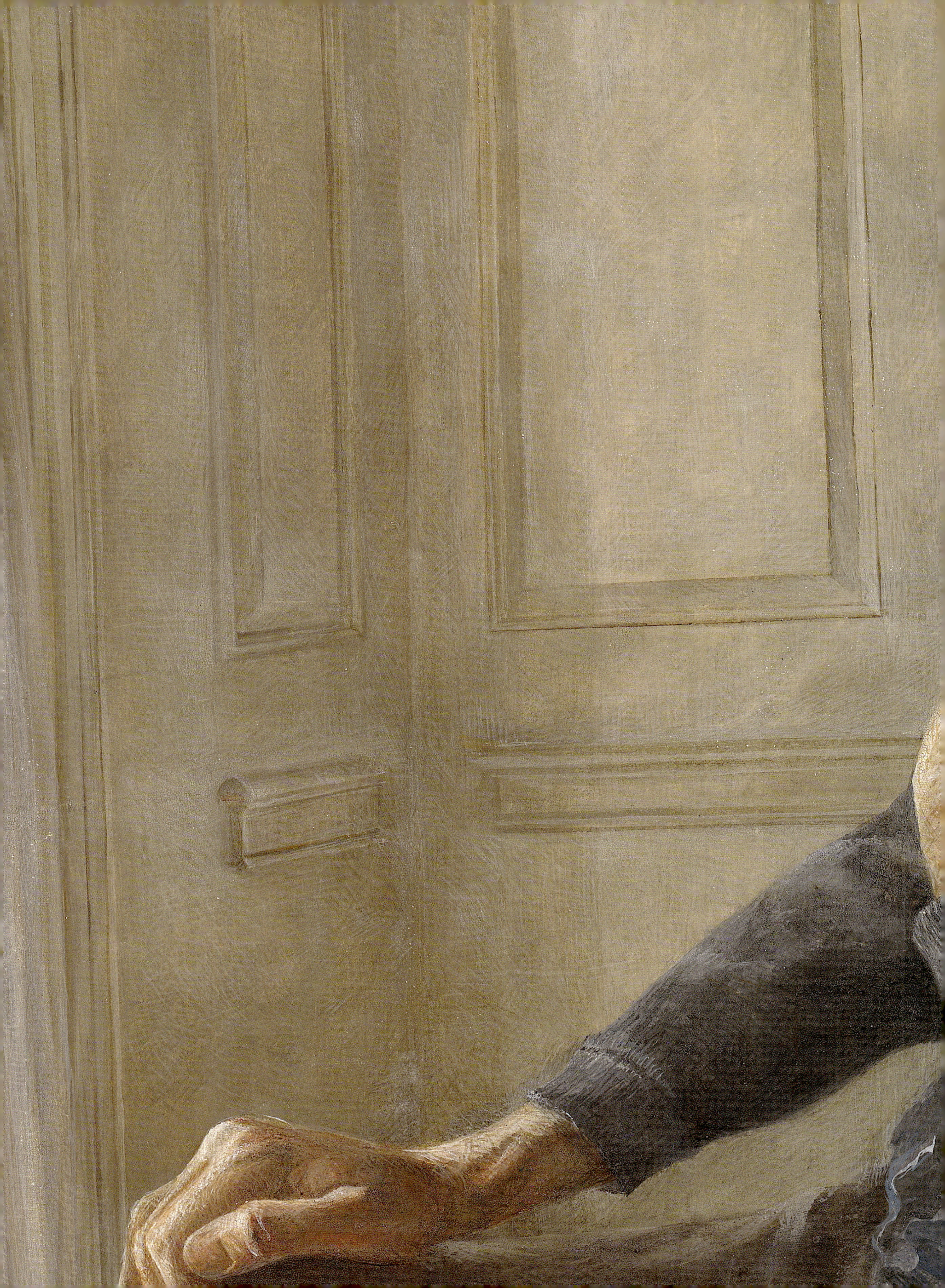

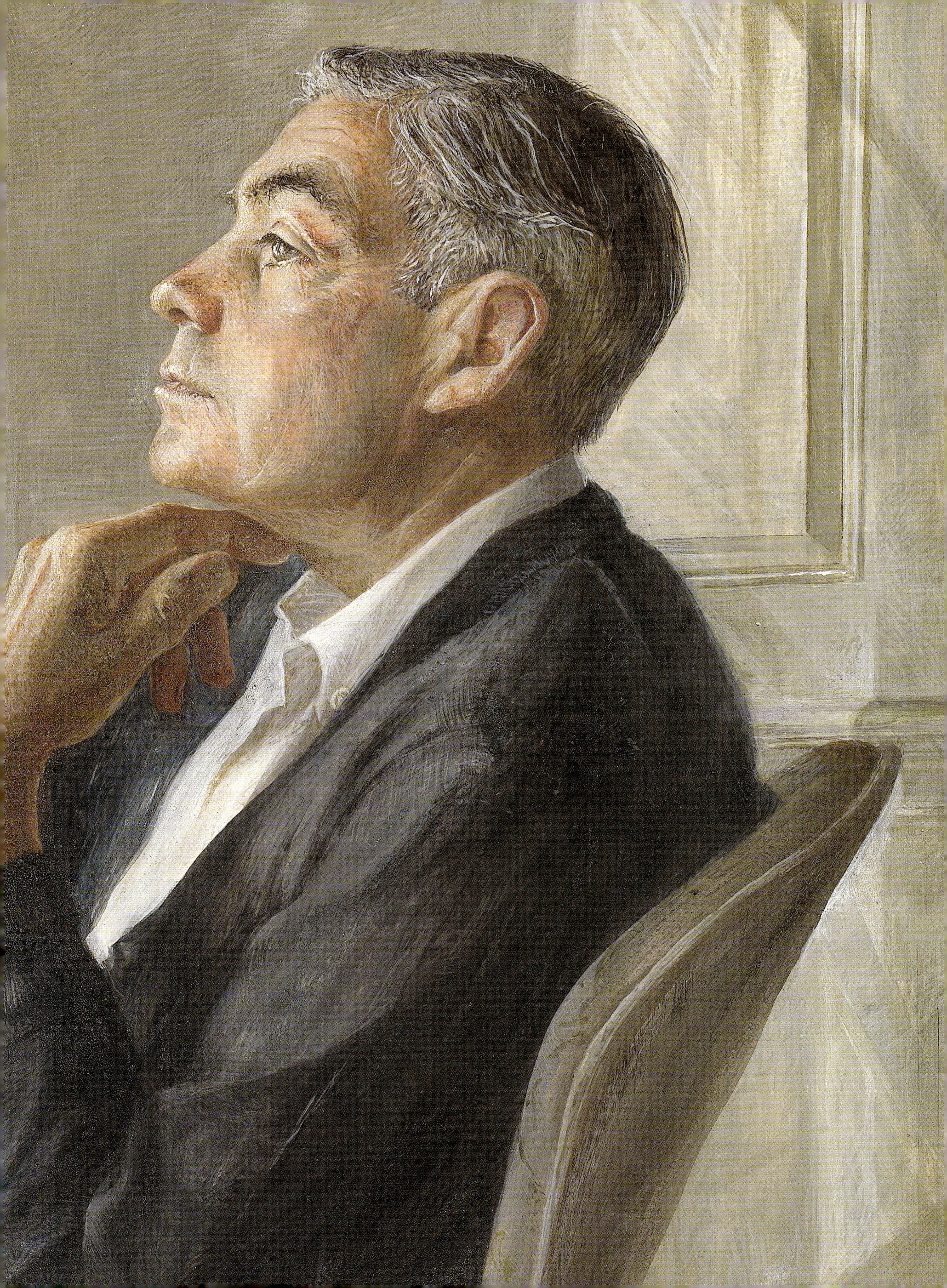

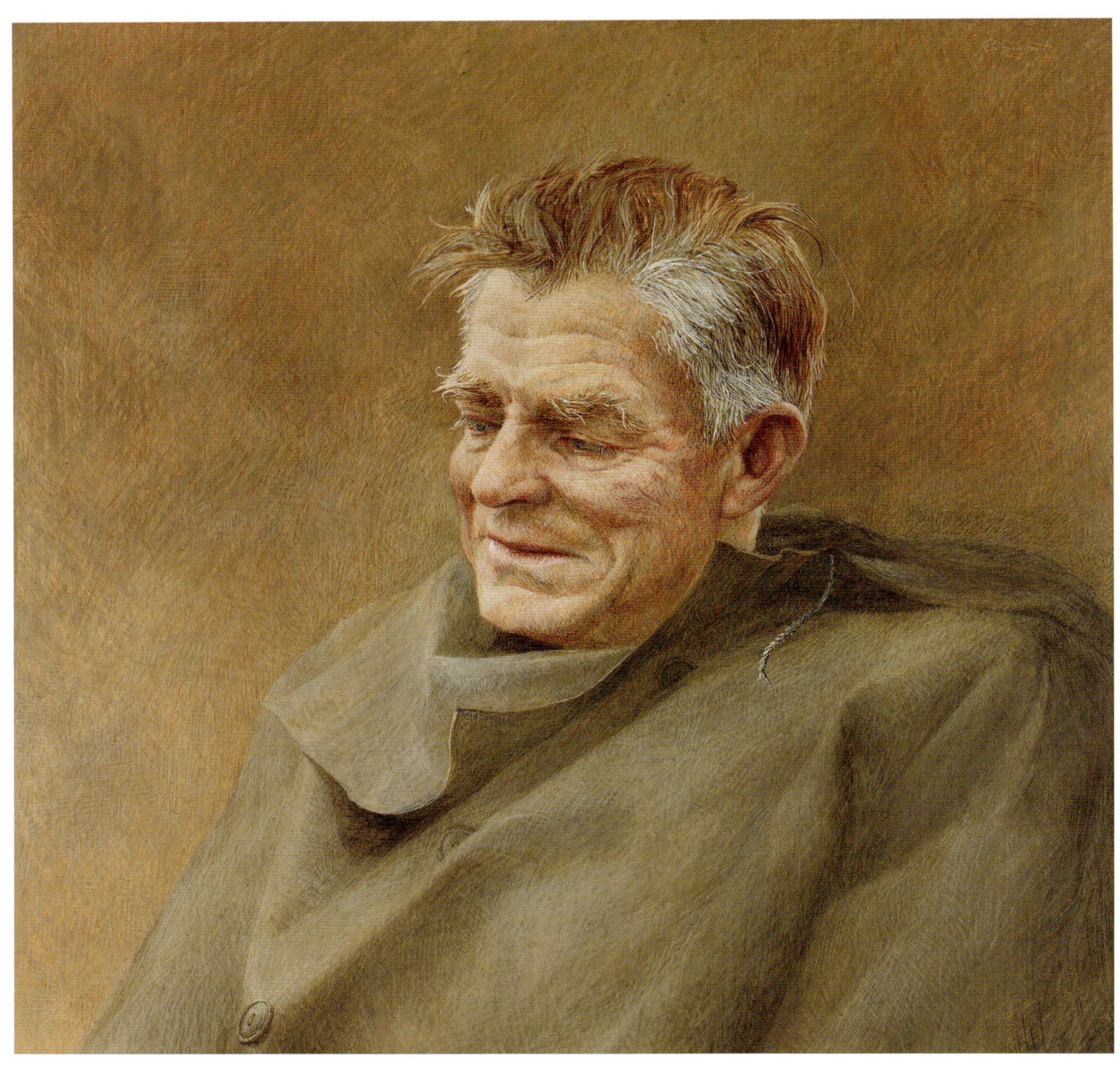

41
***HENRY BELIN DU PONT, JR.*, 1971**

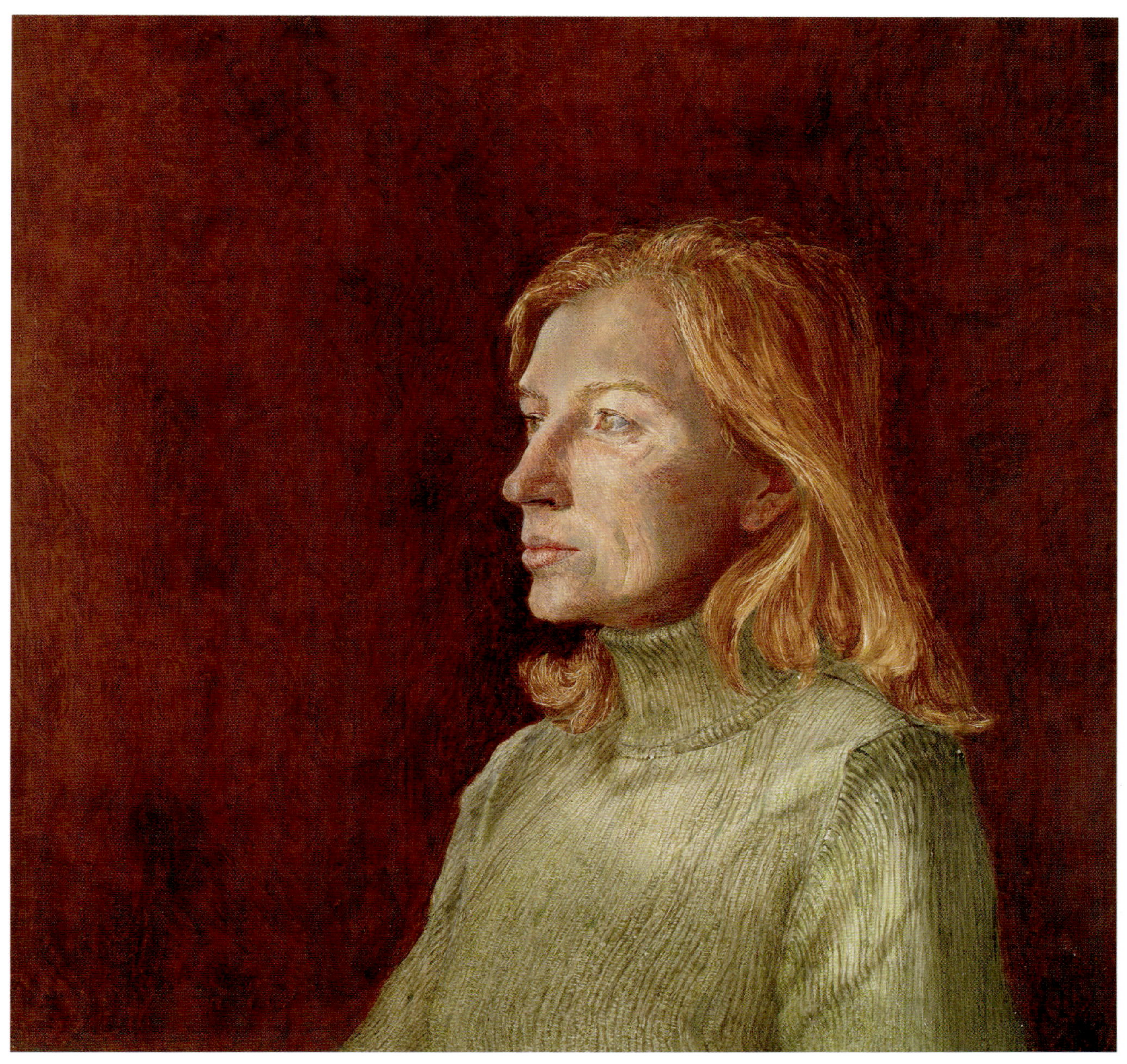

42

***PORTRAIT OF DD MATZ*, 2007**

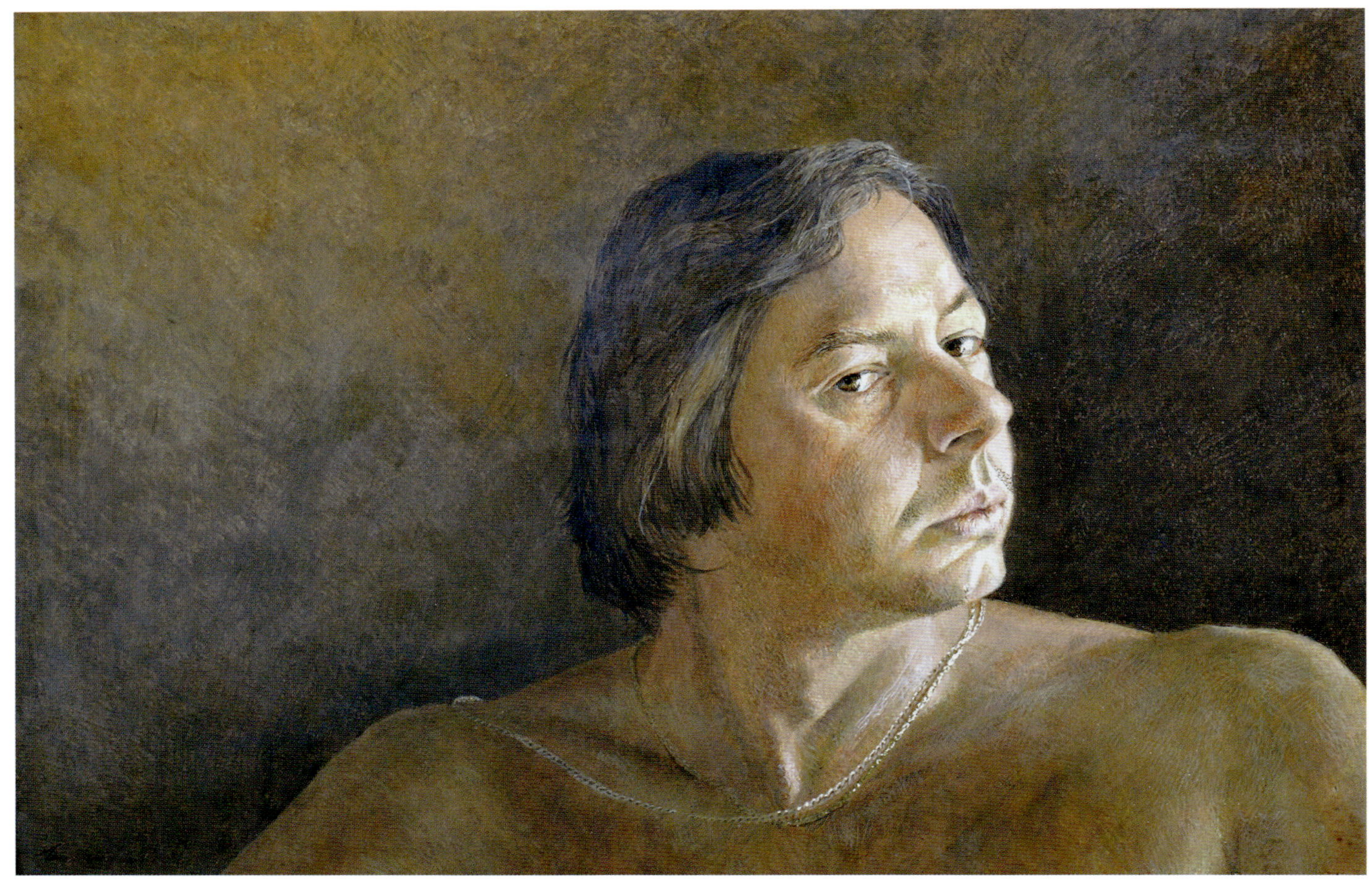

43
***MONTSDEOCA*, 1977**

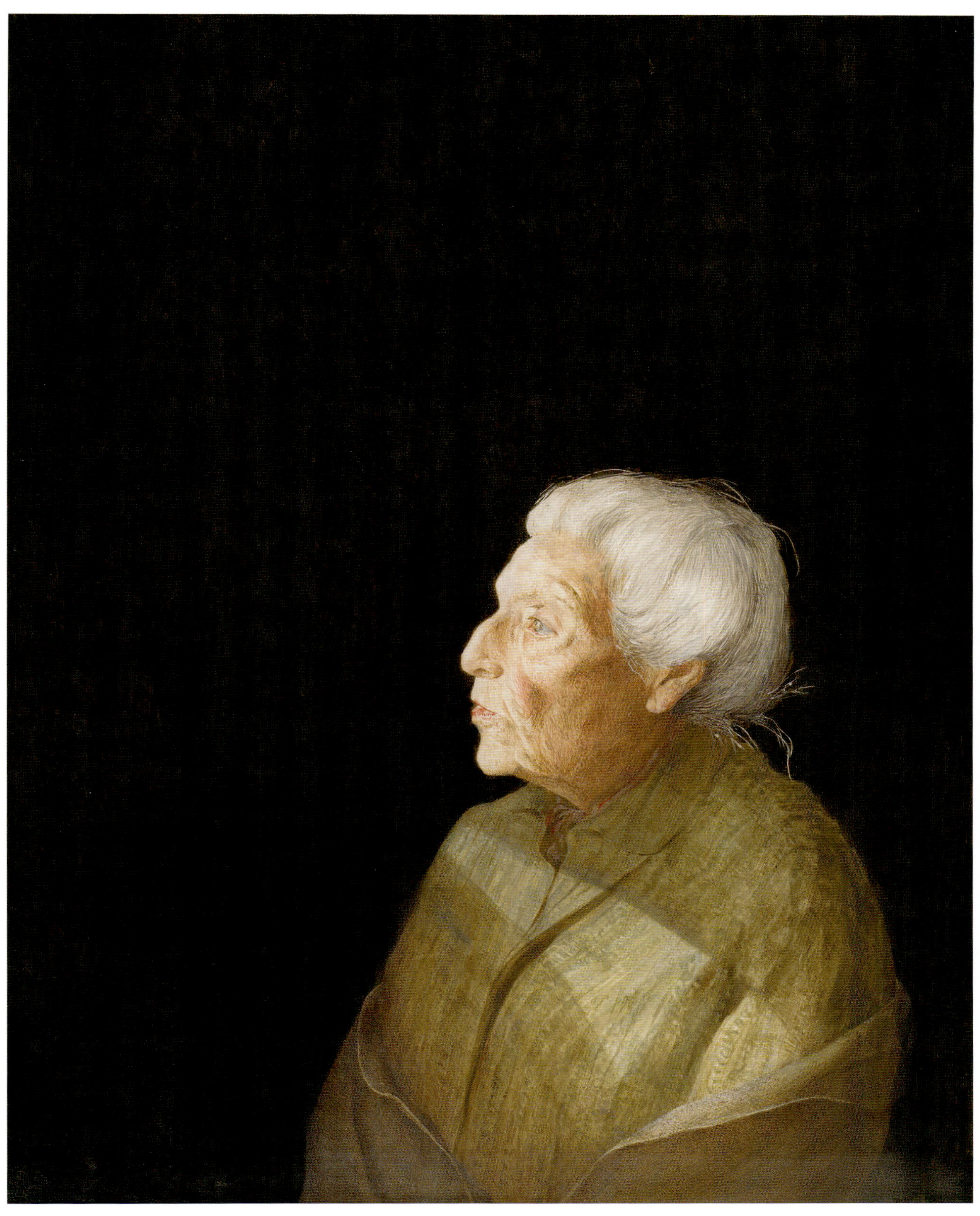

44
***BARONESS*, 1997**

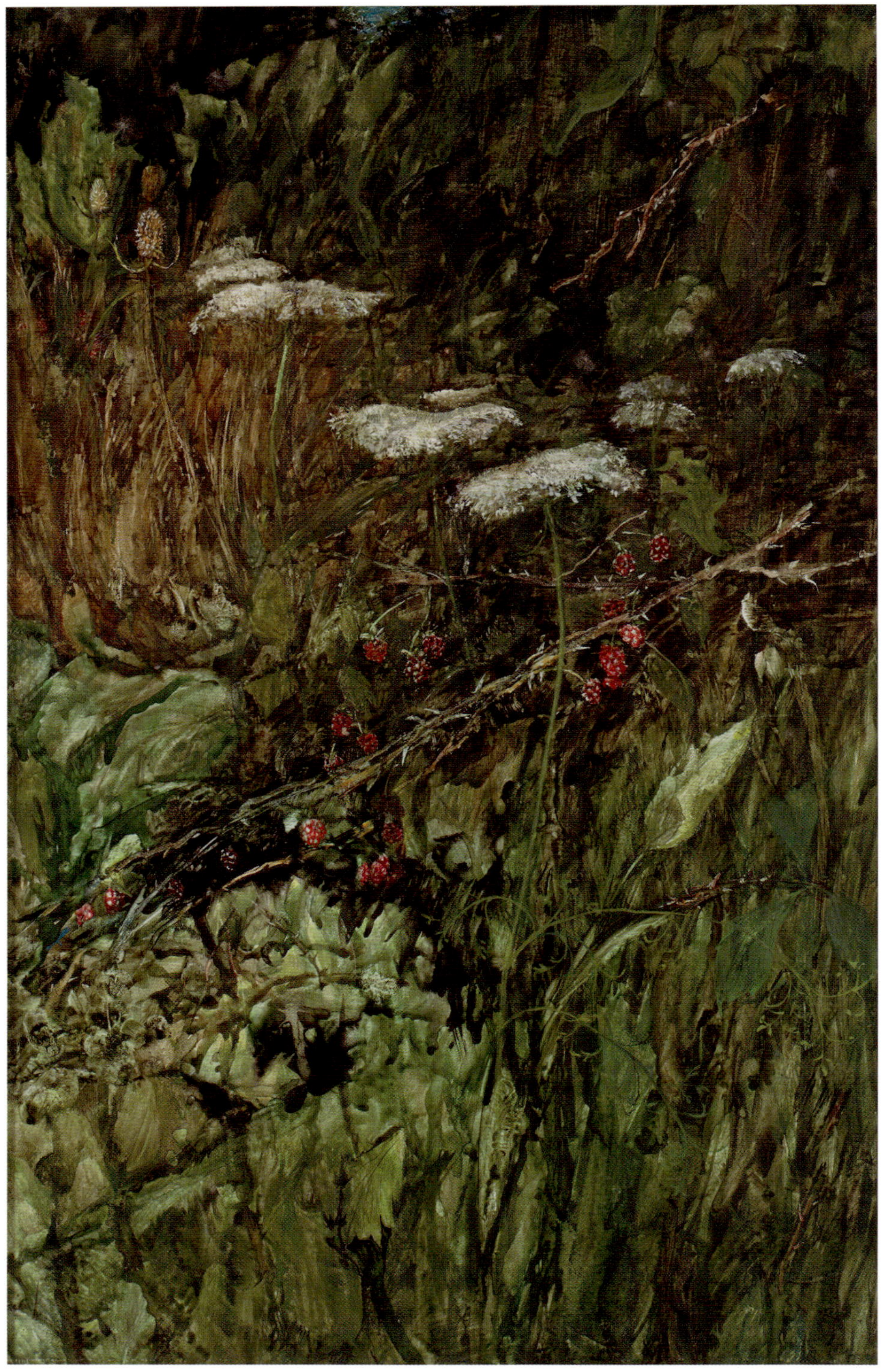

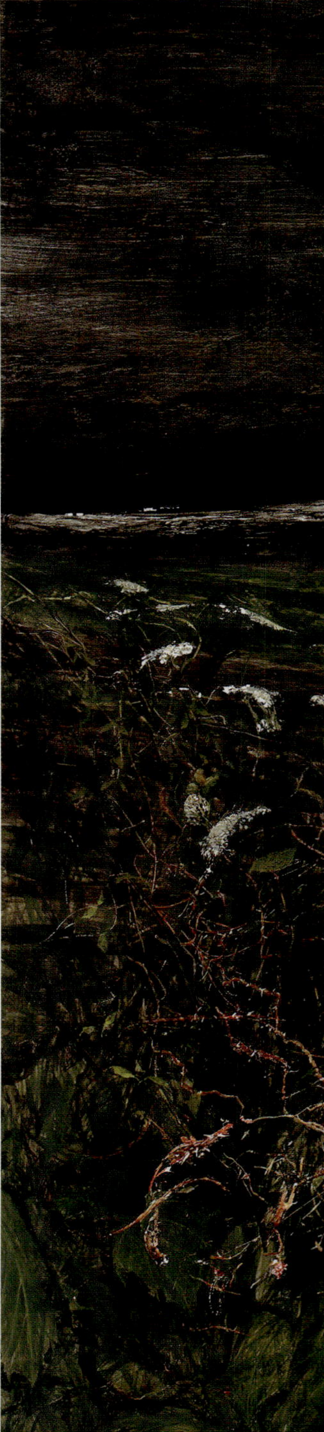

45
UNDER THE FENCE, STUDY FOR *THE CROSSING*, 2009

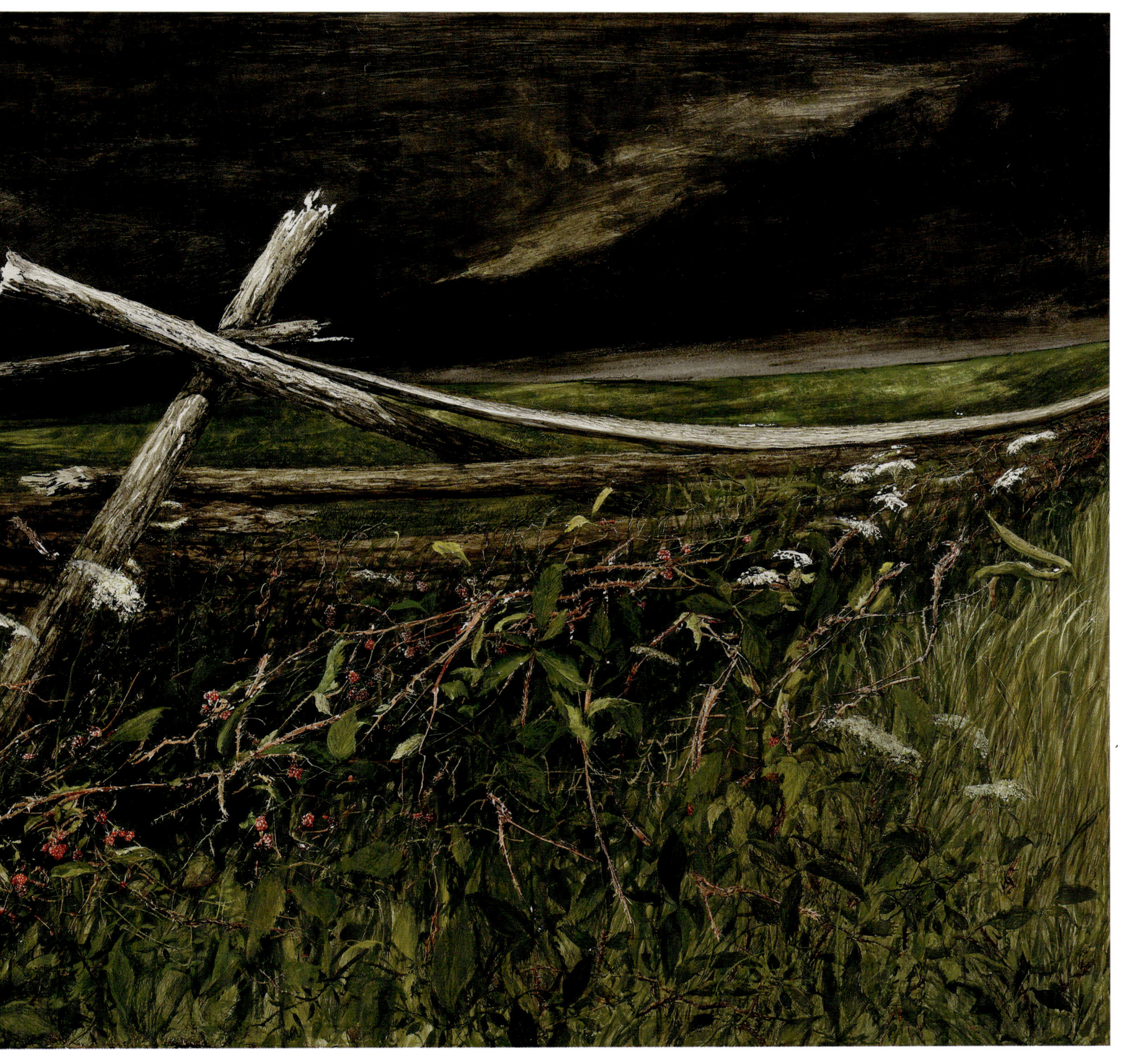

46
***THE CROSSING*, 2009–10**

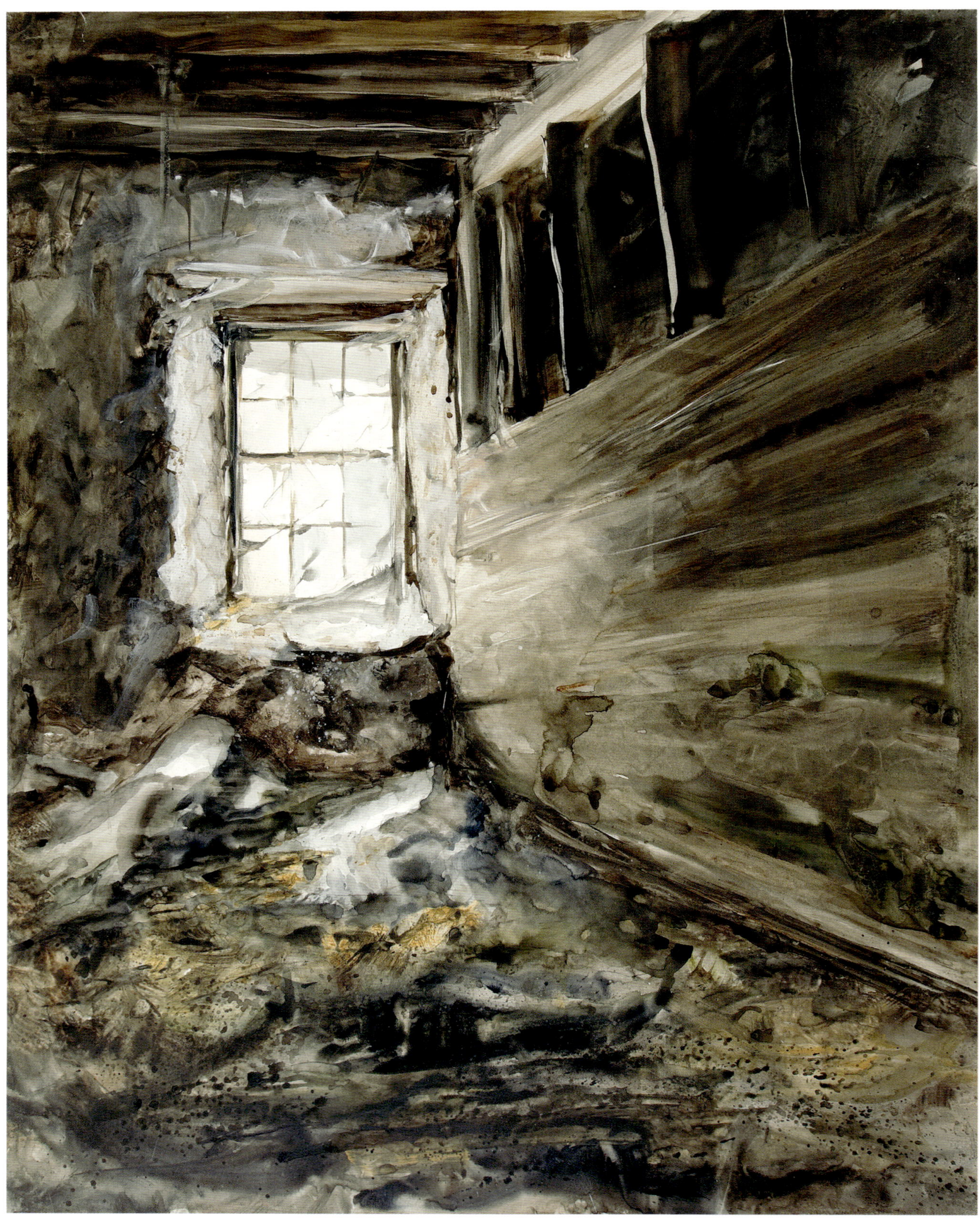

47
UNTITLED (*BARN INTERIOR*), CA. 1990

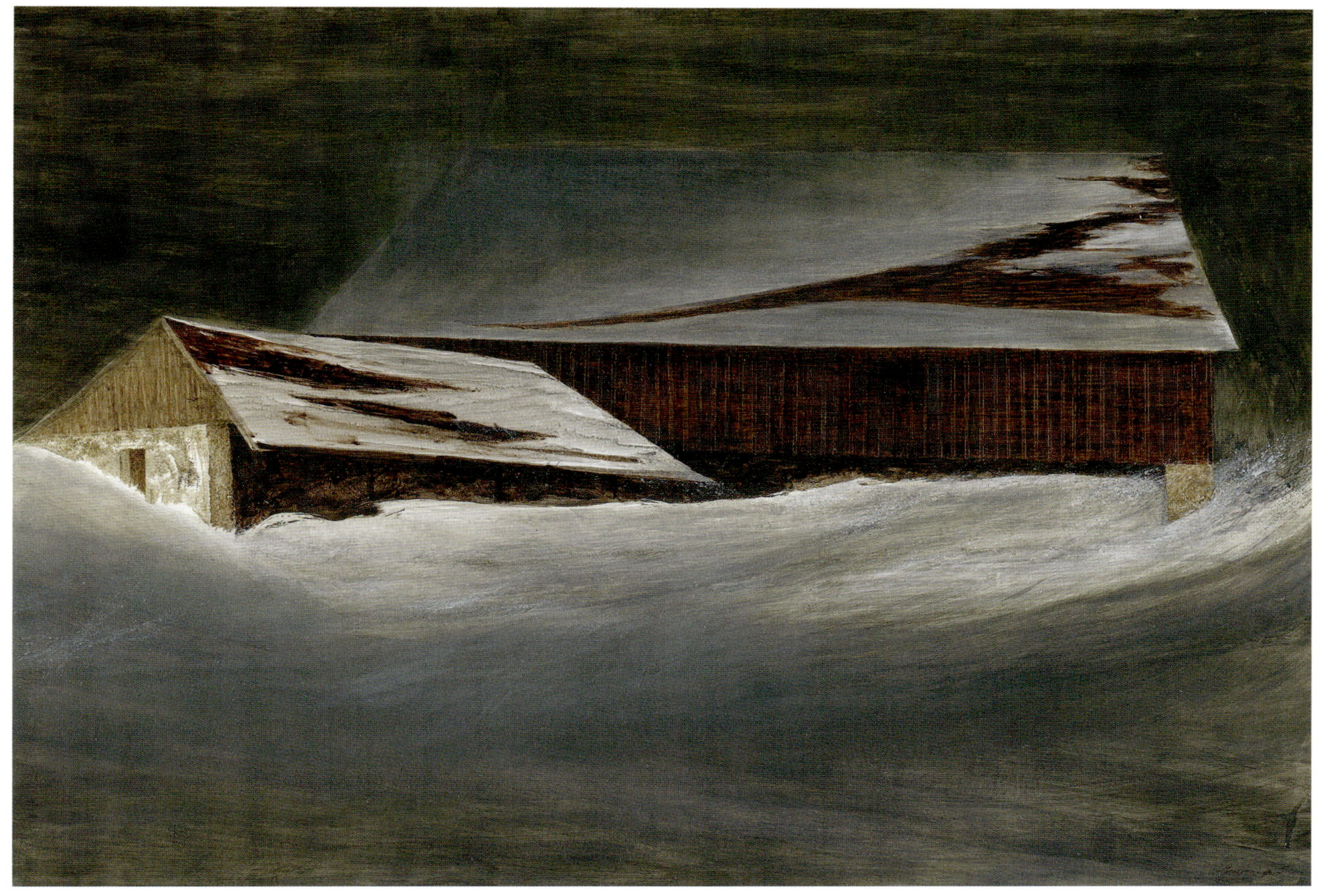

48
***ROGUE WAVE*, 2010**

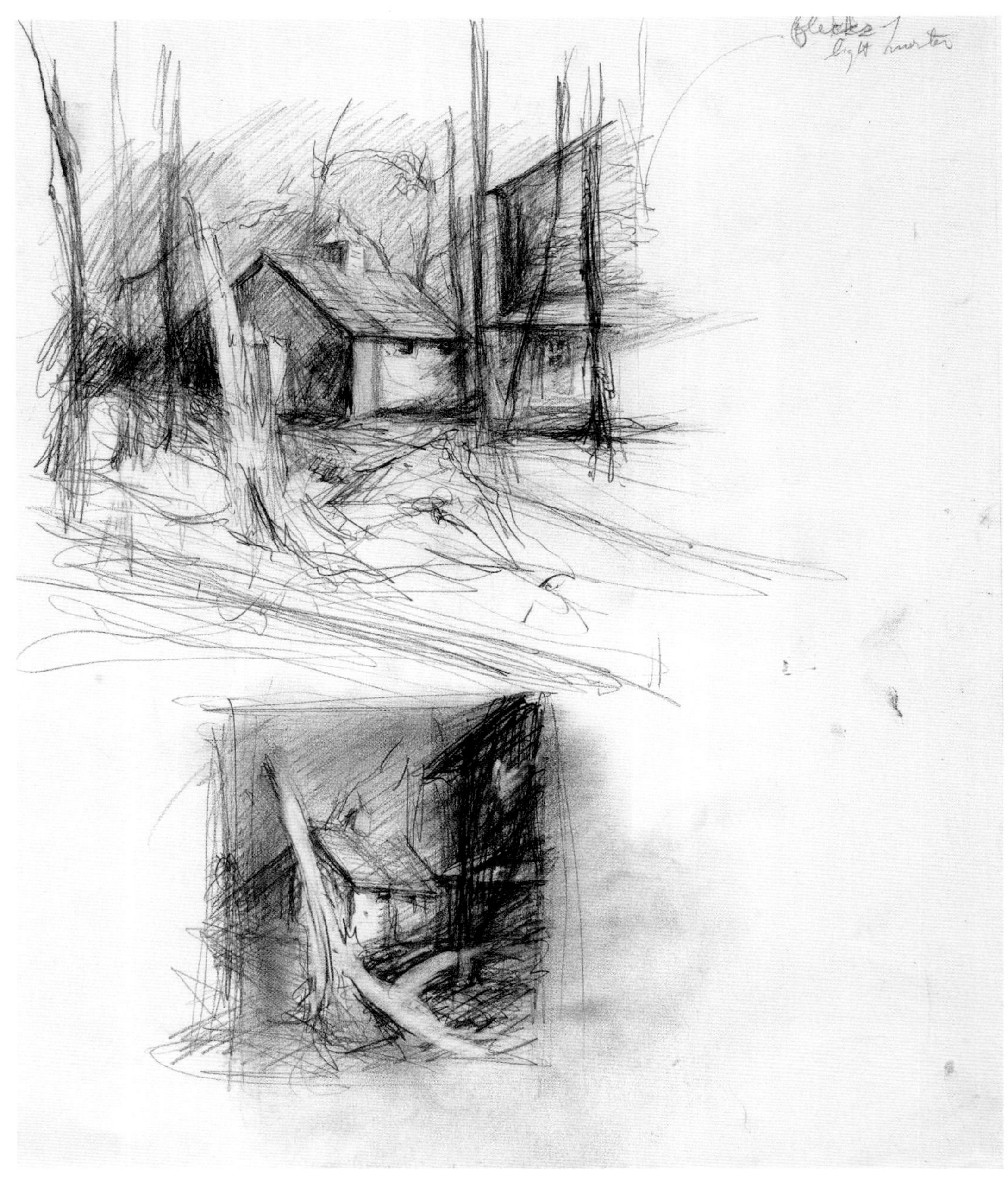

49
STUDY FOR *REQUIEM*, 2010

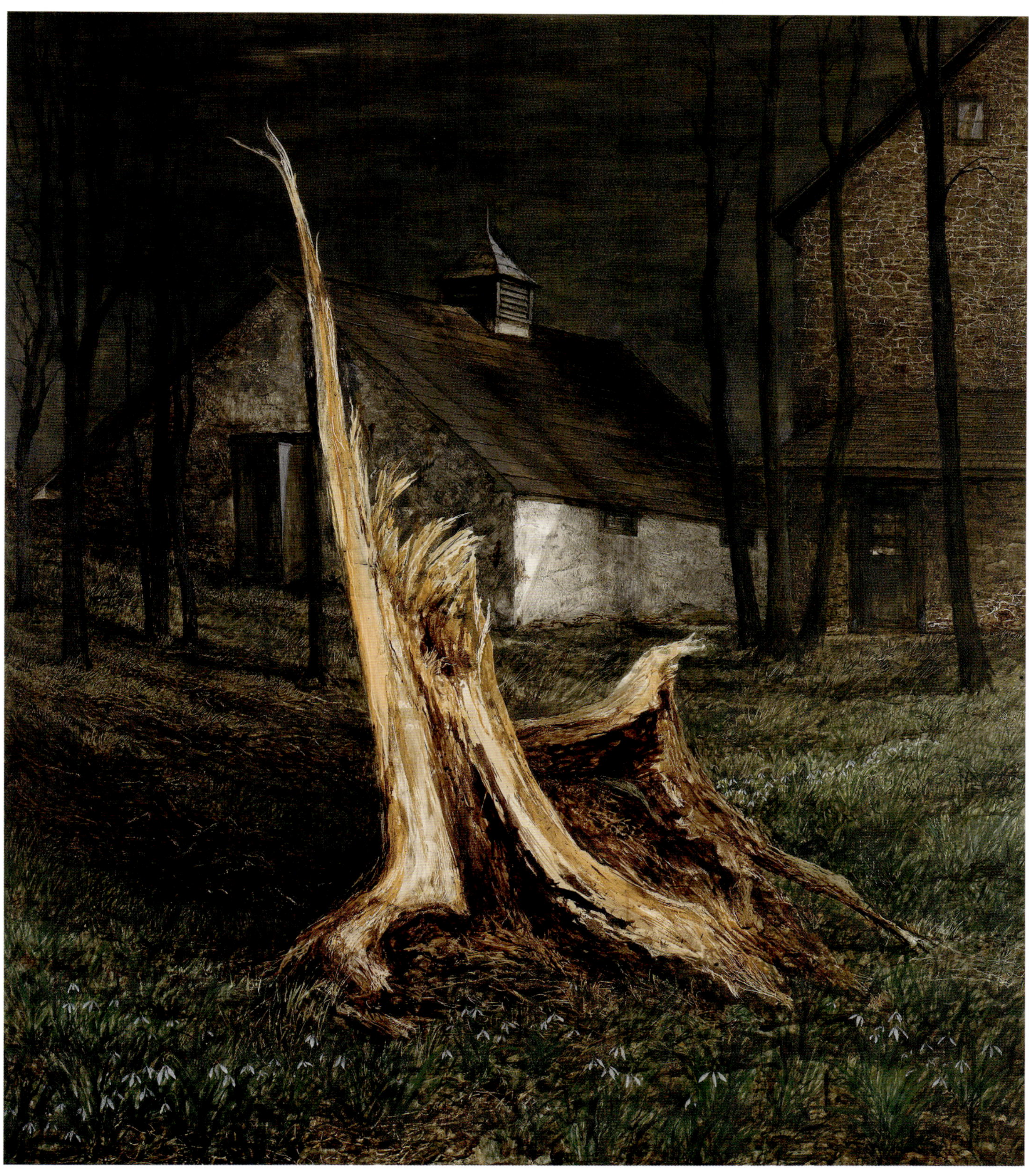

50
***REQUIEM*, 2010**

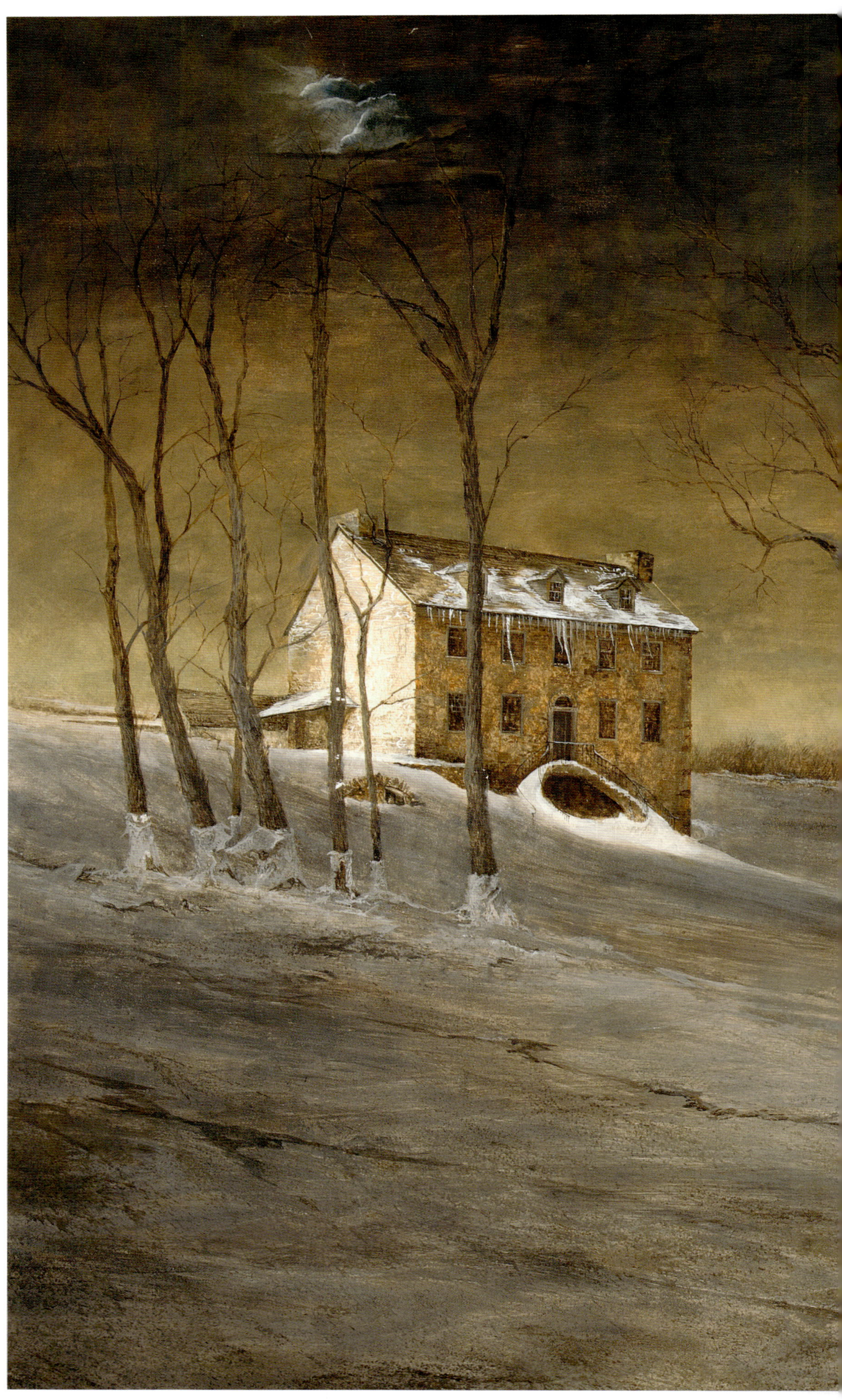

51
***ICE SHOES*, 1996**

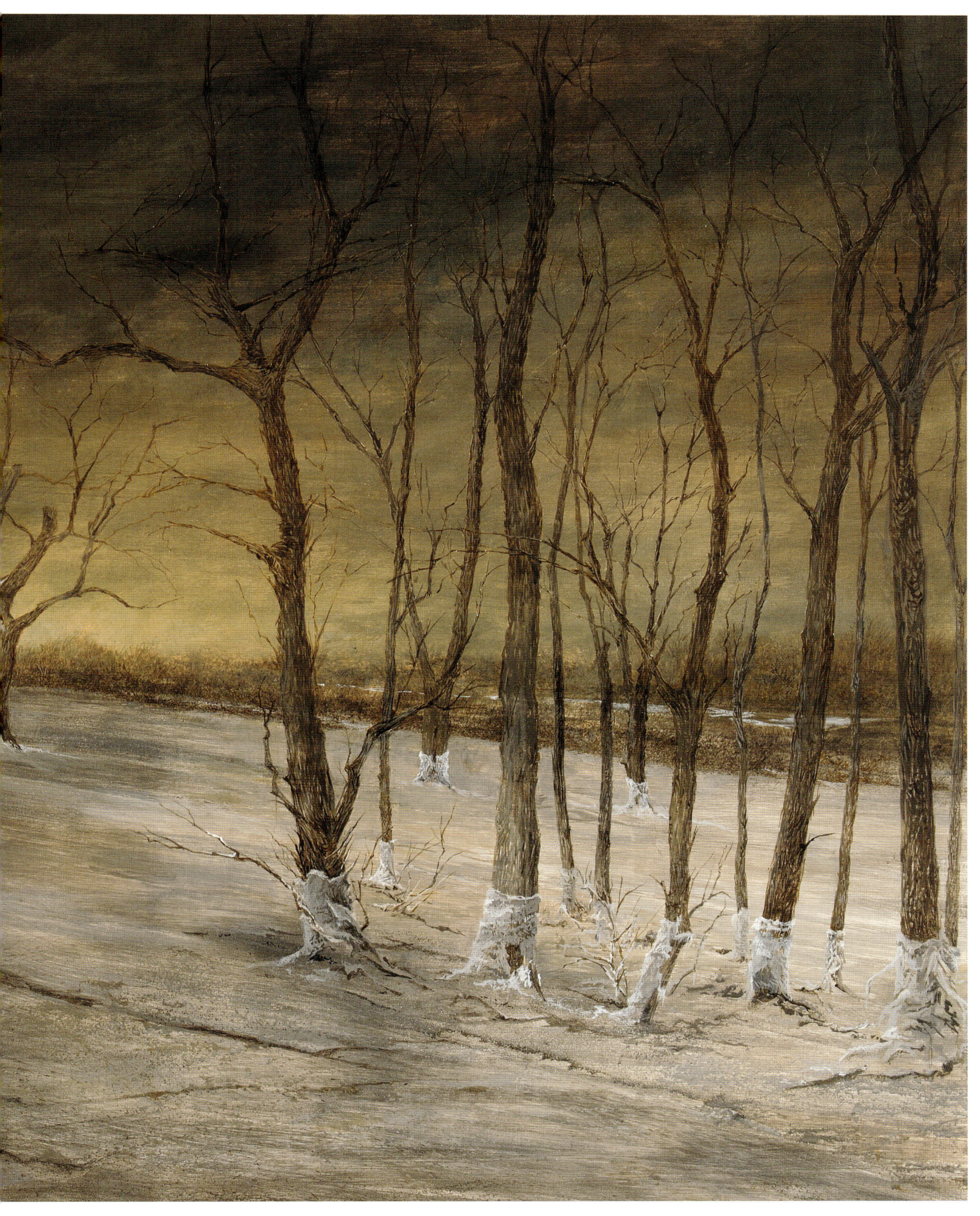

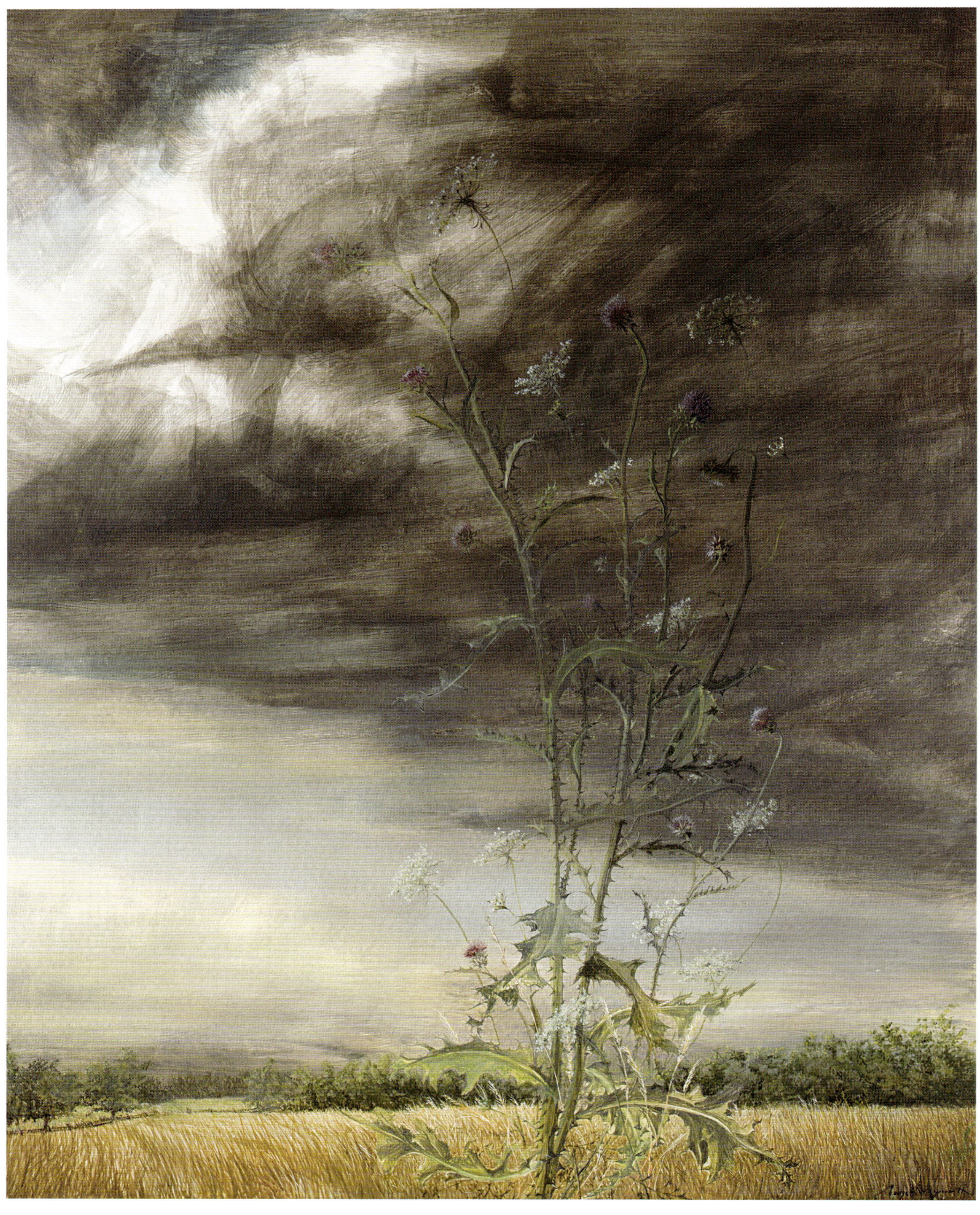

52
***STORM*, 2004**

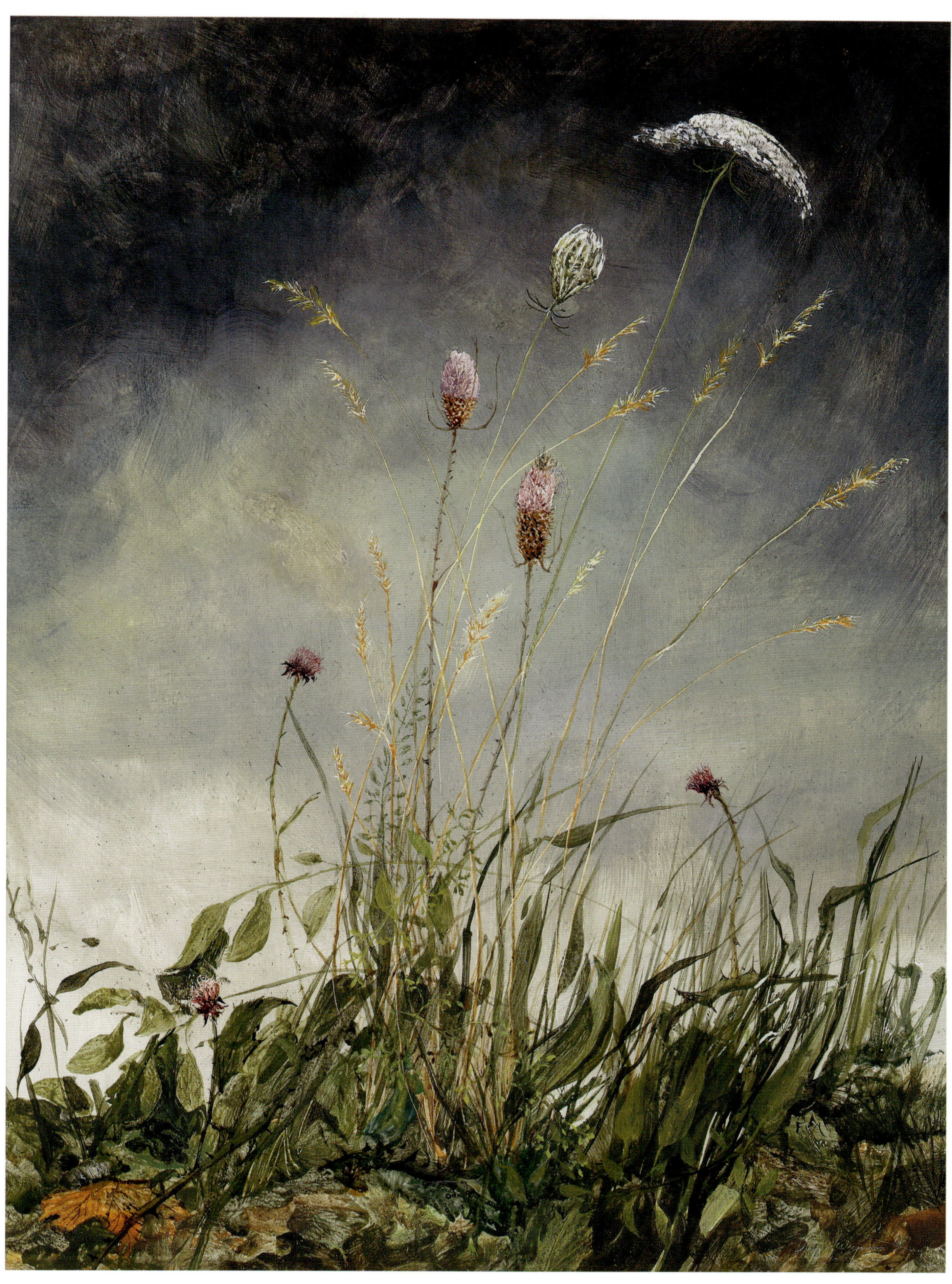

53
BEFORE MOWING, 2009

54

PARTY LINE, 2001

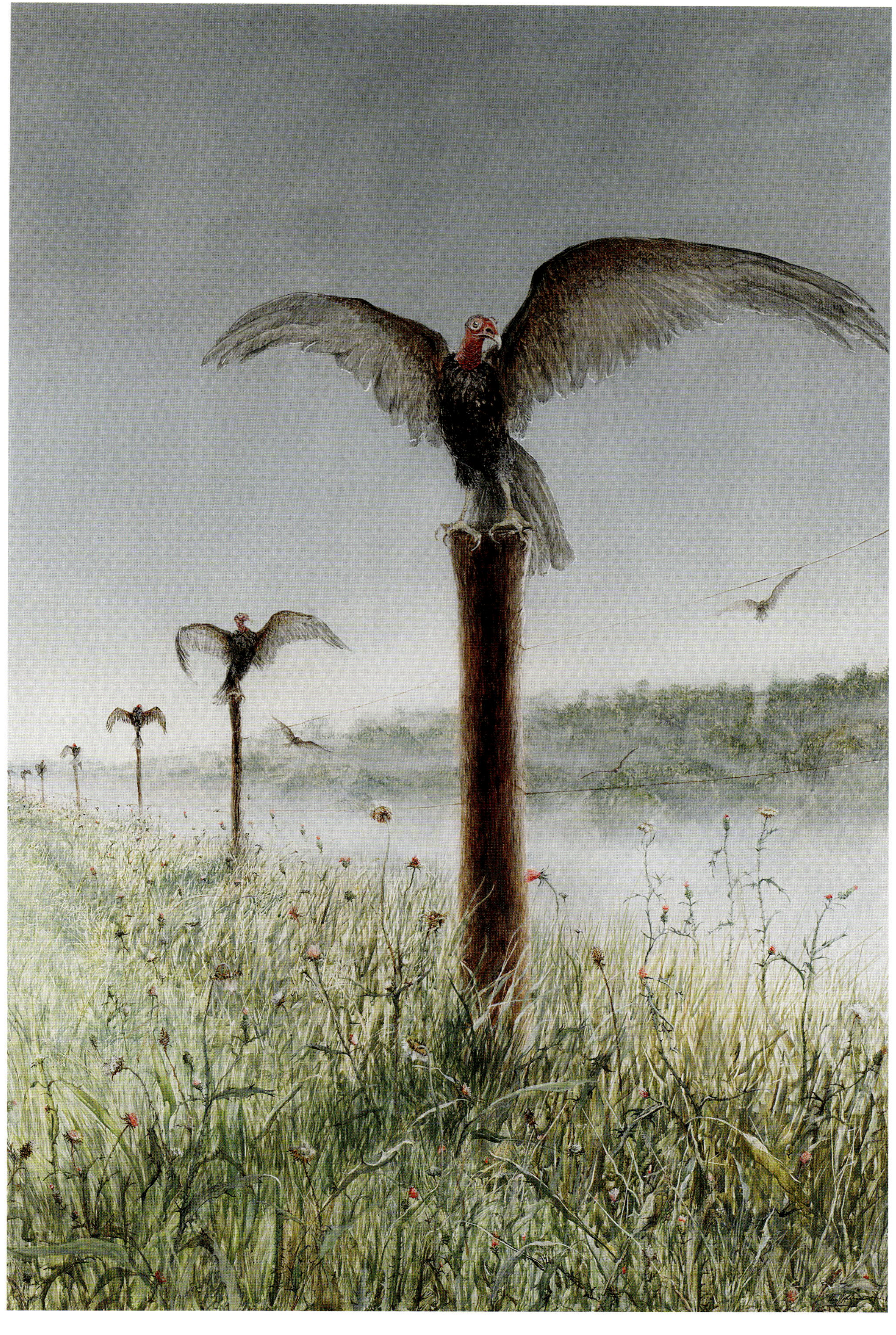

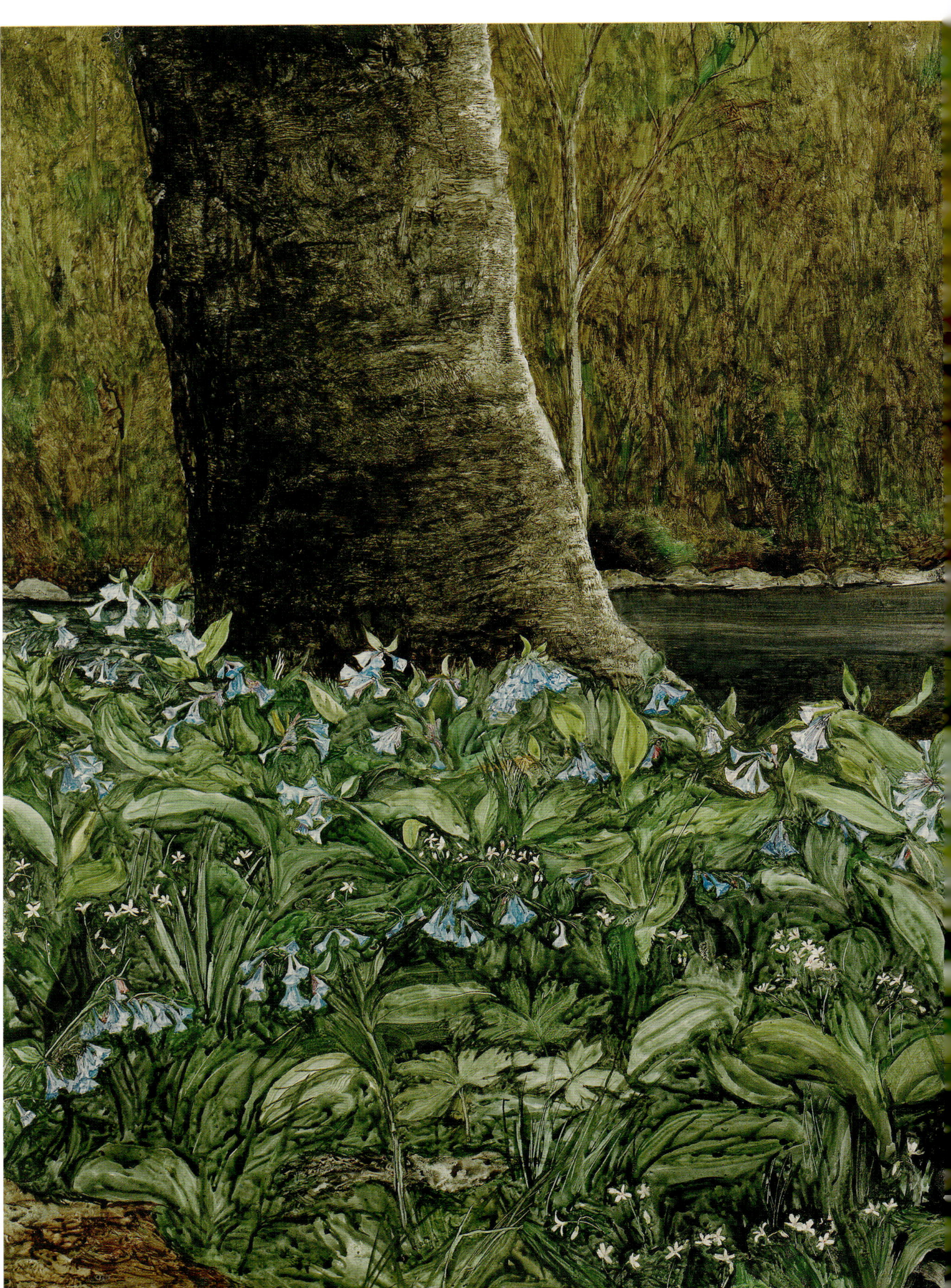

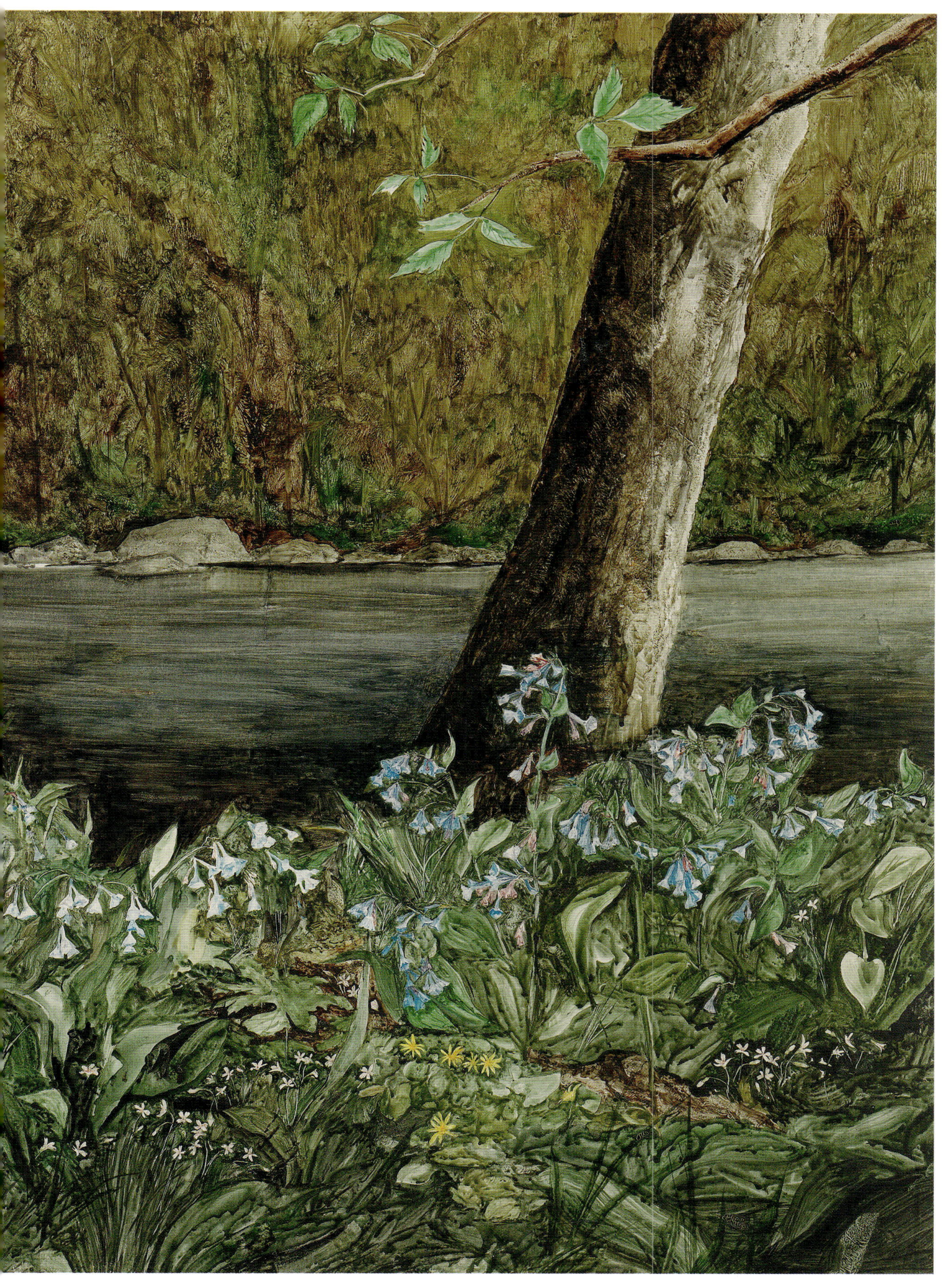

55
INDIAN HANNA, 1990

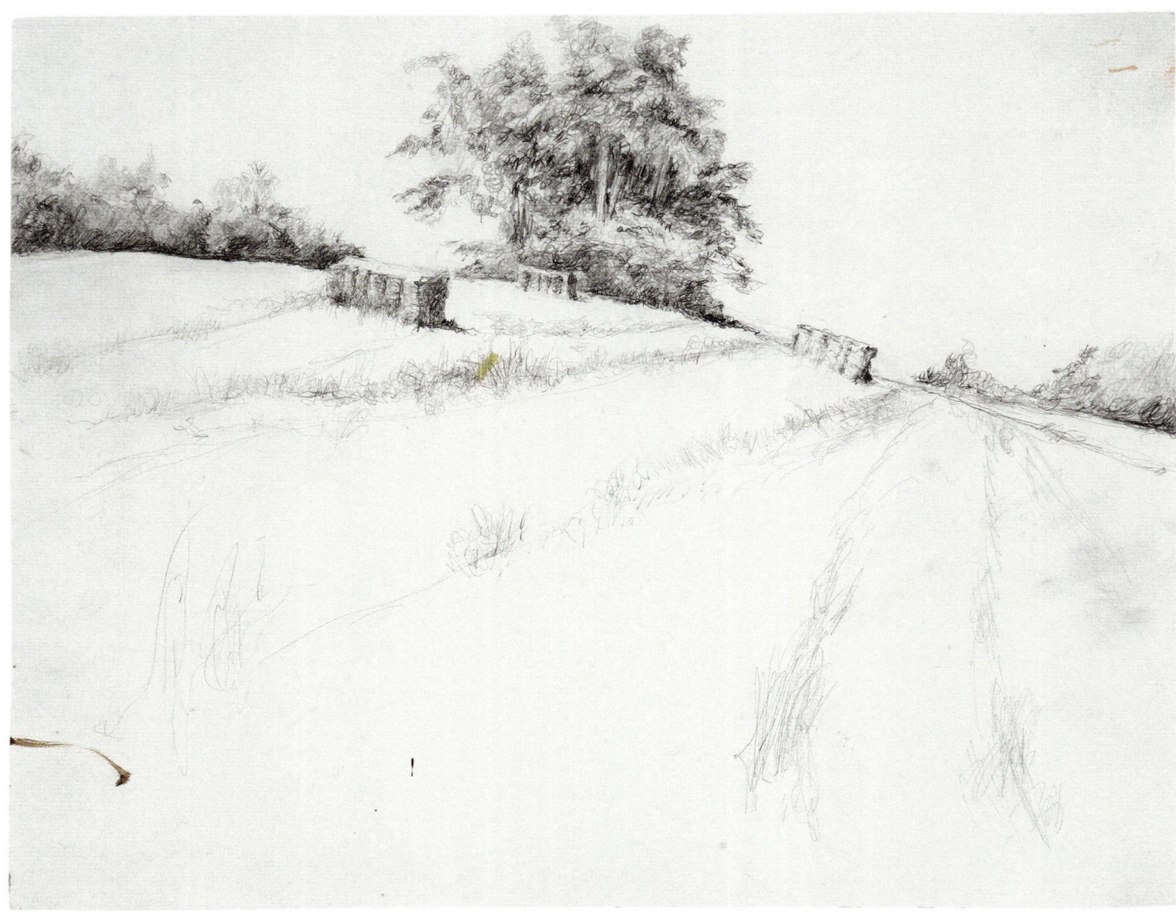

56
STUDY FOR *FIRST CUTTING*, 2004

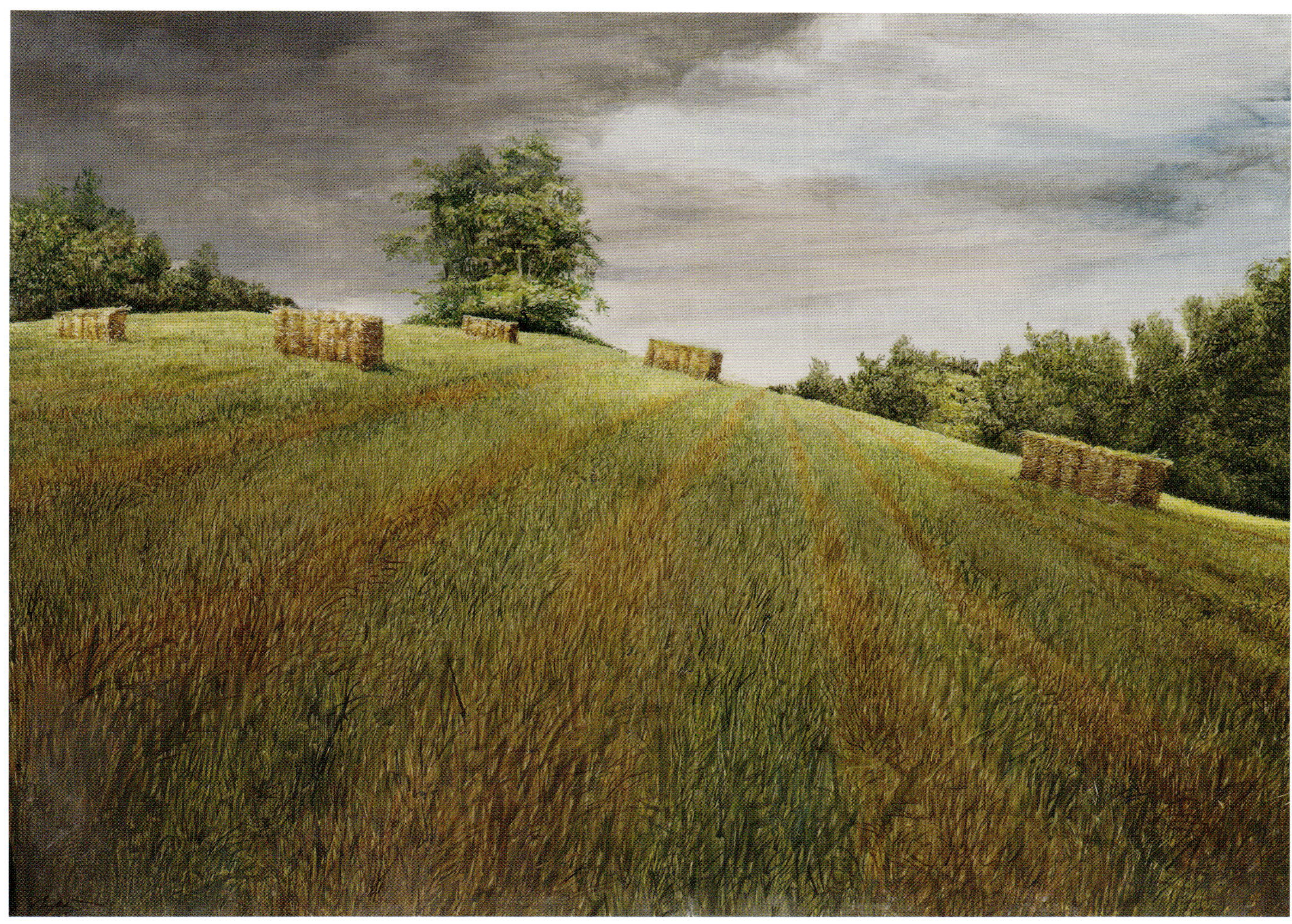

57
FIRST CUTTING, 2004

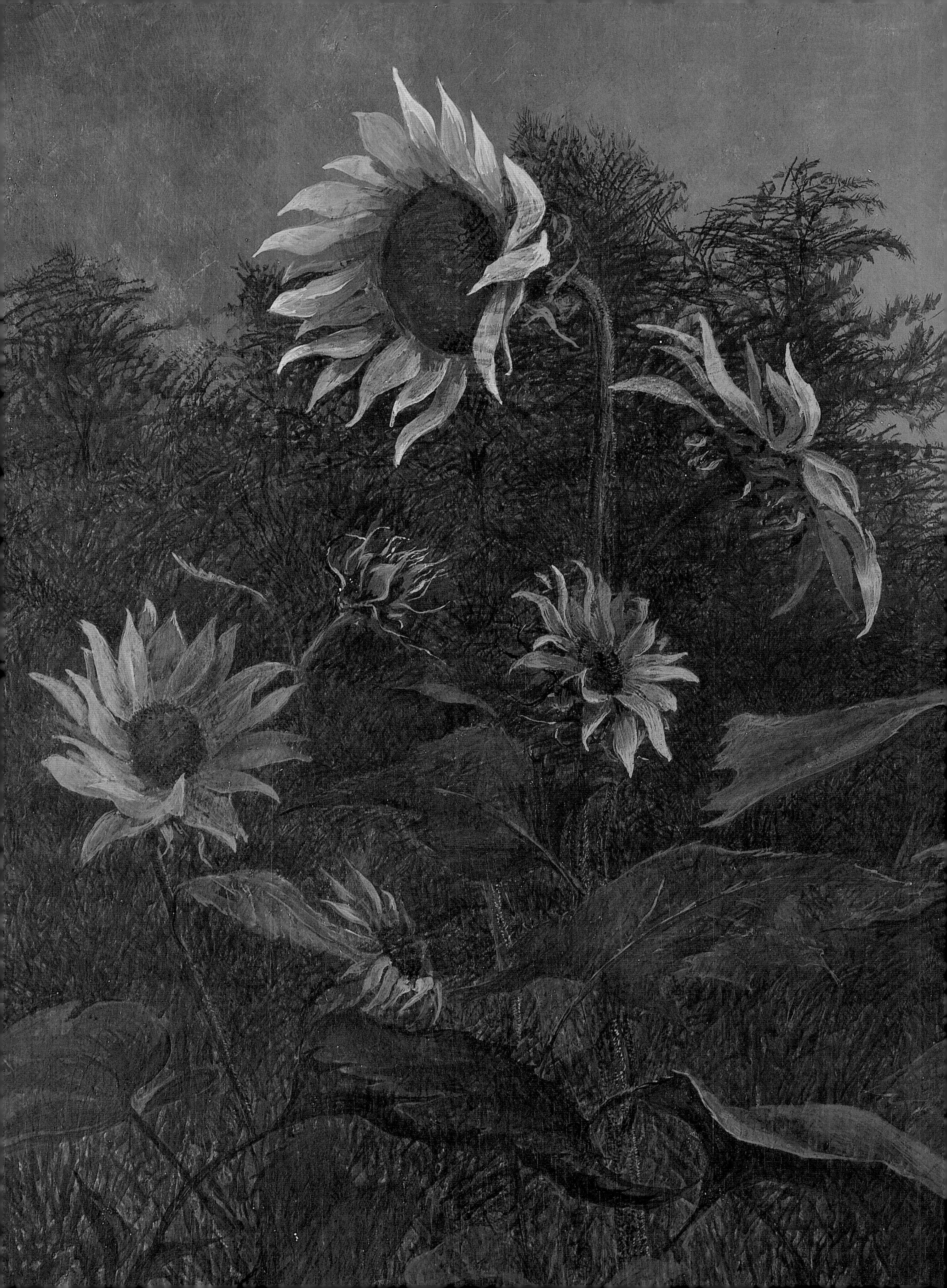

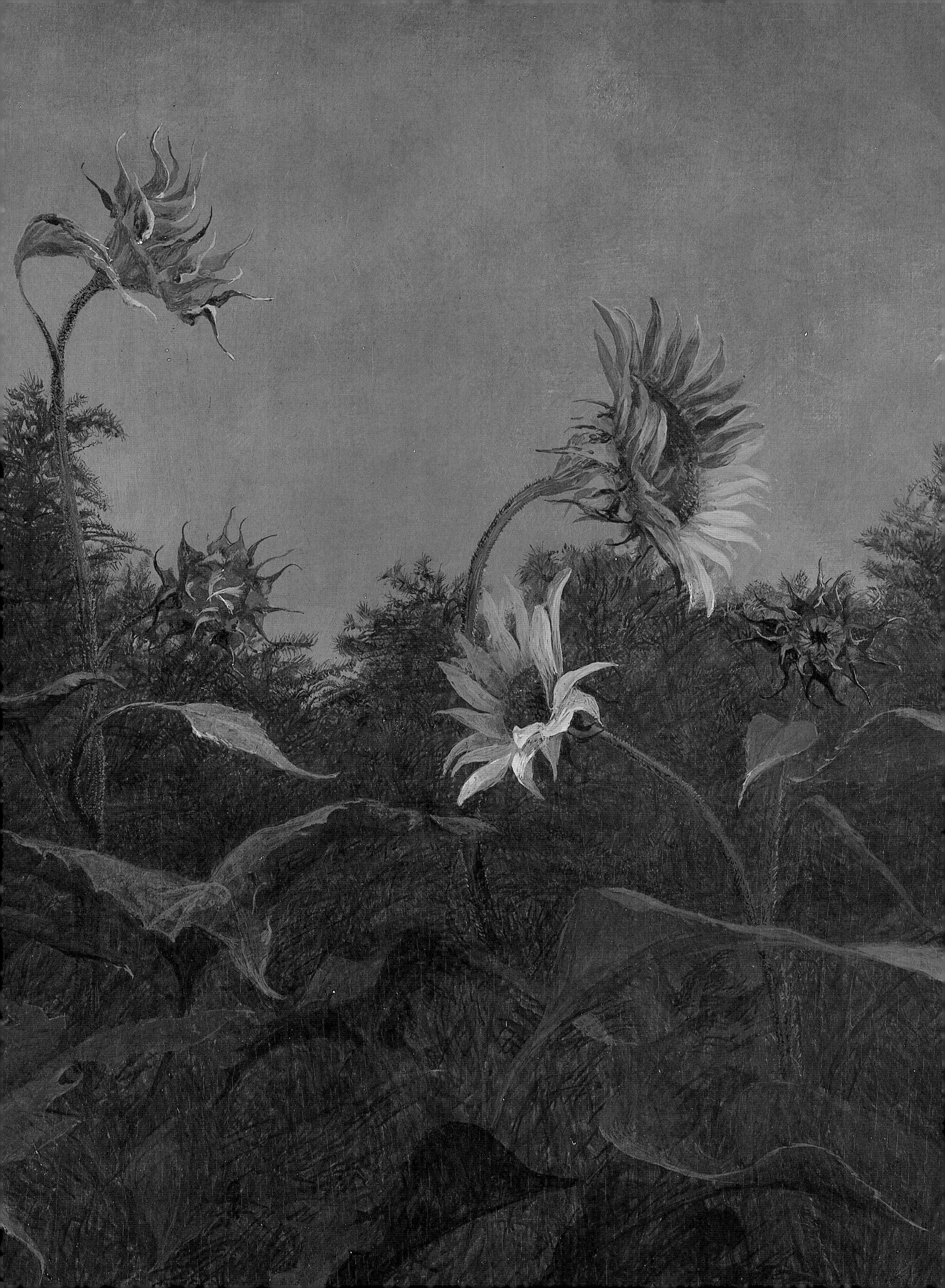

58
***NIGHT LIFE*, 2000**

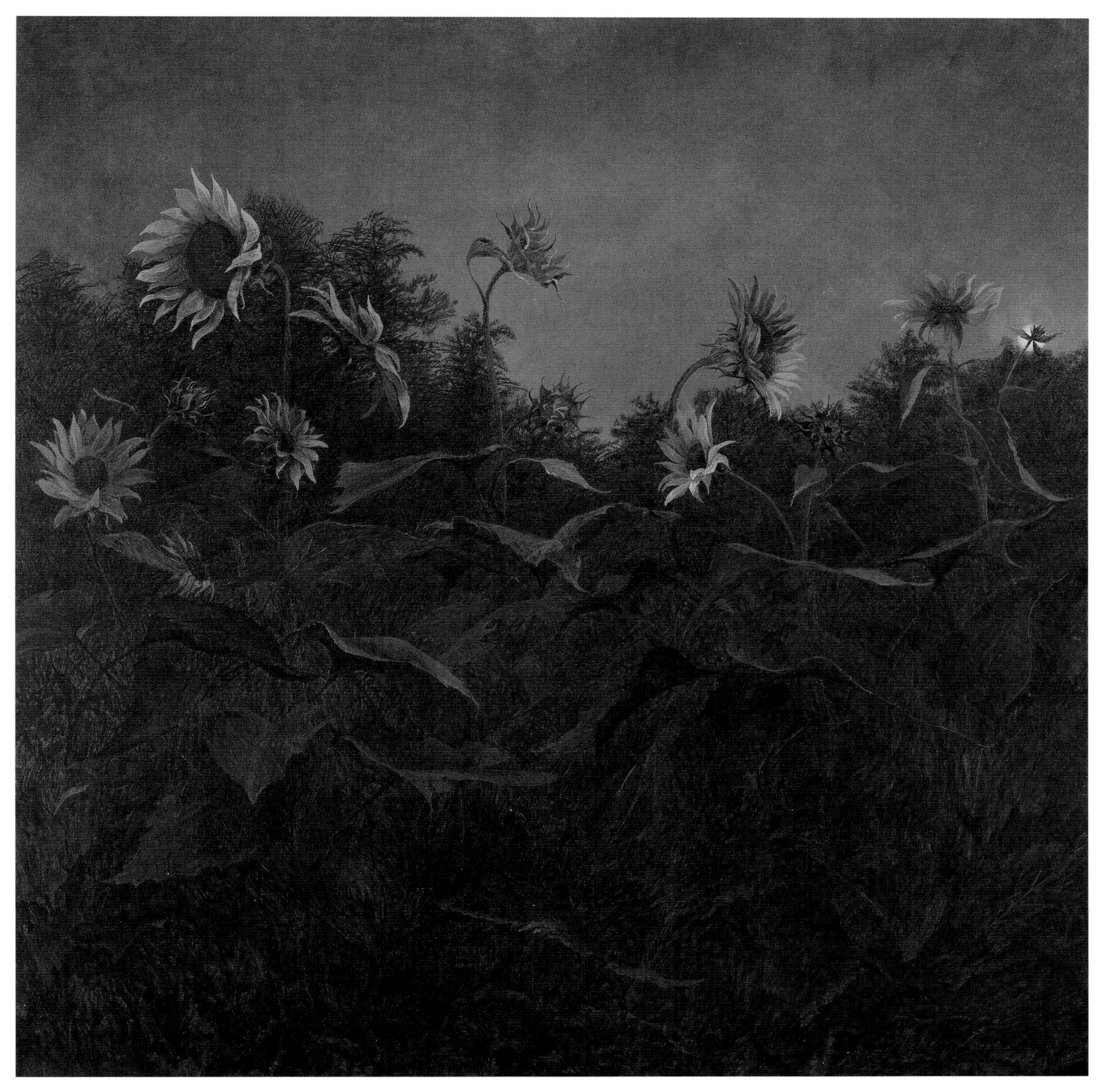

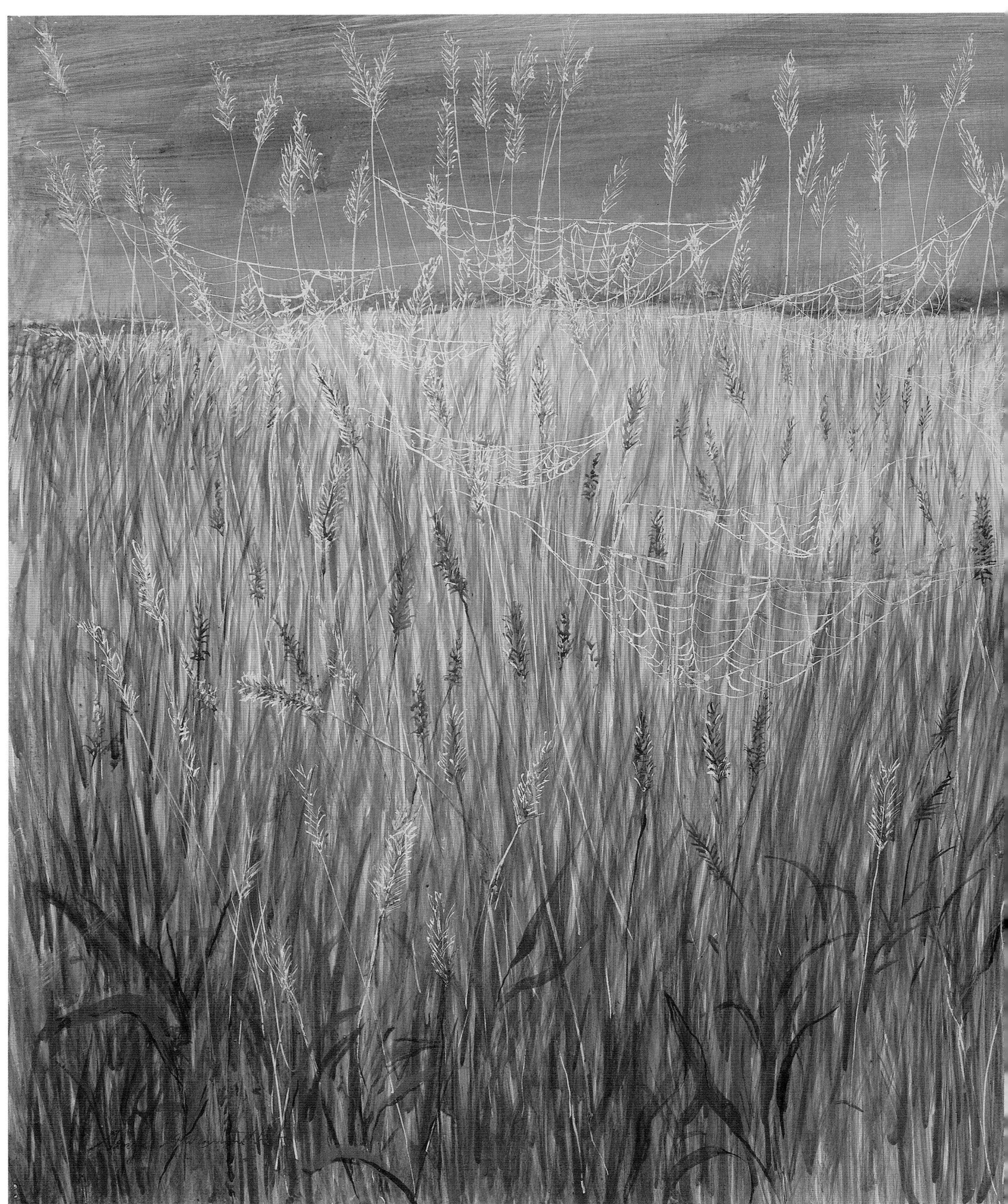

59
WWW, 2002

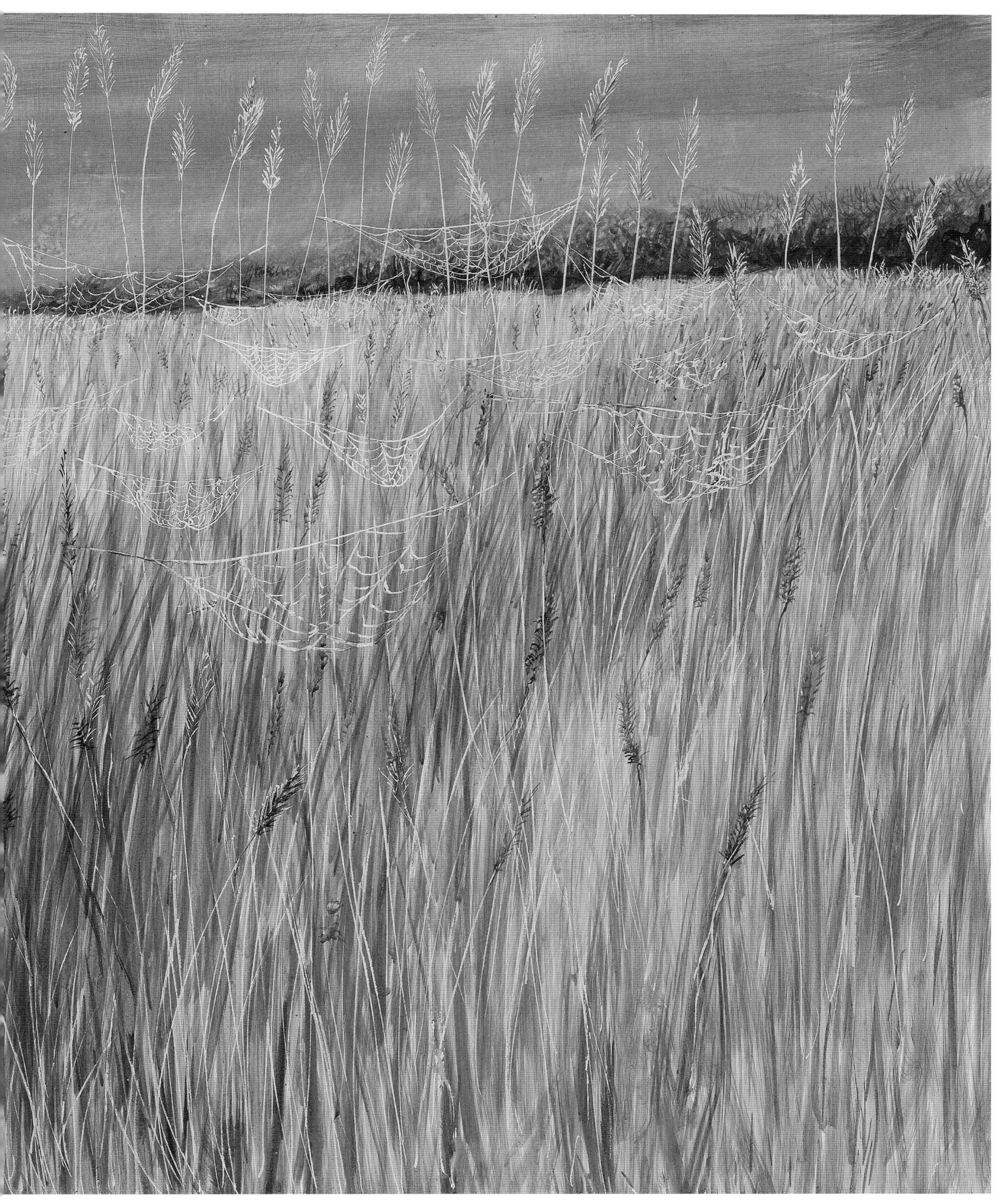

60
WEBSITE, 2003

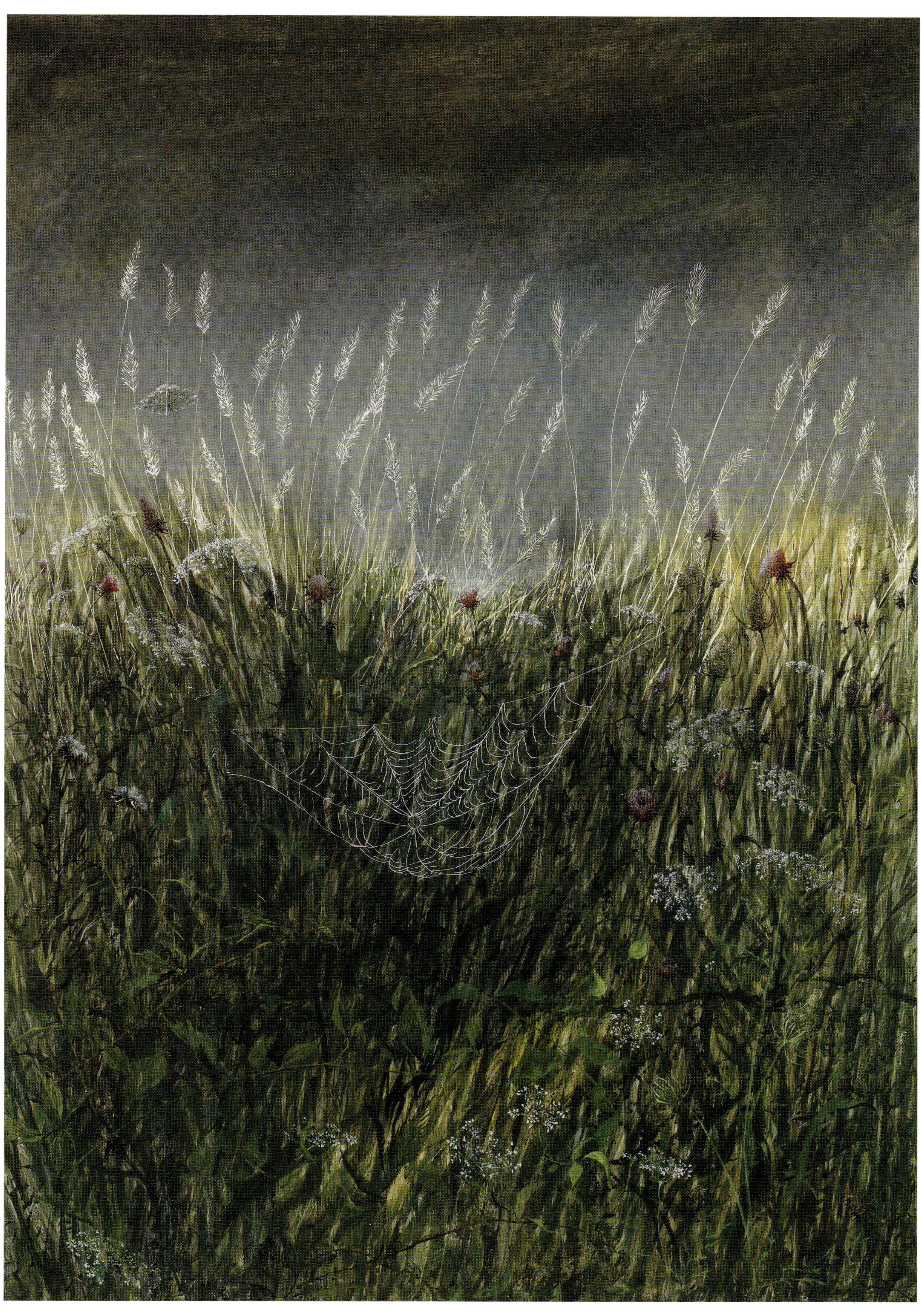

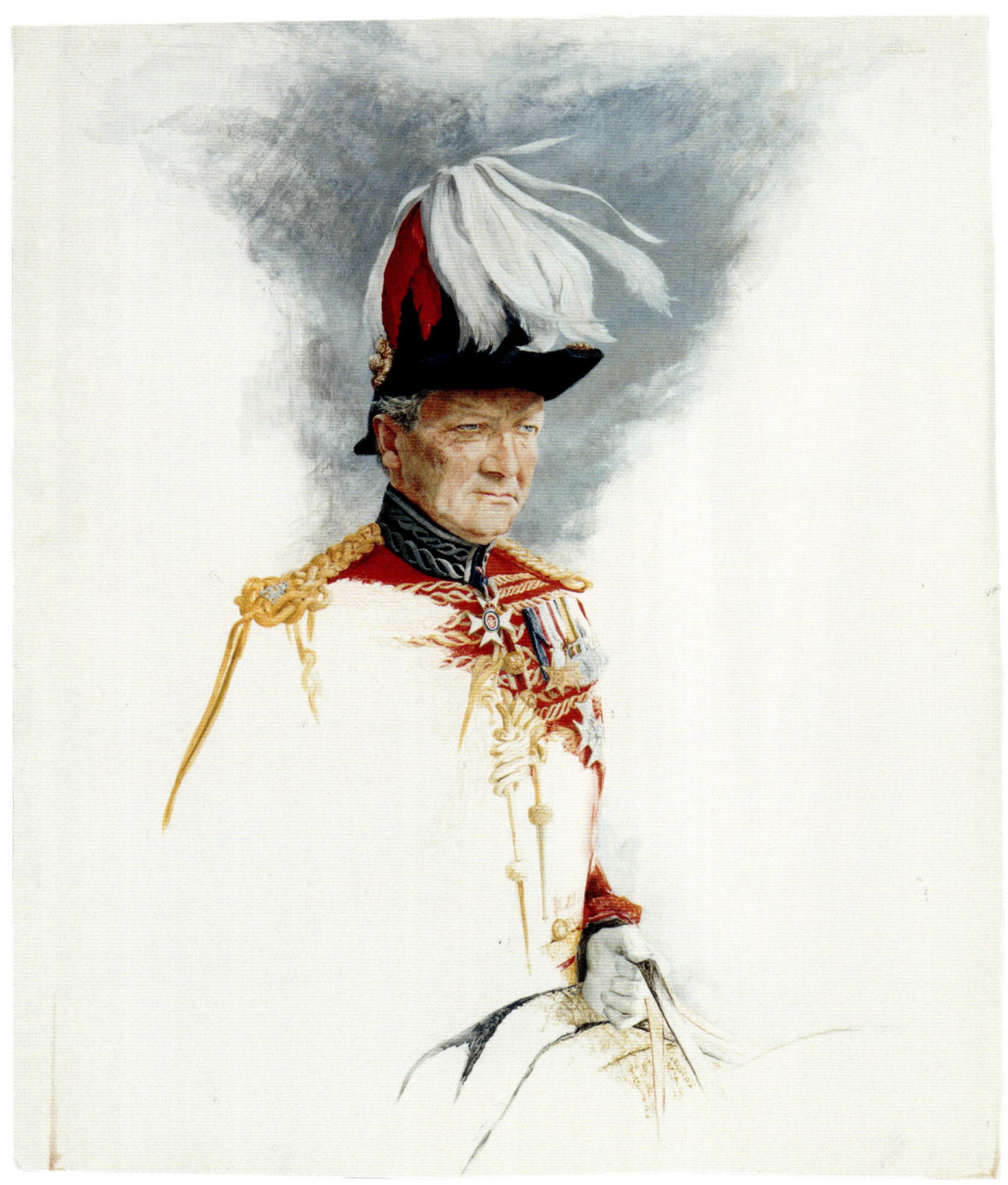

61
THE EARL OF WESTMORLAND, MASTER OF THE HORSE, 1980

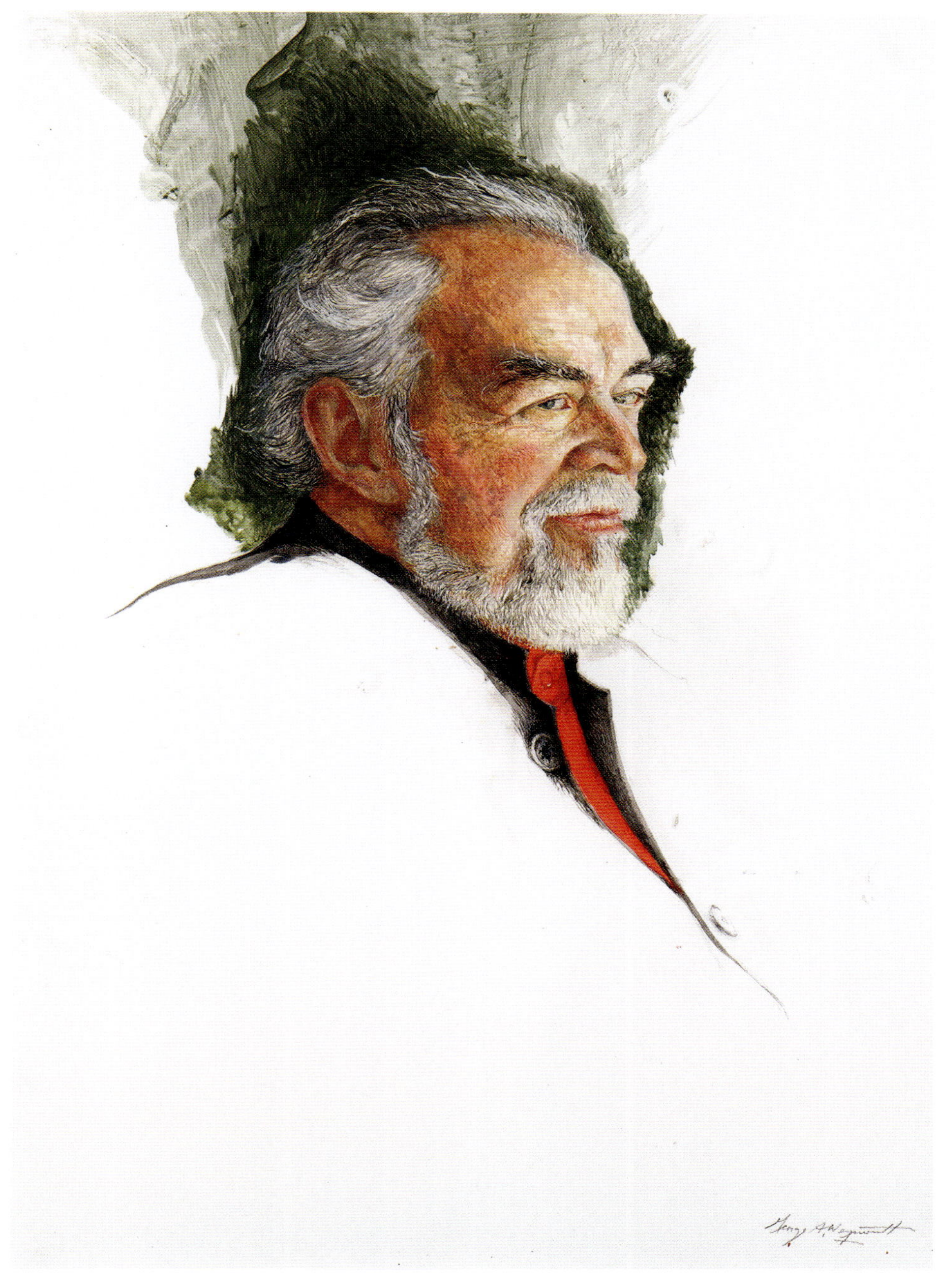

62
PORTRAIT OF HERBERT V. KOHLER, JR. ("THE CHAIRMAN"), 2012

63
MELANIE IN REPOSE, 2011

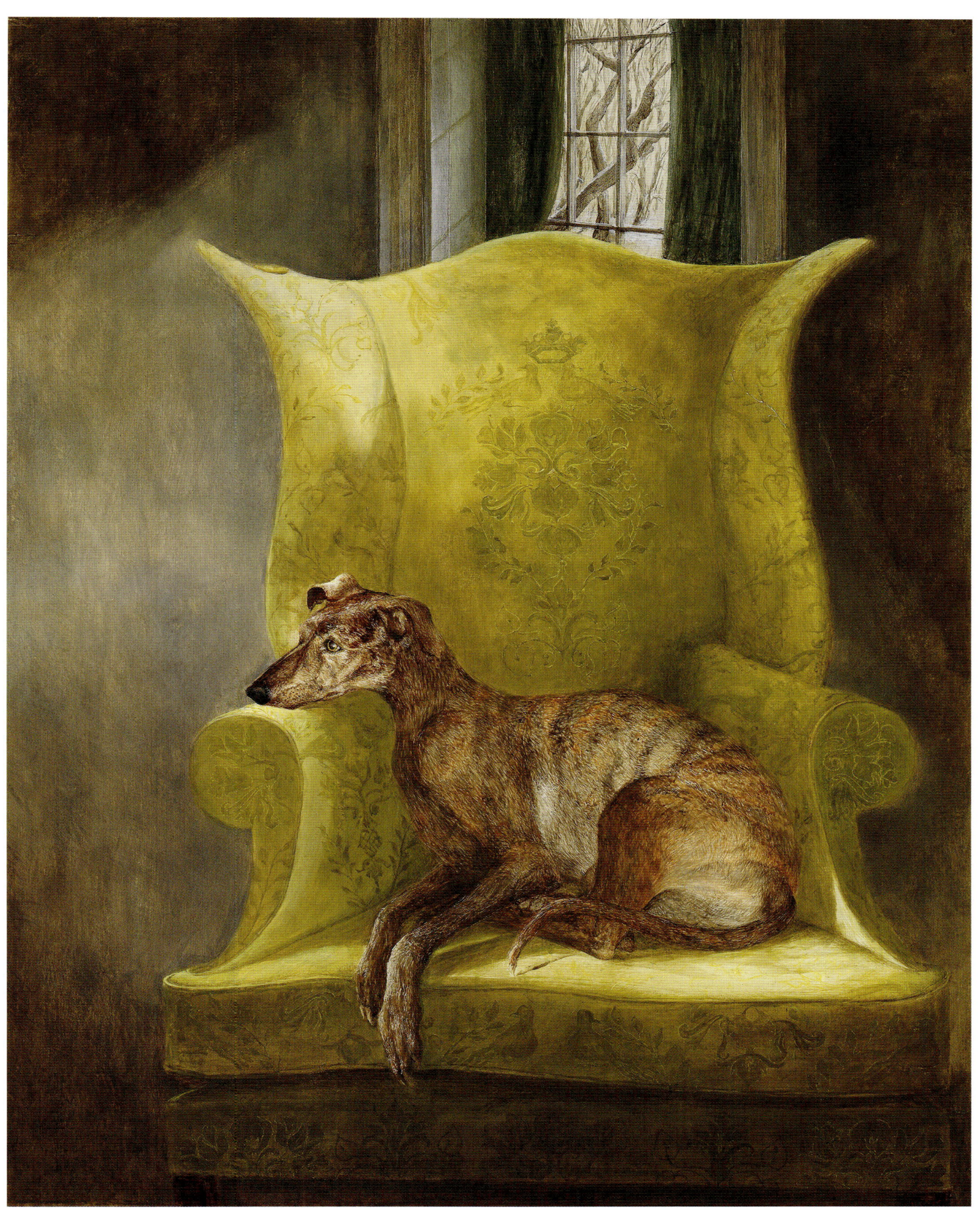

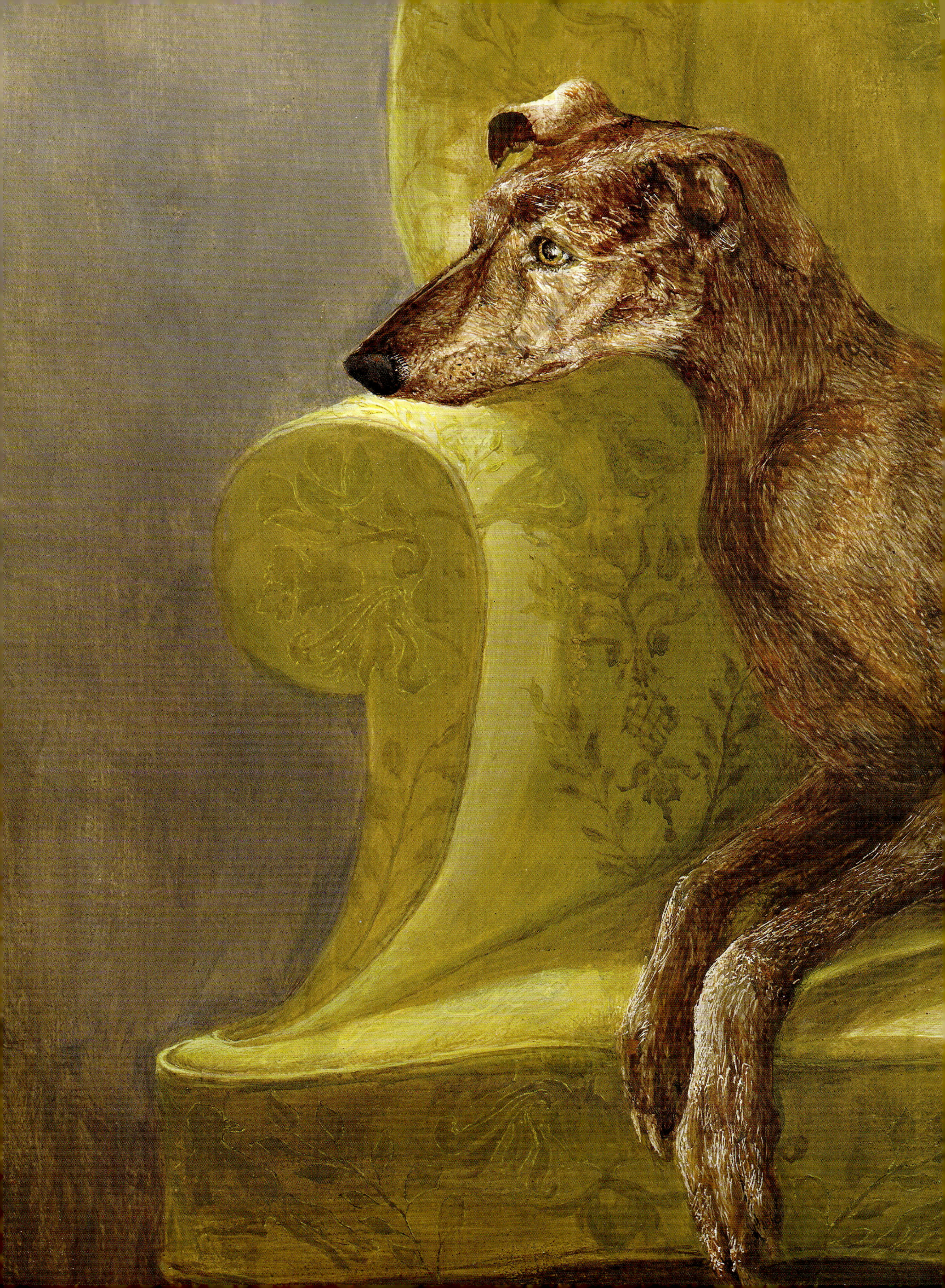

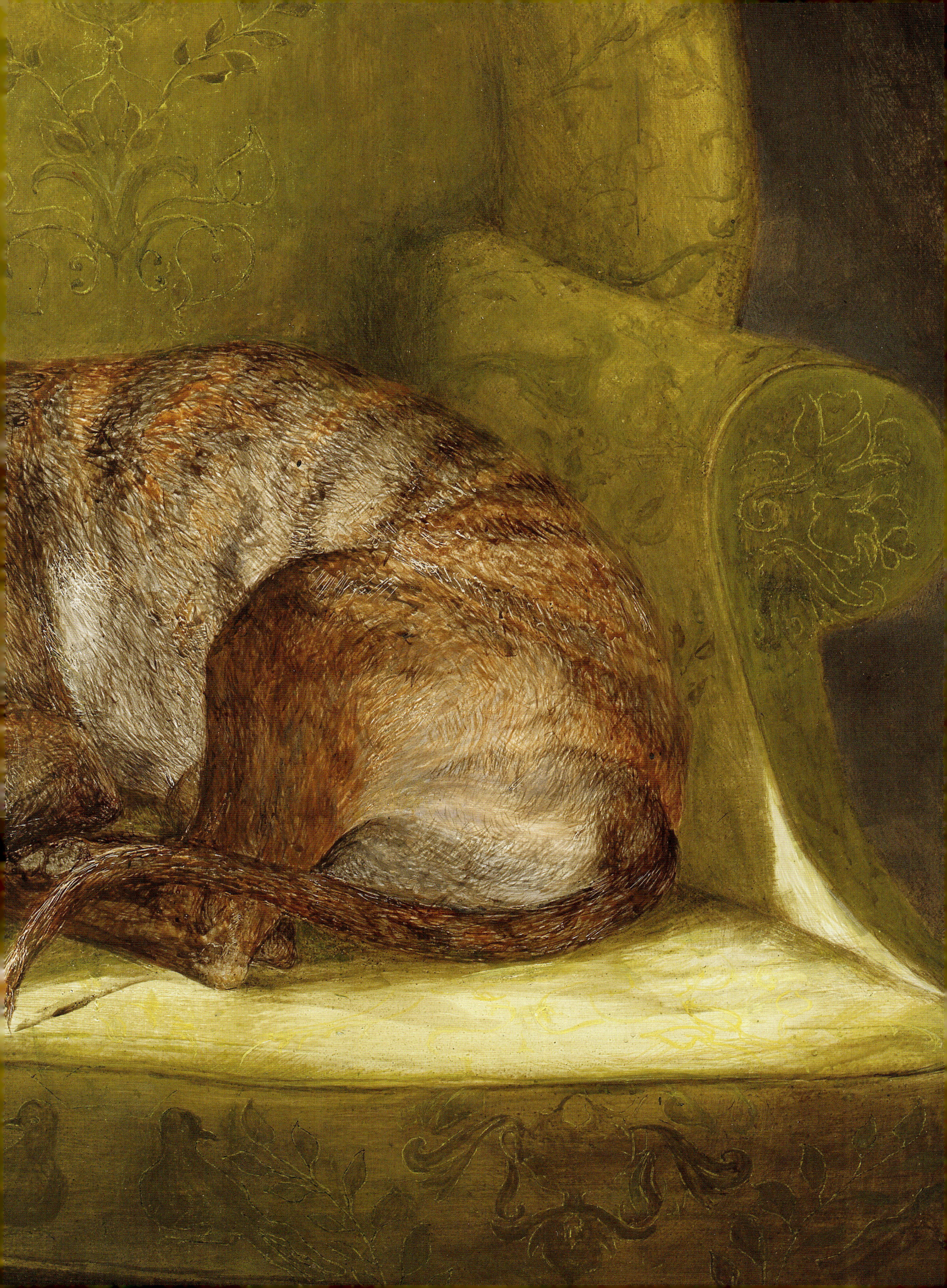

64
SWELTER, 2011

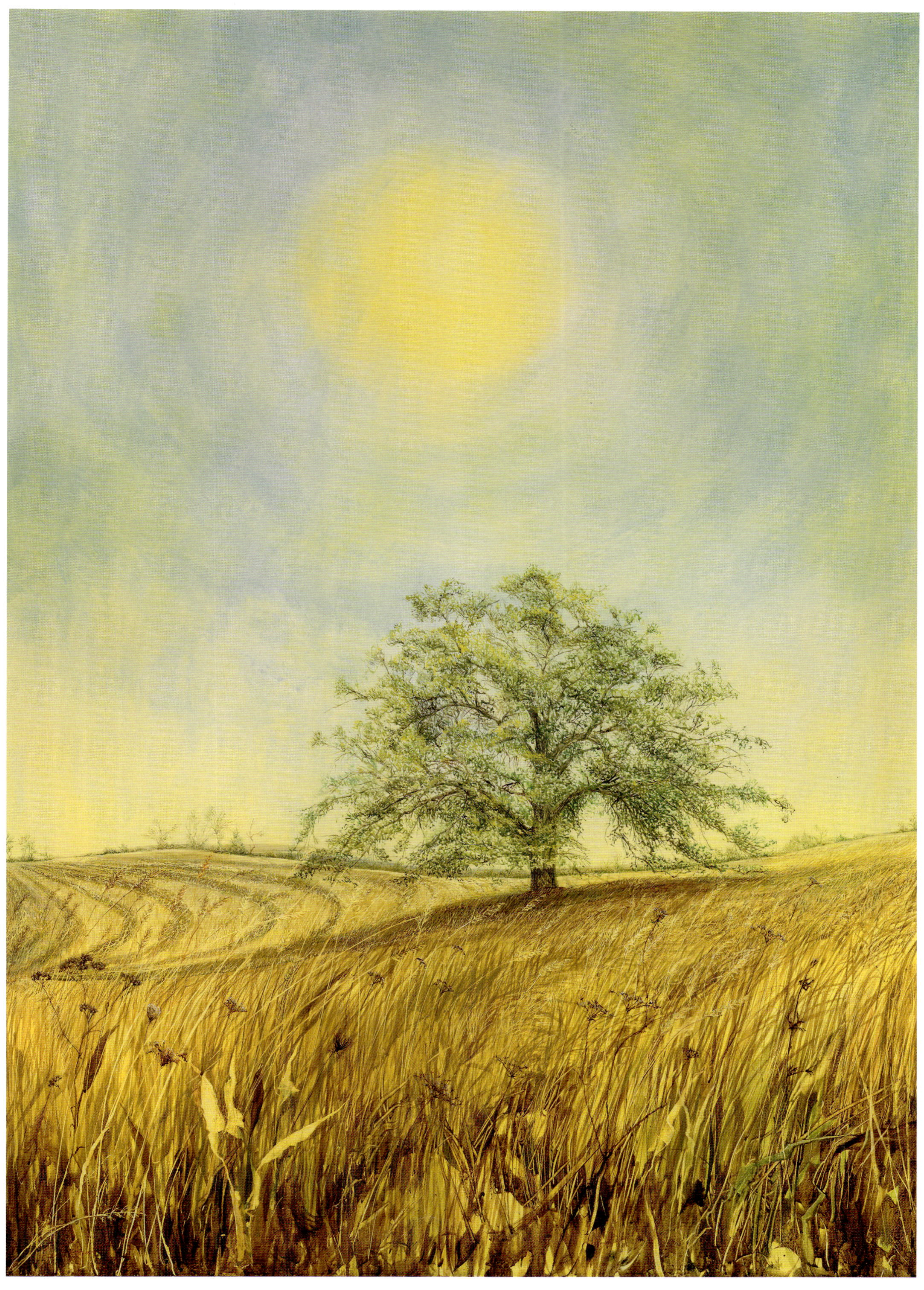

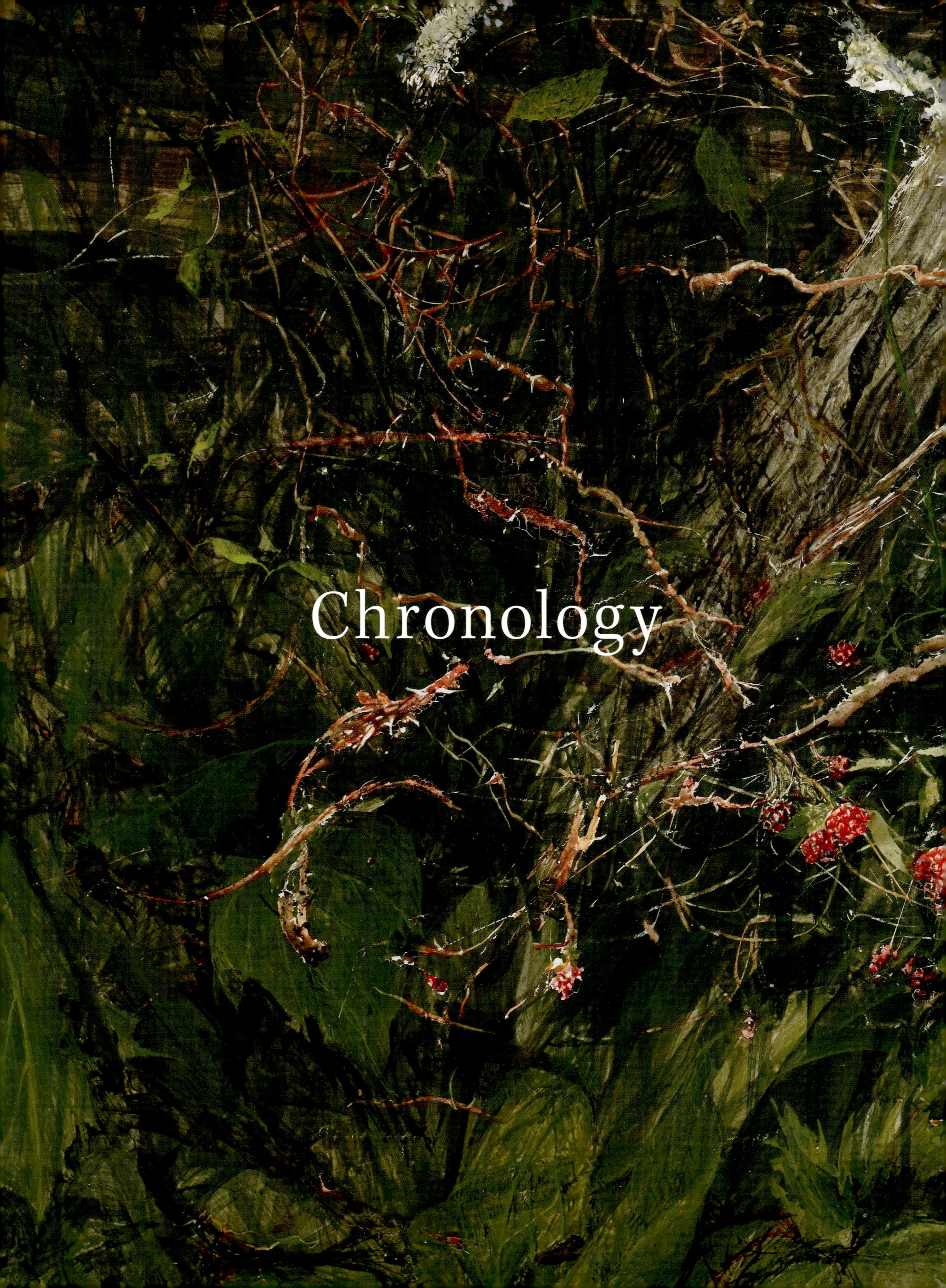

Chronology

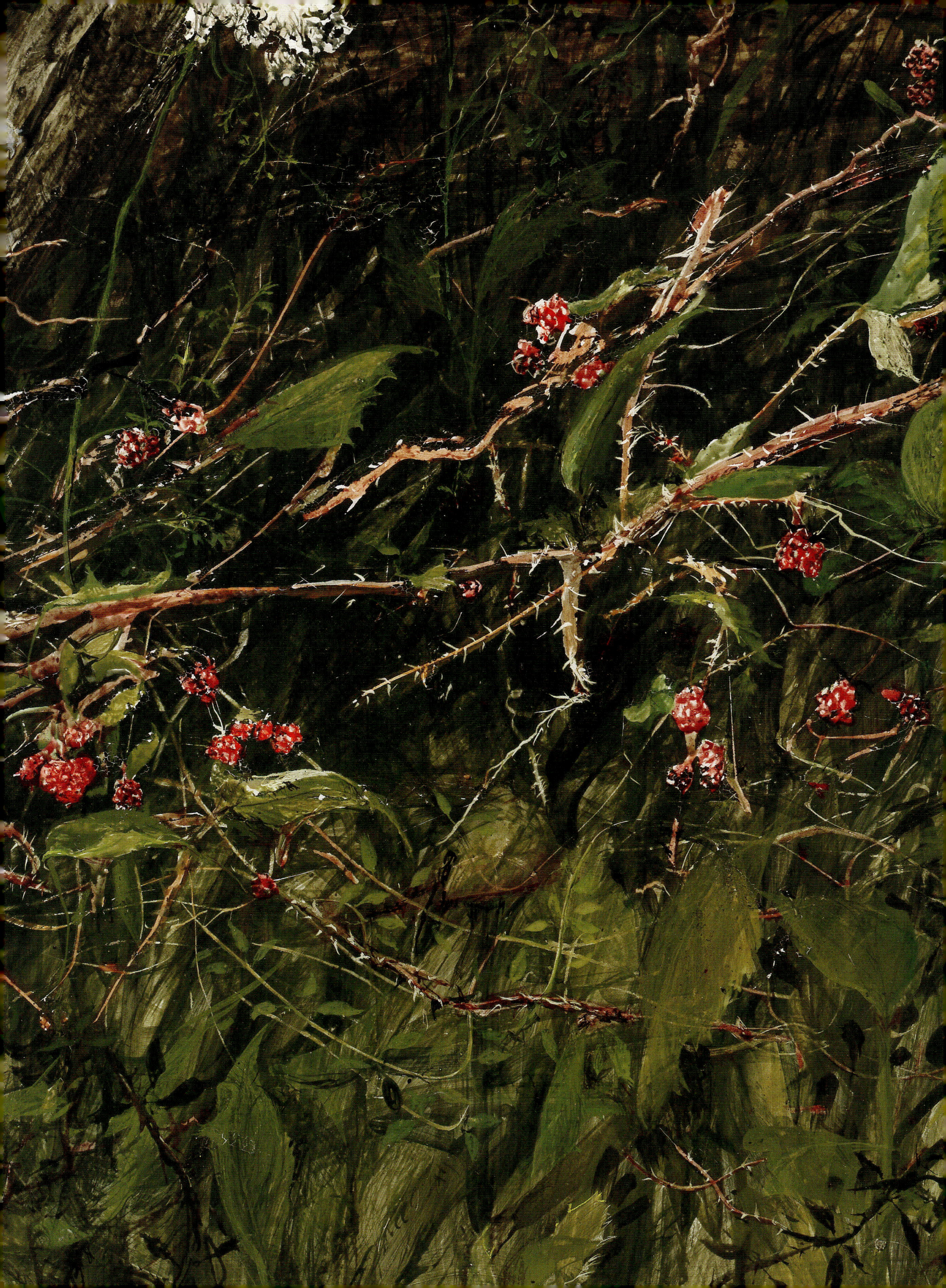

CHRONOLOGY

GAIL STANISLOW

Chronologies and essays found in earlier catalogues on George Weymouth were the logical place to begin a comprehensive review of his life and career. Foremost among these was *George A. Weymouth: A Retrospective* (Chadds Ford, PA: Brandywine River Museum, 1991). *George Weymouth: Landscapes and Portraits of the Brandywine* (Milwaukee: Haggerty Museum of Art, Marquette University, 2001) was also a good source of information. Exhibition catalogues and checklists in which his work appeared were also consulted in the research on his exhibition history and other details of Weymouth's life.

Numerous periodicals, newspaper clippings, photographs, and archival materials from Weymouth's office at the Brandywine Conservancy & Museum of Art, where he was chairman of the board from the institution's inception until his death, were provided by his administrative assistant, Rita Razze, and were invaluable in compiling the Chronology. Additionally, the Brandywine Conservancy's institutional archives and the Museum's Curatorial Department files were sources of a wealth of information and photographs. Archival materials from the Conservancy's Walter and Leonore Annenberg Research Center's collections—in particular the Ann Wyeth McCoy Collection, a gift from her children, one of whom was AnnaB McCoy—were likewise very helpful in locating information, exhibition catalogues and checklists, and photographs.

Other archives contacted for material for the Chronology were those of the National Gallery of Art, Washington, DC; the National Air and Space Museum Archives, Washington, DC; Yale University Archives, New Haven, Connecticut; the Westtown School Archives, West Chester, Pennsylvania; and Hagley Museum and Library Digital Archives, Wilmington, Delaware.

Much information was gained from conversations with Weymouth's son, McCoy (Mac) du Pont Weymouth, and with Weymouth's former wife, AnnaB McCoy. Mary Landa of the Andrew Wyeth Office provided insights not found elsewhere about Weymouth's relationship with the Wyeths. In addition, James Dean, the founding director of the NASA Art Program, very kindly clarified and gave more detail on how Weymouth came to be chosen as one of the first group of artists in the beginning years of that program.

Brandywine Conservancy staff members were also consulted and helped with other aspects of Weymouth's life. David Shields, Associate Director of Land Conservation, helped with details about Weymouth's involvement in several Conservancy activities, and he and his staff provided facts about Weymouth's property and easements in addition to supplying important photographs. Additionally, David Shields's book on the King Ranch's Pennsylvania farms, *Catalyst for Conservation* (Chadds Ford, PA: Brandywine Conservancy, 2011), coauthored by Bill Benson, pointed out how Weymouth began the effort to save the Buck and Doe Run Farms and to create the Laurels Preserve as early as 1972, and how it was ultimately accomplished. Christine Podmaniczky, Curator of N. C. Wyeth Collections and Historic Properties, helped with several entries in the Chronology.

Finally, the online service Newspapers.com proved to be of inestimable value as a source of information and verification of many events in Weymouth's life. Numerous articles from the *Wilmington* (Delaware) *News Journal* and the *Philadelphia Inquirer* from the 1930s to recent years were consulted for specific dates and details to supplement other sources.

UNLESS OTHERWISE NOTED, ALL PHOTOGRAPHS WERE PROVIDED BY THE BRANDYWINE CONSERVANCY & MUSEUM OF ART.

1936 George Alexis Weymouth is born in Philadelphia to George Tyler Weymouth (1904–1990), an investment broker, who founded Laird & Company in Wilmington, Delaware, and Dulcinea (Deo) du Pont Weymouth (1909–1981) on June 2. He grows up in Greenville, Delaware. His mother studied at the Art Students League of New York and was herself an artist. She encouraged Weymouth's pursuit of art.

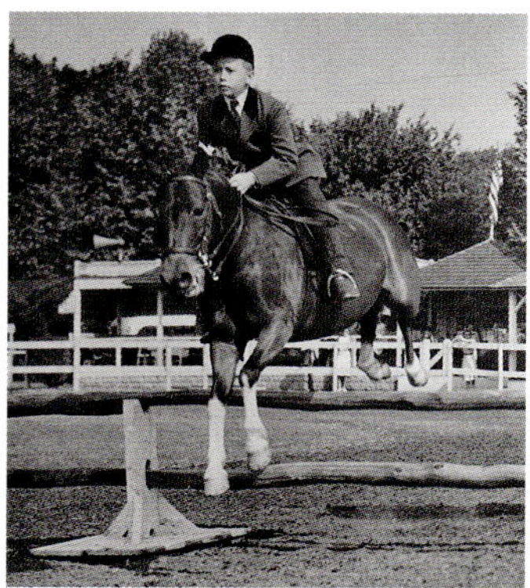

FIG. 1
George A. ("Frolic") Weymouth, age six, on his horse. Mr. and Mrs. Mac Weymouth. Photograph by Freudy, New York.

He is nicknamed "Frolic," after a family pet—a name he used for the rest of his life.

1938–49 Weymouth's parents are very involved with horses and encourage him in this pursuit from a young age. As early as 1938, when Weymouth is not quite two years old, he competes in his first horse show in Wilmington as one of many children in the lead line class for ages fifteen months to six years. He and his brother and sister continue to compete in local horse shows, several of which are held on his parents' estate in Greenville, until 1949. Horses occupy a large part of his life until his death.

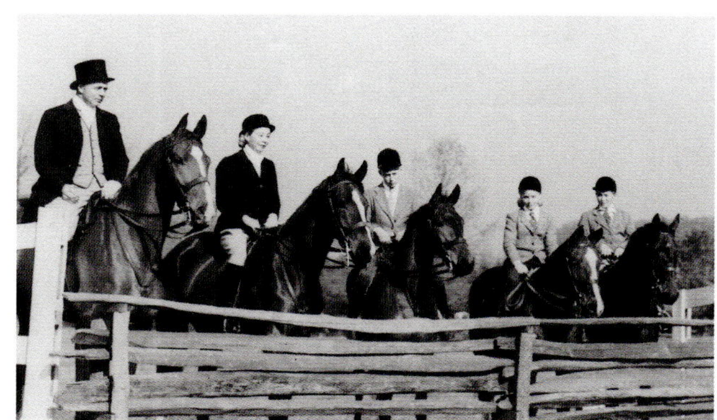

FIG. 2
The Weymouth family on their horses, 1946; left to right: George T., Dulcinea, Eugene, Patricia, and George A. Hagley Museum and Library

1942–48 Attends A. I. du Pont Elementary School until spring 1945.

Attends Westtown School, West Chester, Pennsylvania, 1945–49. His seventh-grade teacher at Westtown commented in Weymouth's file about his "very obvious superiority in the arts."

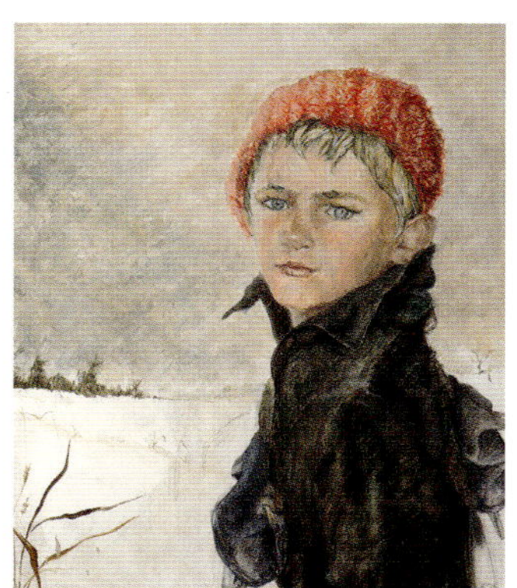

FIG. 3
George A. Weymouth, *Frozen Pond*, 1957
Oil on panel,
16 × 14 inches
Mr. and Mrs. Michael M. Ledyard. Photo by Rick Echelmeyer.

1949–54 At age thirteen, Weymouth enters St. Mark's School, a preparatory school in Southborough, Massachusetts, where he studies painting with Kleber Hall (Blaugrund essay, fig. 4).

1954–58 Introduced to Andrew Wyeth (1917–2009) by his aunt Murton du Pont Carpenter. He takes a painting, *Frozen Pond*, 1957 (fig. 3), to show Wyeth.

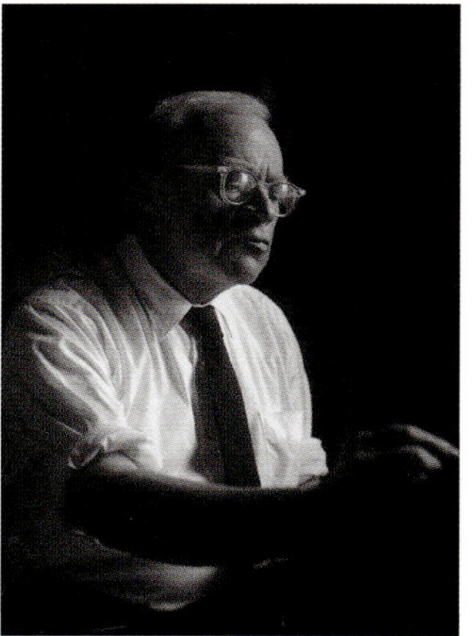

FIG. 4
Deane Keller, painter and professor in the Yale University Department of Art, with whom Weymouth studied during his college years. Yale University Archives.

Attends Yale University and earns a degree in American Studies, Class of 1958. Studies life drawing with Deane Keller (1901–1992) and also attends anatomy sessions at the medical school; begins painting in oil.

Becomes an avid polo player during this time, playing on the Yale team and being chosen as captain for most of his years there. He is also one of a team of college all-stars who travel to England to compete in international tournaments.

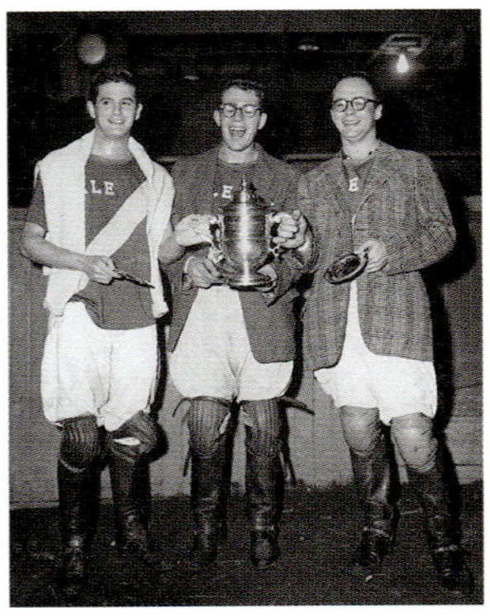

During the summers, he plays polo for local teams, playing first for Maule Farms and then helping to form a new club, the Brandywine Polo Association, in 1957. He is elected as the club's first president that year and captains the team to many victories for the next fourteen years.

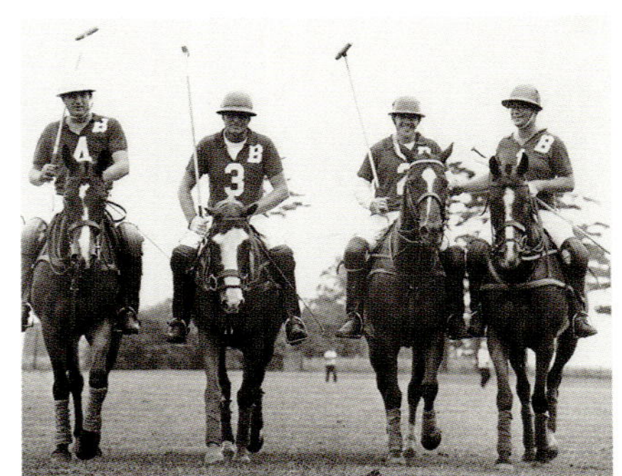

FIG. 5
The Yale polo team with trophy, 1957. Weymouth is on the right. Mr. and Mrs. Mac Weymouth.

1958–59 Andrew Wyeth and his brother-in-law Peter Hurd (1904–84) visit Weymouth while he is painting an oil portrait of his grandfather, Eugene Eleuthère du Pont (plate 10). Noticing that he is using oil paint the same way as they use tempera, Wyeth and Hurd introduce him to the techniques of tempera painting.

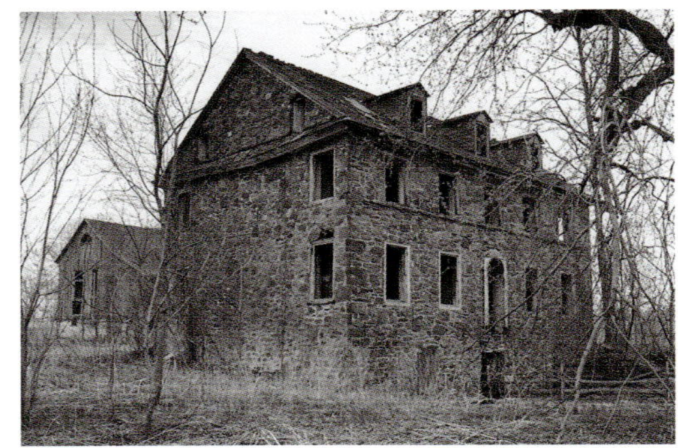

FIG. 6
Brandywine polo team. Weymouth is on the right. Mr. and Mrs. Mac Weymouth.

1959 Paints his first tempera, *Charfoot* (plate 4), an equestrian scene.

1961 Purchases an abandoned eighteenth-century Georgian-style stone house with a large barn on about 125 acres (increased through later purchases to nearly 250 acres) of pasture and thick woodland, once the homeland of the Lenni Lenape Native Americans. He begins restoration of the house and names it "The Big Bend," the Lenni Lenape name for the sharp curve of the Brandywine River flanking the property. He also adopts one of the Lenapes' tribal symbols, the turtle, as a logo for the estate.

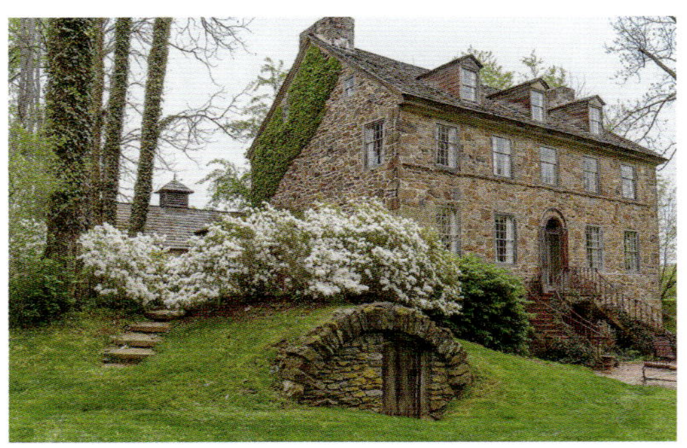

FIG. 7
The Big Bend, previously Twaddell Mill, before restoration by Weymouth.

Soon after restoring the house, Weymouth purchases his first carriage, wanting to keep the historic ambience of the estate. This begins a passion for carriages and coaching that lasts until the end of his life. He begins acquiring antique coaches and carriages, eventually becoming an expert "whip," or driver, and at one time owning more than one hundred of them. He is a prominent member of such organizations as the Coaching Clubs of America and England, the Four-in-Hand Club, and others. His carriages are the highlight of Newport Coaching Weekend, the Devon Horse Show, Old Saratoga Carriage Parade, and more.

FIG. 8
The Big Bend after restoration. Photograph by Jim Graham. © Jim Graham

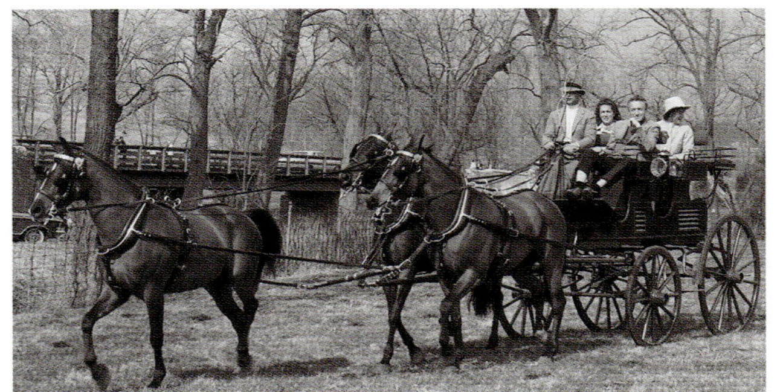

FIG. 9
Weymouth driving one of his coaches with Anna Brelsford McCoy and Andrew and Betsy Wyeth. Ann Wyeth McCoy Collection, Brandywine River Museum of Art, Walter and Leonore Annenberg Research Center.

He marries Anna Brelsford McCoy (AnnaB), daughter of John W. McCoy (1910–1987) and Ann Wyeth McCoy (1915–2005), and niece of Andrew Wyeth.

Weymouth is one of five who purchase the Brandywine Polo Club, which has two polo fields, an arena, stables, and a clubhouse. Weymouth, still president of the club as well as captain of the team, trains, sells, and rents polo ponies with the club manager while continuing to play the sport himself until back problems force him to give it up in the early 1970s.

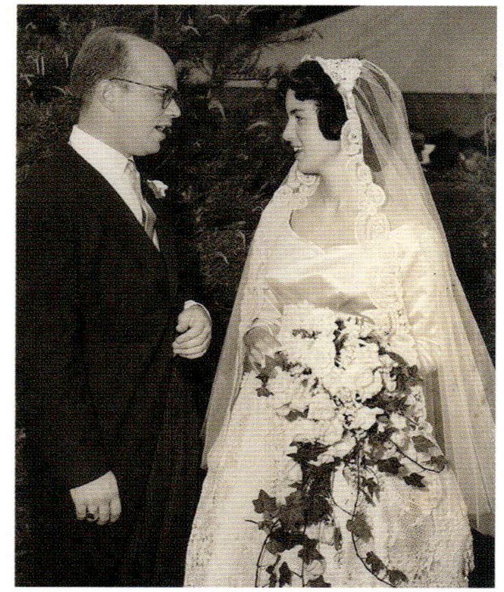

FIG. 10
Anna Brelsford McCoy and George A. Weymouth on their wedding day (May 13, 1961). Ann Wyeth McCoy Collection, Brandywine River Museum of Art, Walter and Leonore Annenberg Research Center.

1962 Exhibits seventeen paintings in the exhibition *Paintings by Richard Layton / Reynolds Thomas / George Weymouth* at the Wilmington Society of Fine Arts, Wilmington, Delaware, February 23–March 18.

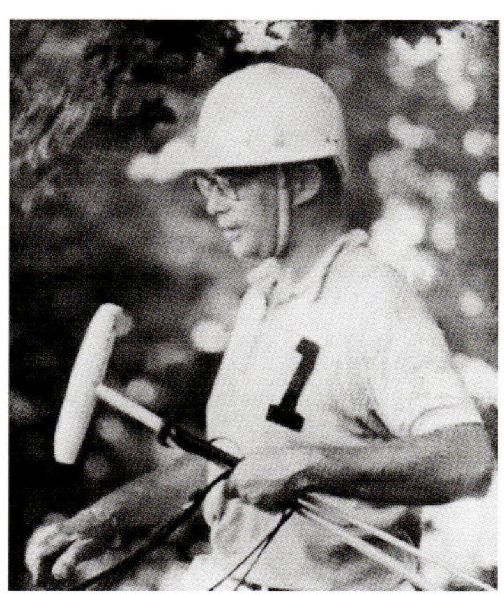

FIG. 11
Weymouth playing polo. Brandywine Polo Club.

1963 Upon the recommendation of Andrew Wyeth, James Dean (director of the newly formed NASA Art Program) chooses Weymouth to be one of the first group of eight artists selected for the program. Peter Hurd and John McCoy are also selected. They are invited to Cape Canaveral, Florida, to witness and record the last launch of the Mercury program on May 15, 1963. Weymouth paints three watercolors, *On the Beach* (Rishel essay, fig. 6), *The Start*, and *Pathways*. Other major artists invited to participate in subsequent years include Robert Rauschenberg, Andy Warhol, and Jamie Wyeth, among many others.

Paints *The Way Back* (plate 17) in tempera, an iconic work that is both a self-portrait and a portrait of his home, The Big Bend.

1963–65 Weymouth is represented by Emanuel J. Rousuck at Wildenstein & Co., New York.

1964 Paints the tempera *Gathering Storm* (plate 19), a portrait of Ethel Roach (Blaugrund essay, fig. 17).

Paintings by George Weymouth, a solo exhibition of thirty-four works, is held at Meredith Long & Co. Gallery, Houston, Texas, December 5, 1964–January 5, 1965.

1965 Weymouth's three NASA watercolors are included in the National Gallery of Art exhibition *Eyewitness to Space*, a presentation of works from the NASA Art Program, March 14–May 23. The exhibition then tours across the country for the next several years.

1966 *Paintings by George Weymouth*, a solo exhibition of thirty works, is held at the A. B. Closson Jr. Gallery, Cincinnati, Ohio, October 12–31.

Exhibits four works in *Loan Exhibition of Paintings by the Wyeth Family* at the Parrish Art Museum, Southampton, New York, July 30–August 22.

Paints the tempera *Eleven O'Clock News* (plate 25).

1967 Responding to concerns of Chadds Ford citizens, including Andrew Wyeth, about a proposed industrial site near the heart of the village, Weymouth, accompanied by William Prickett Jr. and Francis I. du Pont, spearheads the formation of the Tri-County Conservancy. Their purpose is twofold: to protect and preserve the land surrounding the Brandywine watershed in southeast Pennsylvania to Wilmington, Delaware, and to build an art museum to showcase the works of artists of the region. They raise funds and purchase the threatened forty-one-acre meadow in Chadds Ford, followed by the purchase of the 1860s Hoffman's Mill. The mill would become the Brandywine River Museum of Art.

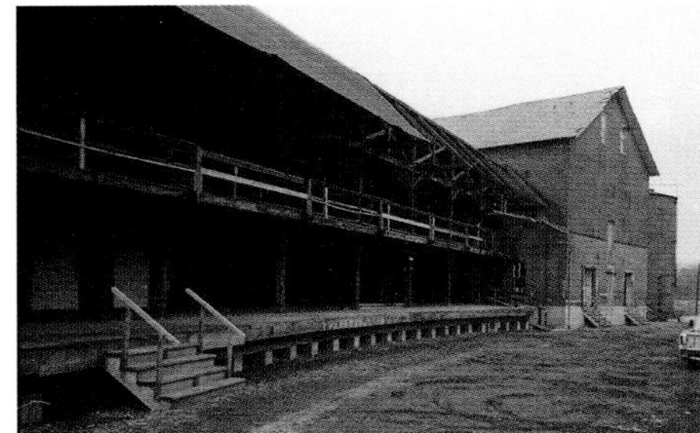

FIG. 12
Hoffman's Mill, side view, before renovation.

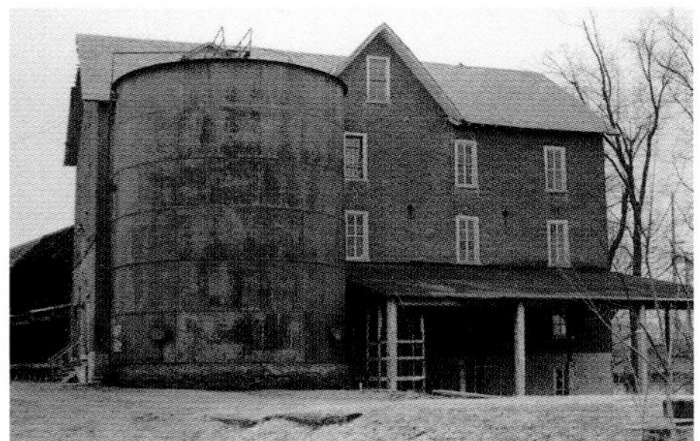

FIG. 13
Hoffman's Mill, shown before its renovation as the Brandywine River Museum of Art.

Paints portrait of Governor William W. Scranton (plate 40).

1968 Eight works by Weymouth are included in the Chadds Ford Historical Society exhibition *Chadds Ford Art Heritage, 1898–1968*, September 7–15, held in Hoffman's Mill.

George A. Weymouth, a solo exhibition of twenty-seven works, is held at the Country Art Gallery, Locust Valley, New York, May 21–June 5.

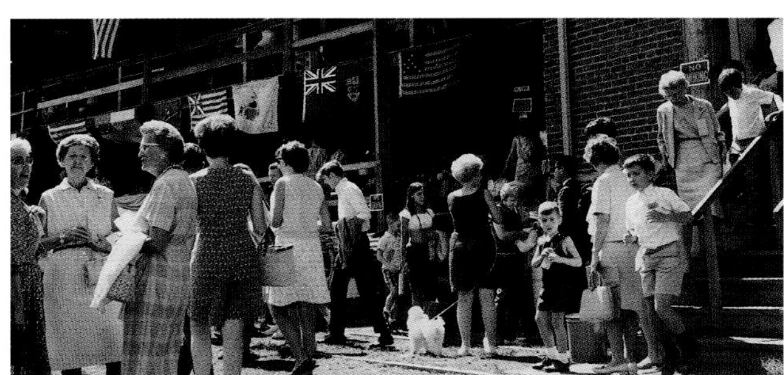

FIG. 14
Visitors at the Chadds Ford Historical Society exhibition *Chadds Ford Art Heritage, 1898–1968*, held in Hoffman's Mill.

Weymouth and AnnaB adopt a son, whom they name McCoy du Pont Weymouth.

1969 Weymouth grants the conservation easement on his Big Bend estate to the Tri-State Conservancy, which becomes the Brandywine Conservancy in later years. His is the first conservation easement the Conservancy receives, and his family and friends soon follow suit.

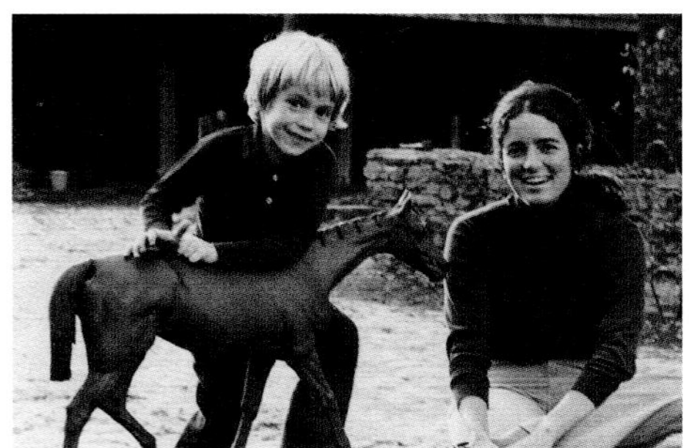

FIG. 15
McCoy du Pont Weymouth ("Mac"), with his mother, Anna Brelsford McCoy, circa 1973. Ann Wyeth McCoy Collection, Brandywine River Museum of Art, Walter and Leonore Annenberg Research Center.

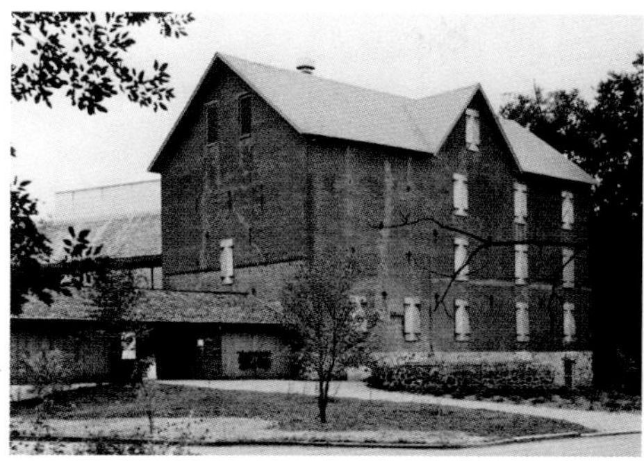

FIG. 16
The Museum after renovation of Hoffman's Mill.

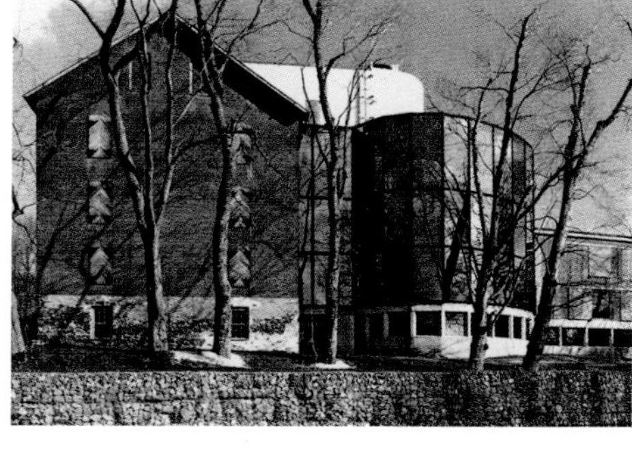

FIG. 17
The Museum after mill renovation, viewed from the river side. Photo by Susan Gray. © www.susangrayart.com

1971 Under Weymouth's guidance, Hoffman's Mill is renovated by architect James R. Grieves of Baltimore. Much of the original mill is kept intact, with art galleries within a three-story, glass-and-steel atrium overlooking the Brandywine River. The Trustees place a marker in a cornerstone of the building dedicating the building to Weymouth.

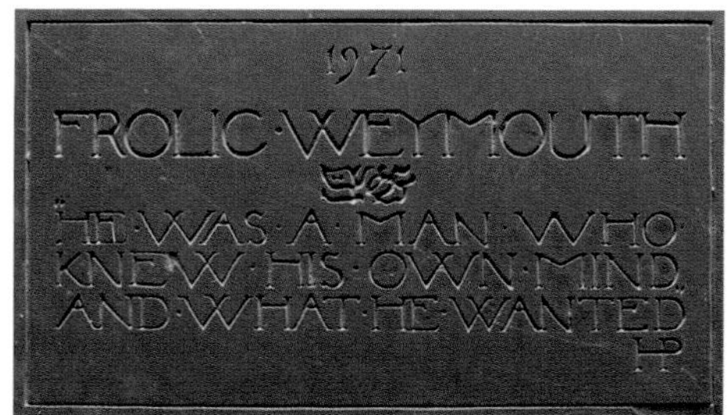

FIG. 18
Plaque honoring George A. Weymouth at the cornerstone of the Museum building.

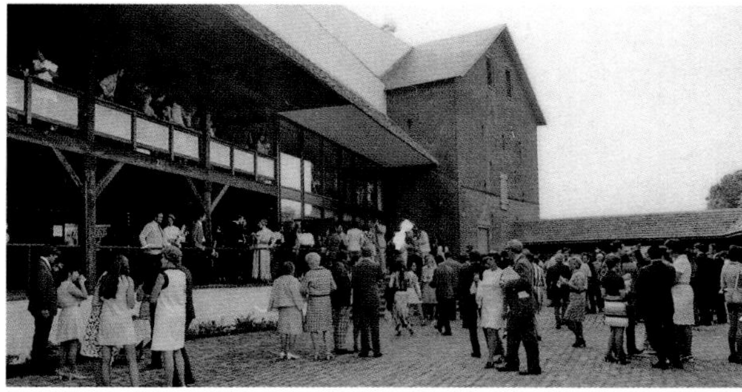

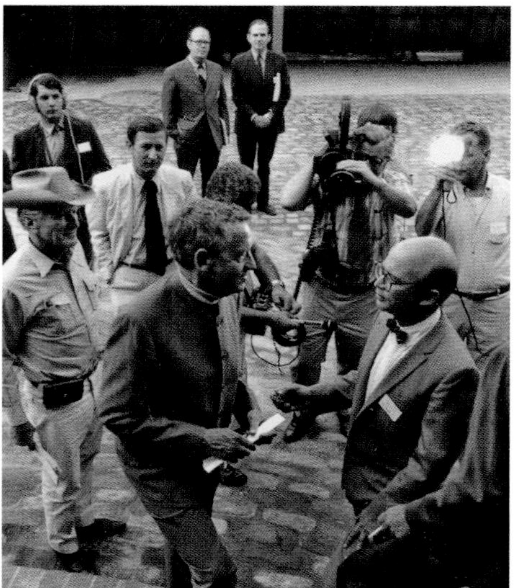

FIG. 19
Visitors to the Museum on the opening weekend.

FIG. 20
Members of the press photographing Andrew Wyeth and George A. Weymouth at the Museum opening June 18, 1971.

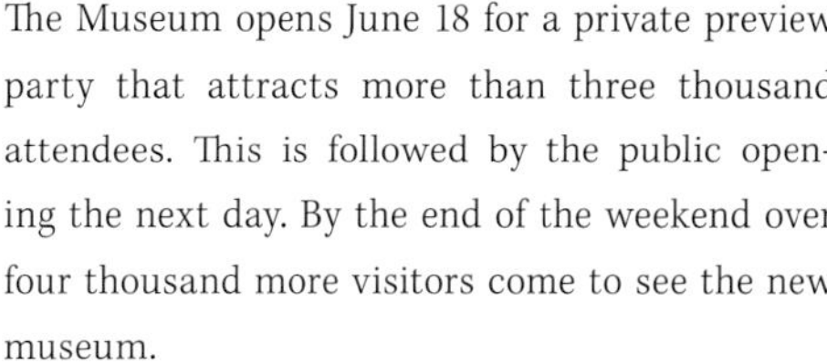

The Museum opens June 18 for a private preview party that attracts more than three thousand attendees. This is followed by the public opening the next day. By the end of the weekend over four thousand more visitors come to see the new museum.

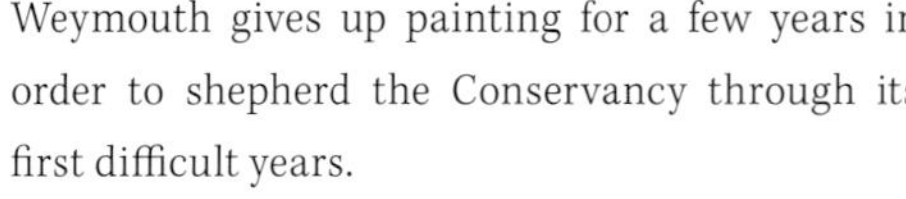

Weymouth gives up painting for a few years in order to shepherd the Conservancy through its first difficult years.

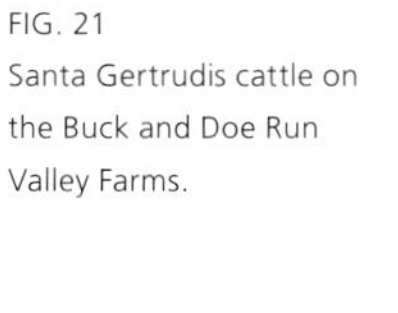

FIG. 21
Santa Gertrudis cattle on the Buck and Doe Run Valley Farms.

1972 Robert Kleberg, of the well-known King Ranch in Texas, invites Weymouth to tour the Buck and Doe Run Valley Farms, the Klebergs' Pennsylvania cattle ranch. Weymouth immediately recognizes the importance of the property, an environmentally sensitive area crucial to protecting the water quality of the Brandywine watershed. Weymouth begins a major effort that continues for the next twelve years to have the property protected.

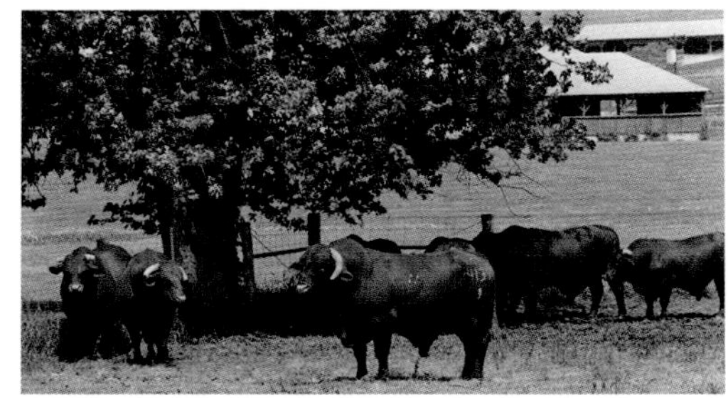

1972–77 Weymouth is appointed by President Nixon to serve on the U.S. Commission of Fine Arts.

1974 Weymouth serves on the Visual Arts Panel of the Pennsylvania Council on the Arts.

He paints the tempera *August* (plate 30), an important work depicting his property, The Big Bend.

1975 Weymouth raises funds to purchase Andrew Wyeth's five paintings of Siri Erickson for the Museum. These works were Wyeth's first series of nudes and an important transition in his artistic career.

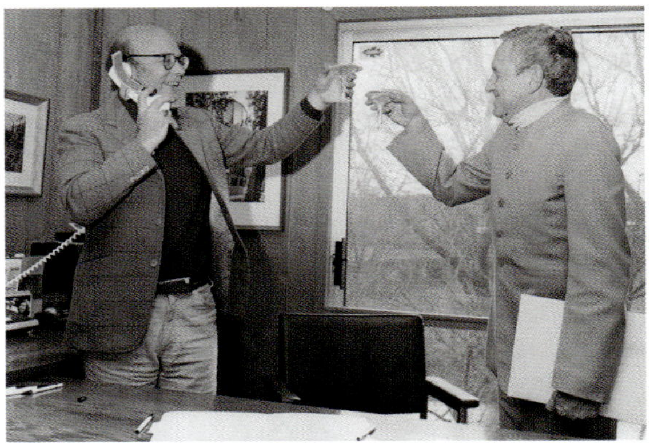

FIG. 22
Andrew Wyeth and Weymouth toast the Museum's acquisition of Wyeth's Siri paintings.

Weymouth is featured in the special February issue of *American Artist* as a member of the Wyeth family of artists in the article "Three Generations of the Wyeth Family" by Susan E. Meyer.

Through the bequest of New York philanthropist Joan Whitney Payson (1903–75), Weymouth's watercolor *Tree Trunks* (1968, plate 37) is given to the Metropolitan Museum of Art.

1976 Weymouth's NASA works are included in the National Air and Space Museum's opening exhibition, *Flight and the Arts*, July 1, 1976–78. (NASA's art collection had been transferred to the NASM and became part of its permanent collections in 1975.)

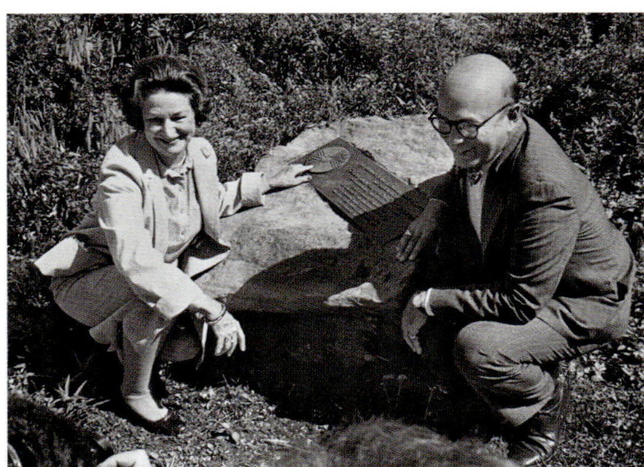

FIG. 23
Weymouth and Lady Bird Johnson viewing campaign dedication plaque honoring Ford Draper and Henry A. Thouron.

1979 Weymouth names Lady Bird Johnson as the Conservancy's Honorary Chairperson for the Museum's first endowment campaign. She visits the Museum and dedicates the surrounding gardens to Ford Draper and Henry A. Thouron, former Trustees.

Initiates the Carriage Parade at Winterthur Museum, Garden & Library's Annual Point-to-Point Steeplechase races. (In 2016, his friends organize and lead the parade with his coach and horses in memoriam.) The event expands to become a weekend-long series of activities for coaching groups, and includes a competition and other related events.

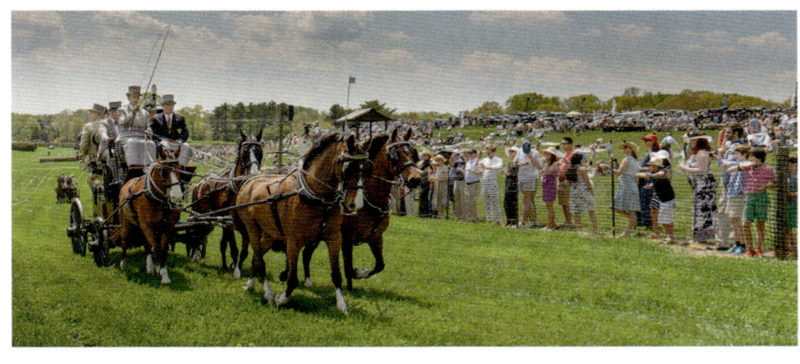

FIG. 24
Weymouth leads the carriage parade at Winterthur's Point-to-Point Steeplechase races. Photograph by Jim Graham. © Jim Graham.

Separated in 1977, Weymouth and AnnaB divorce.

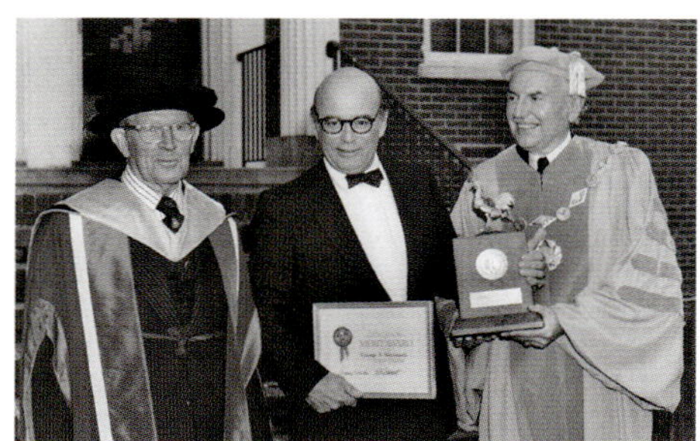

FIG. 25
Executive Director James H. Duff and Weymouth with Amanda K. Berls and Ruth A. Yerion.

1980 Weymouth oversees donation of thirty-eight major paintings to the Museum by art collectors Amanda K. Berls and Ruth A Yerion. This gift significantly expands the Museum's collections of landscapes, still lifes, and portraits.

1981 Weymouth receives the University of Delaware Merit Award for Community Service.

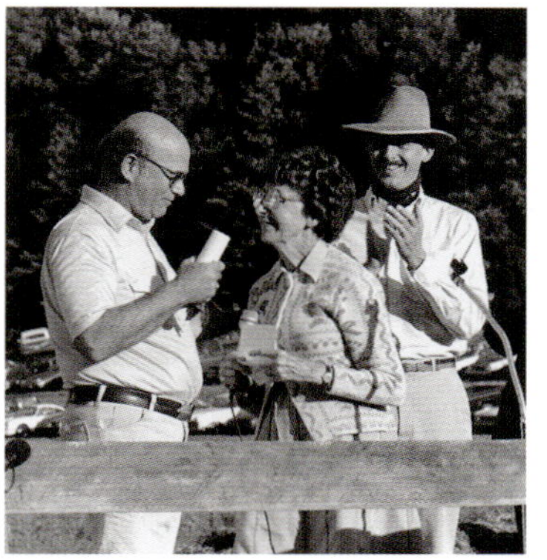

FIG. 26
Weymouth receives the University of Delaware's Merit Award for Community Service from university president E. A. Trabant and unidentified official.

1982 Through the generosity of the Wyeth family and their long-standing friendship with Weymouth and belief in his mission for the Conservancy, the N. C. Wyeth House and Studio and surrounding land are acquired by the Conservancy. Carolyn Wyeth, one of N. C. Wyeth's daughters, has life tenancy in the house.

Weymouth begins the tradition of a carriage parade at the Radnor Hunt Races annual "Race for Open Space," a benefit for the Conservancy.

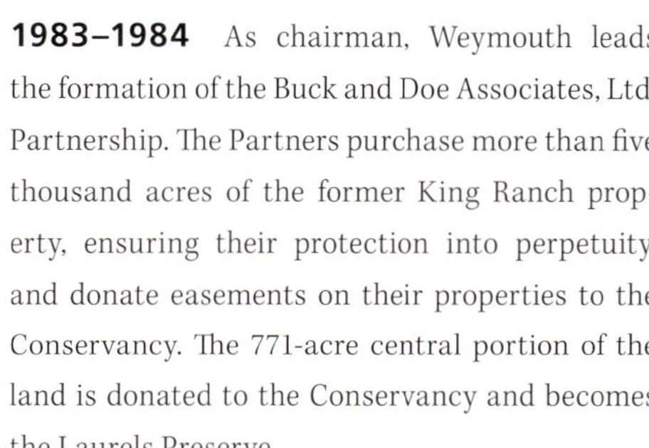

FIG. 27
Weymouth receives the deed to the Laurels Preserve from Mrs. E. Miles Valentine while Executive Director Duff and others applaud.

1983–1984 As chairman, Weymouth leads the formation of the Buck and Doe Associates, Ltd. Partnership. The Partners purchase more than five thousand acres of the former King Ranch property, ensuring their protection into perpetuity, and donate easements on their properties to the Conservancy. The 771-acre central portion of the land is donated to the Conservancy and becomes the Laurels Preserve.

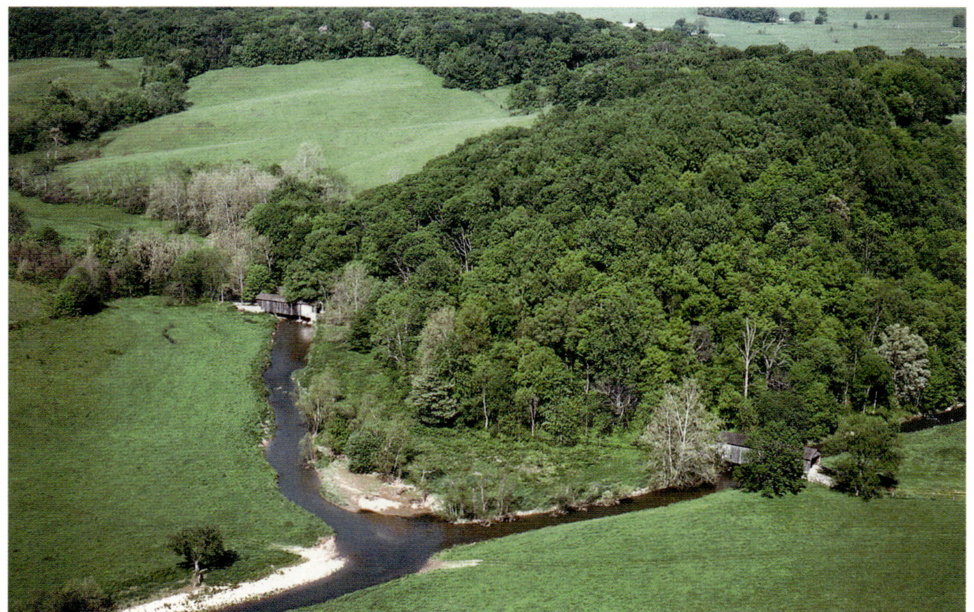

FIG. 28
Aerial view of the Laurels Preserve.

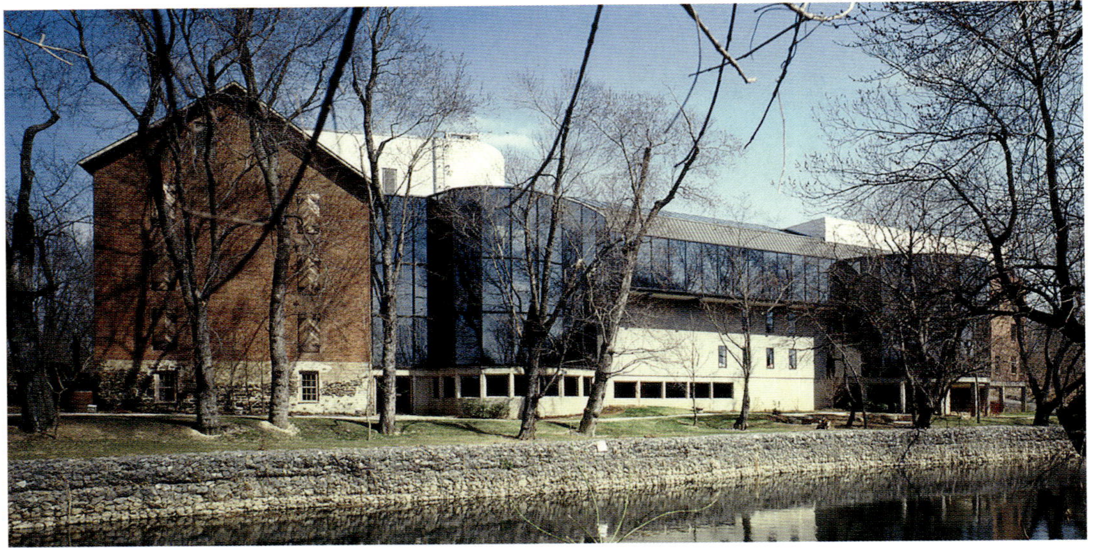

FIG. 29
Brandywine River Museum of Art with 1984 addition.

1984 After a fundraising campaign led by Weymouth and James H. Duff, executive director of the Conservancy and the Museum, they preside over the Museum's first expansion, which provides new galleries and a café.

Six works by Weymouth are included in *Flower Painting: An American Tradition*, an exhibition at the Brandywine River Museum of Art, Chadds Ford, Pennsylvania, July 2–September 9.

1985 Paints portrait of Delaware Governor Pierre S. du Pont IV.

In May, Weymouth takes his horses and coach to Europe for over three months, driving one thousand miles in the United Kingdom and one thousand miles in France, with the help of his long-time coaching assistant and stable manager, Robert Morhard-Longstaffe. Highlights of the trip include meeting Queen Elizabeth when she presented them with a coaching award and attending Royal Week at Ascot.

1987 Weymouth is featured in the article "George A. Weymouth," by editor M. Stephen Doherty, in the January 1987 issue of *American Artist*.

At a press conference, Weymouth announces plans for an exhibition, *An American Vision: Three Generations of Wyeth Art*, organized by the Museum, which will travel to the USSR, Japan, Italy, and England, and several other museums in the United States. It is the first American art exhibition to travel to the Soviet Union as part of the General Exchanges Agreement signed in 1985.

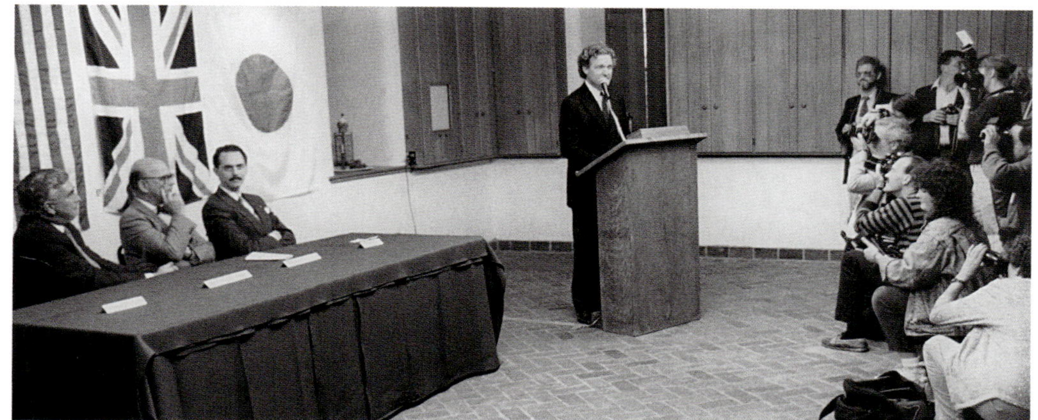

FIG. 30
Press conference announcing the world tour of the *American Vision* exhibition.

1988 Paints portrait of Prince Michael of Kent (Blaugrund essay fig. 25).

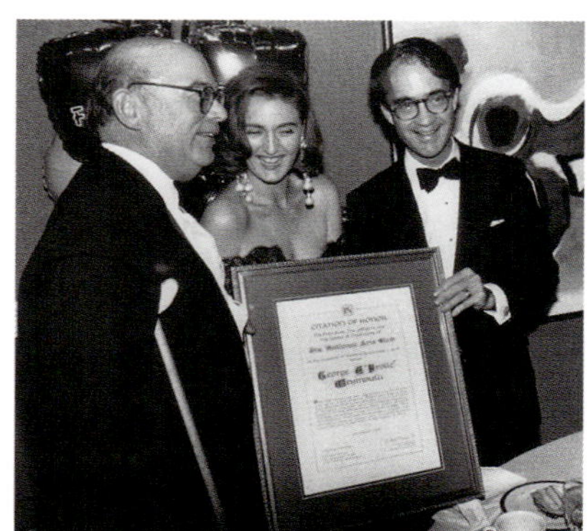

FIG. 31
Weymouth receiving the National Arts Club Award from club president O. Aldon James, Jr. National Arts Club, New York; photo by C. Zumwalt. National Arts Club.

1989 Receives the National Society of Fund Raising Executives Outstanding Fund Raising Volunteer Award.

1990 Weymouth is awarded the National Arts Club's Citation of Honor and is the honoree at the club's 92nd Anniversary Benefit Ball in New York in November.

1991 The Museum's exhibition *George A. Weymouth—A Retrospective* opens on June 9 and runs through September 2. This retrospective exhibition is organized by the Museum to celebrate its twentieth anniversary. The exhibition travels to the Jacksonville Art Museum, October 3–November 10.

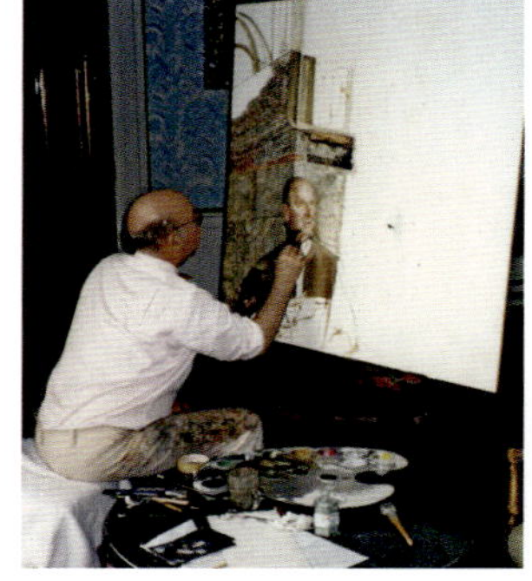

FIG. 32
Weymouth painting portrait of H.R.H. Prince Philip. Collection of Mr. and Mrs. Mac Weymouth.

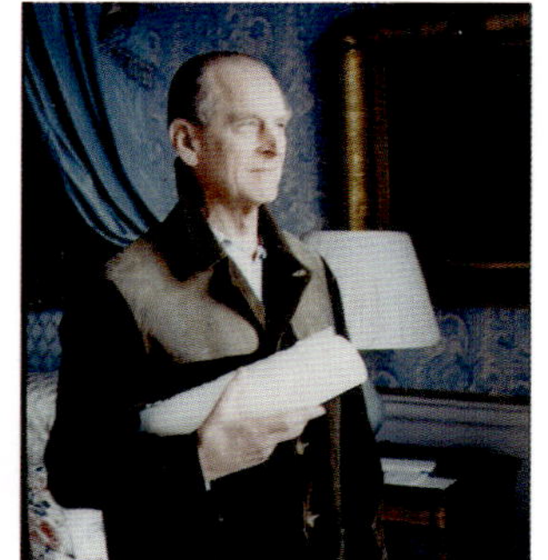

FIG. 33
H.R.H. Prince Philip posing for portrait. Collection of Mr. and Mrs. Mac Weymouth.

1995 Weymouth paints portrait of Prince Philip, Duke of Edinburgh (Blaugrund essay, fig. 1). He depicts the prince, whom he met in England through coaching circles, standing in the recently fire-damaged section of Windsor Castle, holding plans for its repair and restoration.

Inspired by private chapels he had visited in Europe, Weymouth oversees the building of an open-air stone structure (Blaugrund essay, fig. 14) at The Big Bend. He allows family and friends to use the chapel for their marriage ceremonies.

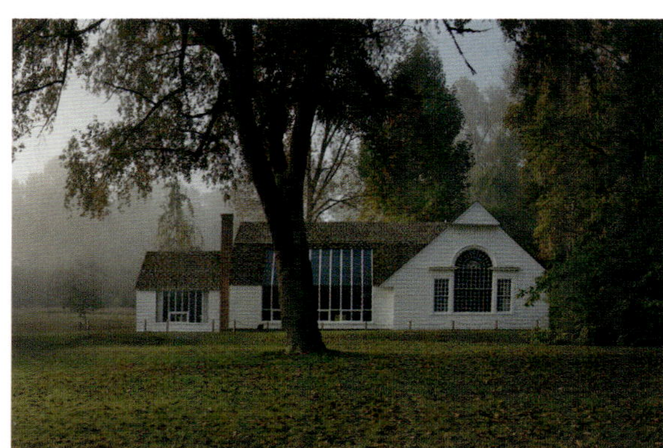

FIG. 34
The N. C. Wyeth Studio. Photo by Carlos Alejandro.

1996 After Carolyn Wyeth dies, the N. C. Wyeth House and Studio become available to the Conservancy. After restoration, the studio opens to the public.

1997 Weymouth and his gardens, many of which he designed, are featured in the article "The Collector," by Mac Griswold, in the October 1997 issue of *Garden Design*.

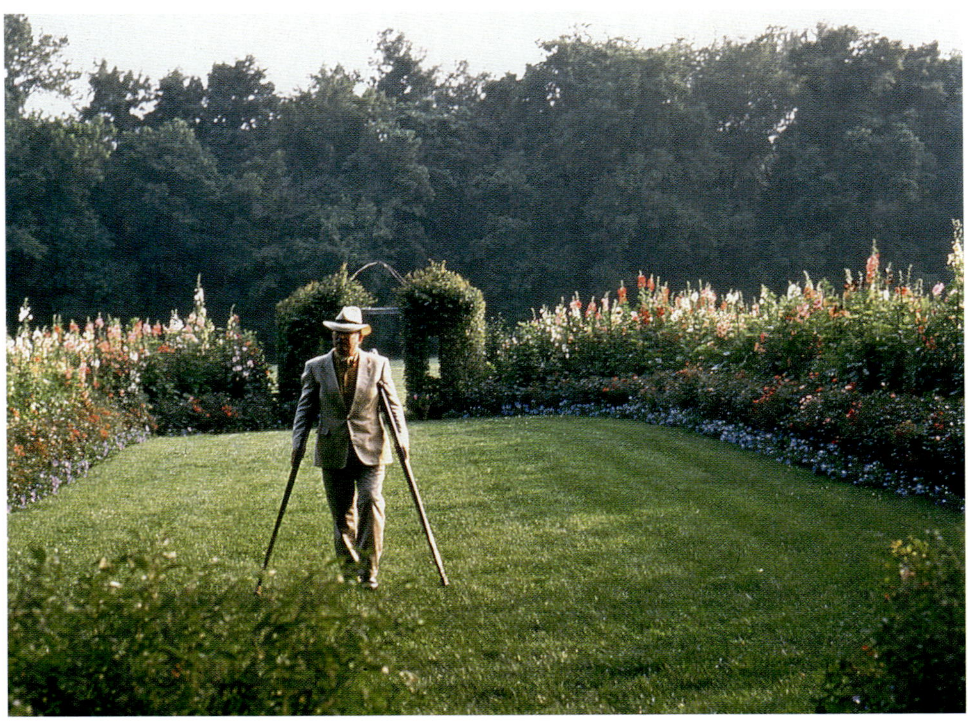

1999 Weymouth's NASA works are included in the traveling exhibition *Artistry of Space: The NASA Art Program*, organized by the Art Train Inc., which travels the nation from 1999 to 2002.

He receives the Cliveden Heritage Preservation award for his preservation work.

2000 Wyeth advises on the exhibition, *The du Pont Family: Two Hundred Years of Portraits*, organized by the Brandywine River Museum of Art, June 10–September 4, which includes seven portraits by him.

After renovations, the N. C. Wyeth House opens to the public for tours.

Weymouth accepts the Garden Clubs of America Special Citation for "Exemplary Service and Creative Vision" in the field of conservation and environmental protection.

Andrew Wyeth paints *The Whip* (Blaugrund essay, fig. 16), a portrait of Weymouth.

2001 *George Weymouth*, a solo exhibition featuring thirty of his works, is held at the Haggerty

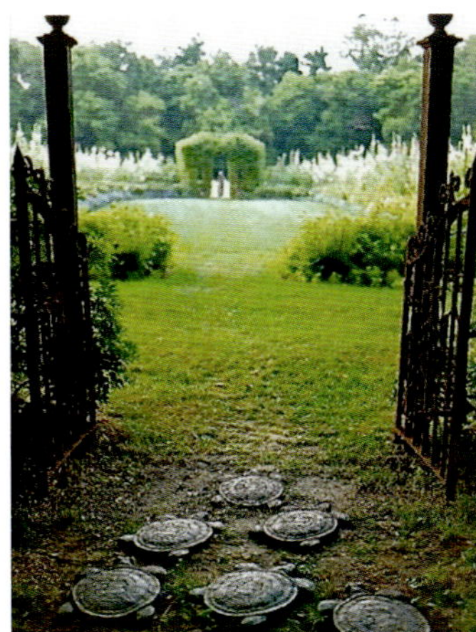

FIG. 35
Weymouth in his garden at The Big Bend. Photo by Kit Latham.

FIG. 36
Turtle stepping-stones in Weymouth's Big Bend garden. Photo by Susan Gray. © www.susangray-art.com

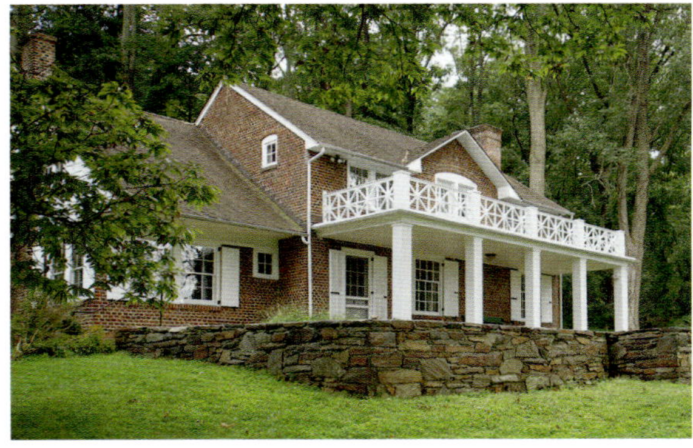

FIG. 37
The N. C. Wyeth House. Photo by Carlos Alejandro.

Museum of Art, Marquette University, Milwaukee, July 19–September 30. A catalogue with text by Curtis L. Carter accompanies the exhibition.

2002 After years of discussion, Weymouth is instrumental in obtaining for the Conservancy an easement on Winterthur Museum, Garden & Library's properties, so they will be protected into perpetuity.

2003 Philadelphia Museum of Art purchases Weymouth's painting *Party Line* (plate 54).

2004 Through Weymouth's and Duff's monumental fundraising campaign, titled Building for a New Century, the Museum opens a second wing, with additional galleries, a library and special collections room, and new storage areas. Across from the Museum, a new building housing the Membership and Development Departments is built in honor of Weymouth. Additionally, a new building for the Facilities Department is constructed, and other buildings on the Conservancy's campus are renovated.

FIG. 38
Trees reflected in the mirrored surface of the Museum's glass-walled addition.

2007 *George Weymouth from the Permanent Collection* (October 5–November 18), with fourteen works by Weymouth, is organized for the Conservancy's fortieth anniversary.

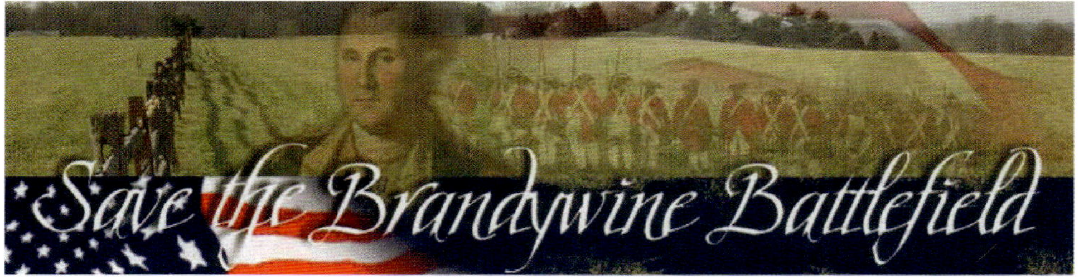

FIG. 39
Graphic designed for the Battlefield Campaign.

With Weymouth serving as chairman, James H. Duff and other Conservancy staff lead the campaign to raise funds for the purchase of Skirmish

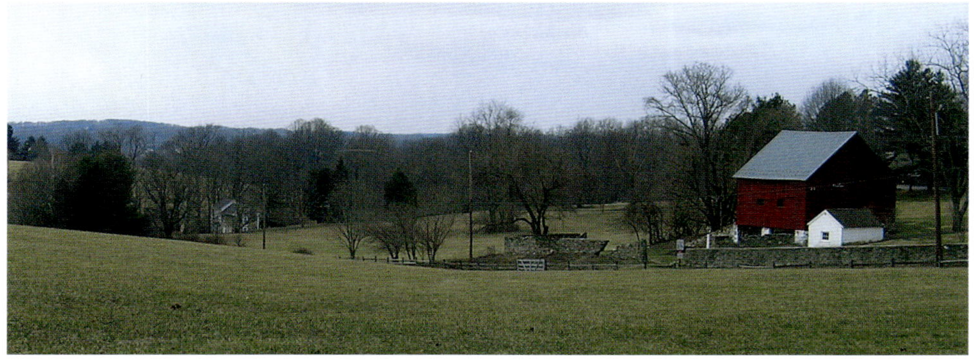

FIG. 40
Skirmish Hill Farm.

Hill Farm, an important hundred-acre section of the Brandywine Battlefield in Chadds Ford. Because the farm is at the center of four other sites already protected by conservation easements, it is dubbed the "center of the doughnut." The Conservancy is successful in raising the amount needed, with donations pouring in from large corporations, foundations, and even schoolchildren.

Weymouth receives an honorary Doctor of Humane Letters from the University of Delaware. The honorary degree is the highest honor the university awards and is given to those "whose contributions to the public good warrant exceptional recognition."

Weymouth is awarded Winterthur Museum, Garden & Library's Henry Francis du Pont Award for his "dedication to the preservation of American art and landscape."

Four works by Weymouth are included in the exhibition *In Tradition—Works by Brandywine Artists*, University Gallery, University of Delaware, Newark, Delaware, April 20–July 20.

2008 The Portrait Society of America awards Weymouth its Leadership in the Arts Award. The society also commissions Alexandra Tyng to paint the society's official portrait of Weymouth.

His work is included in *American Green: Art and Stewardship* at Somerville Manning Gallery in Greenville, Delaware, December 14, 2008–June 3, 2009.

Two works by Weymouth, *The Start* and *On the Beach*, are included in the NASA Art Program's fiftieth anniversary exhibition, *NASA / Art: 50 Years of Exploration*, which opens in October at the Art League of Bonita Springs in Florida and travels around the country under the auspices of the Smithsonian Institute, ending its three-year tour of the country at the National Air and Space Museum from May 28 to October 9, 2011.

2010 Weymouth paints *Requiem* (plate 50), an homage to Andrew Wyeth, who had passed away in 2009.

Weymouth is featured in *100 Artists of the Brandywine Valley* (Atglen, PA: Schiffer, 2010), by Catherine Quillman.

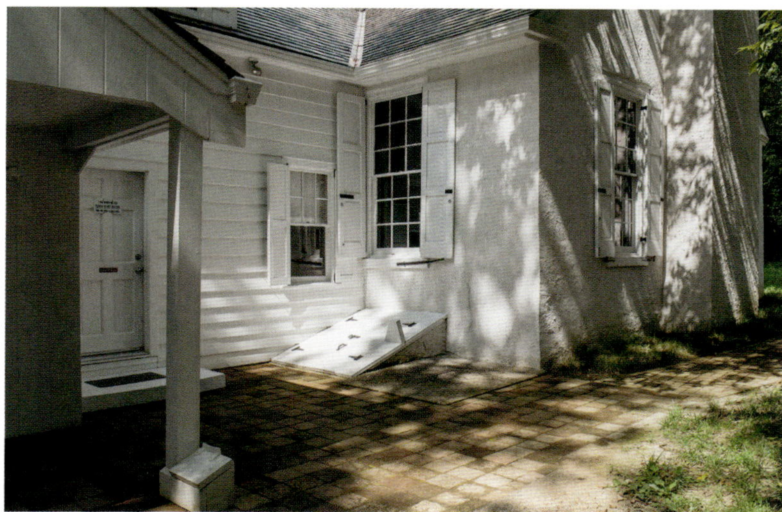

FIG. 41
The Andrew Wyeth Studio. Photo by Carlos Alejandro.

2012 During his years of friendship with the Wyeth family, Weymouth persuades them to donate the Andrew Wyeth Studio to the Conservancy. After renovation and some restoration, guided by Weymouth and Wyeth's sons, Jamie and Nicholas, to ensure its historical accuracy, the studio opens to the public for tours.

2014 Weymouth receives the Lifetime Conservation Leadership Award from the Pennsylvania Land Trust Association.

Richard Mellon Scaife, a former Trustee of the Conservancy, bequeaths half of his extensive art collection to the Museum and half to the Westmoreland Museum of American Art. In addition, the Conservancy is given his nine-hundred-acre estate, Penguin Court, in western Pennsylvania.

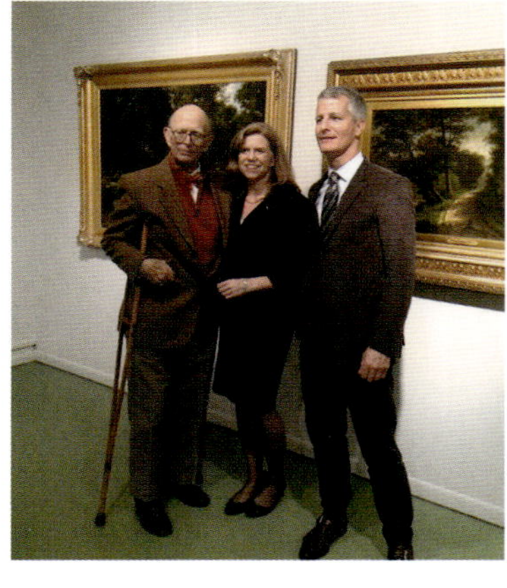

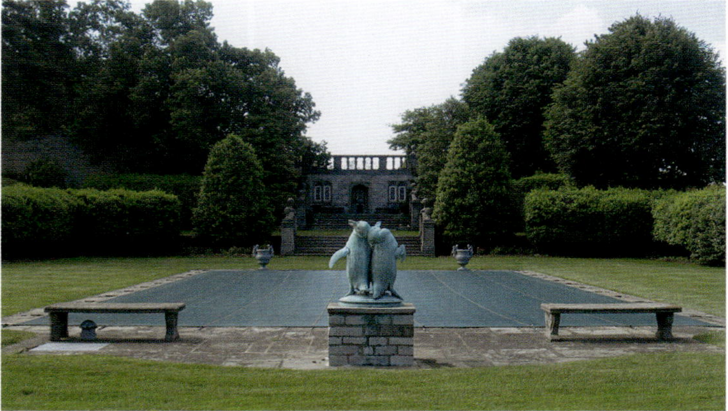

FIG. 42
Weymouth with the Brandywine's Executive Director Virginia Logan and Museum Director Thomas Padon.

FIG. 43
Penguin statue and pool at Penguin Court.

2016 Weymouth travels to Madrid, Spain, for a week at the end of February to attend the opening of the Denver Art Museum's exhibition *Wyeth: Andrew and Jamie in the Studio* at the Museo Thyssen-Bornemisza. While there, he visits the Museo del Prado, and makes a special trip to Toledo to see works by the sixteenth-century artist El Greco, whom he greatly admires.

After a long illness, Weymouth dies on April 24, 2016. The funeral service is held in his chapel at The Big Bend.

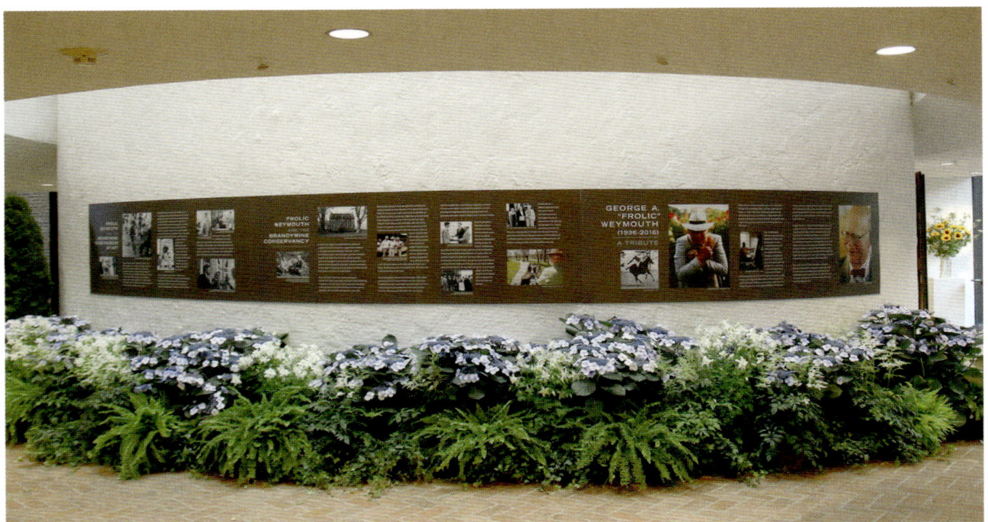

FIG. 44
Memorial display for George A. Weymouth at the Museum.

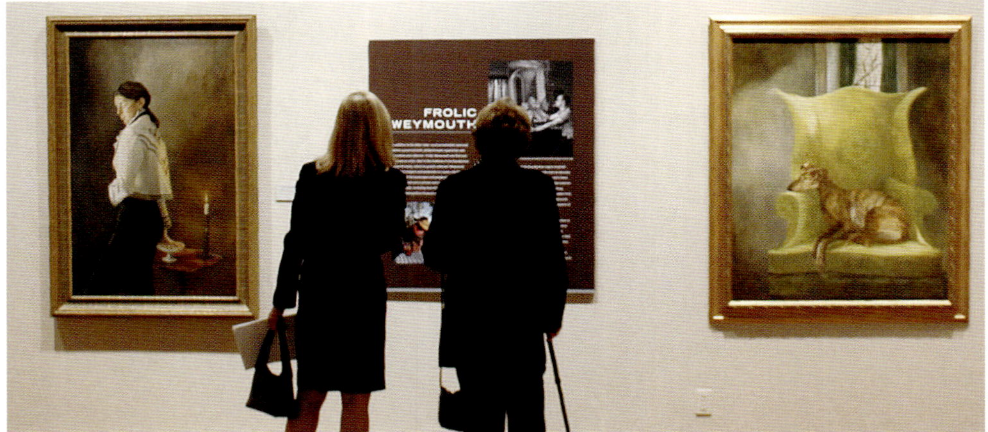

FIG. 45
Visitors to the memorial display.

Weymouth is honored by the Conservancy with a memorial display presenting highlights of his life and career and a selection of nineteen paintings, April 29 to July 3.

2018 *The Way Back: The Paintings of George A. Weymouth* is organized by the Brandywine River Museum of Art, open January 27–June 3. More than sixty works of art by Weymouth are included, and a fully illustrated catalogue is published in conjunction with the exhibition.

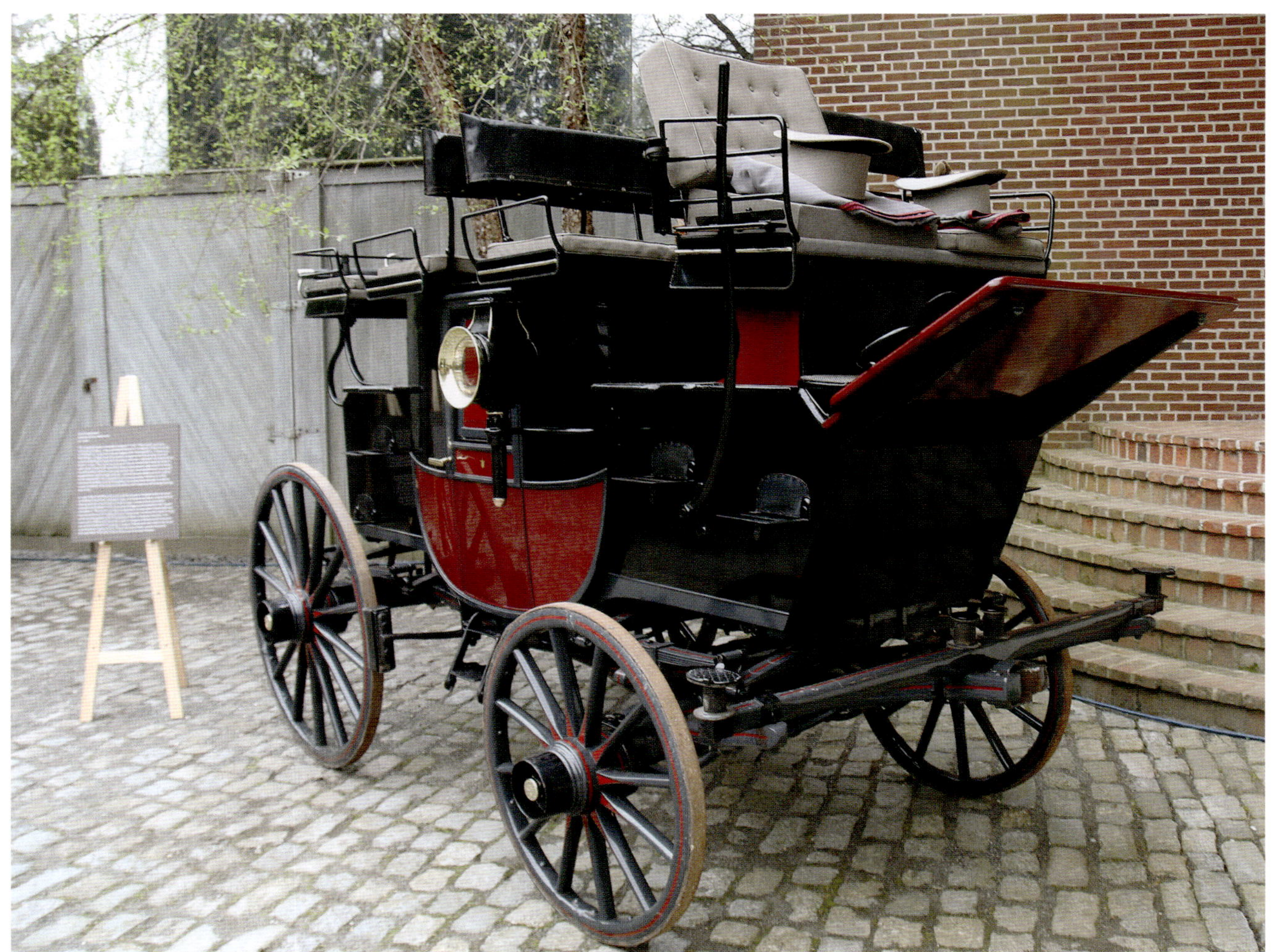

FIG. 46
Weymouth's coach in the Museum courtyard during the memorial display.

WORKS IN THE EXHIBITION

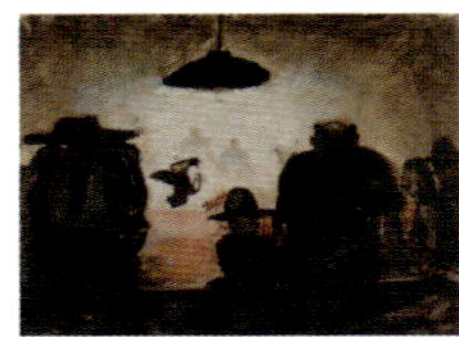

***Chicken Fight*, ca. 1948**
Oil on canvas, 9 × 12 inches
Mac Weymouth
Plate 1

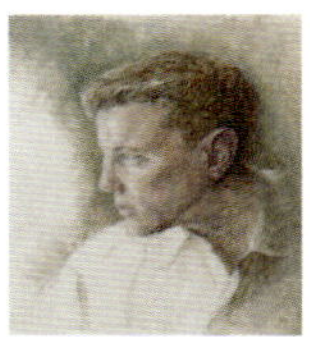

***Anson*, 1956**
Oil on board, 14 × 14 inches
Anson and Debra Beard, Jr.
Plate 3

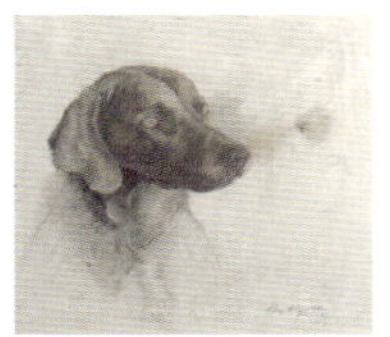

***Chucker*, 1957**
Oil on board, 16 × 16 inches
Private collection
Plate 2

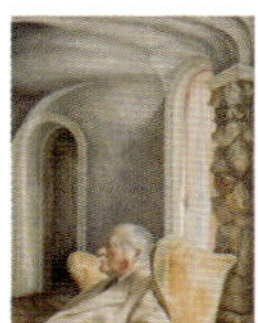

***Eugene Eleuthère du Pont*, 1958**
Oil on panel, 48 × 36 inches
Brandywine River Museum of Art
Gift of Mac Weymouth, 2017
Plate 10

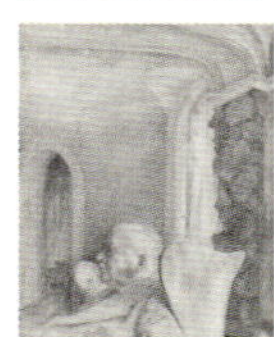

Study for *Eugene Eleuthère du Pont*, 1958
Pencil on paper, 19⅞ × 16½ inches
Mr. and Mrs. Samuel S. Hobbs and family
Plate 9

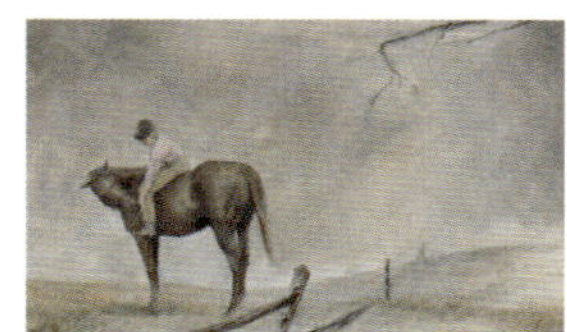

***Charfoot*, 1959**
Tempera on panel, 12 × 14 inches
Private collection
Plate 4

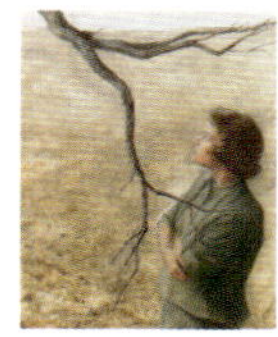

***Field Sparrow*, 1959**
Oil on panel, 17½ × 13¼ inches
Private collection
Plate 5

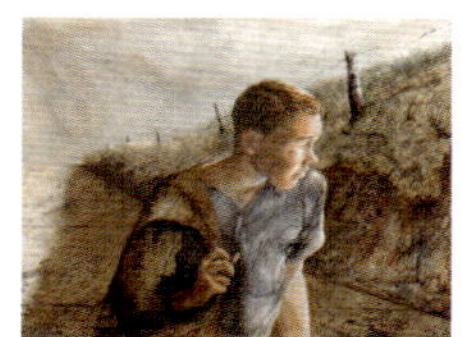

***Pete*, 1959**
Oil on panel, 26¼ × 34 inches
Private collection
Plate 6

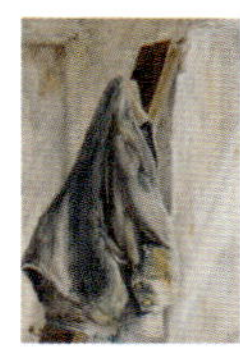

***Jack Campbell's Coat*, 1961**
Watercolor on paper, 20½ × 17¾ inches
Mac Weymouth
Plate 7

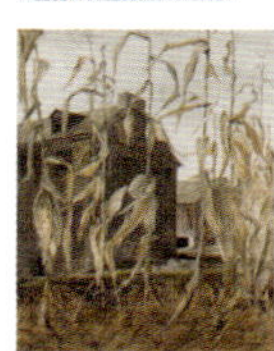

***Cornfields*, 1962**
Watercolor on paper, 21½ × 27½ inches
Mac Weymouth
Plate 11

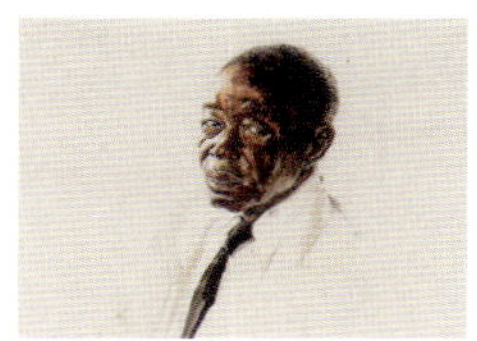

***Mr. Hilton Taylor*, 1962**
Watercolor on paper, 28½ × 17⅝ inches
Mac Weymouth
Plate 24

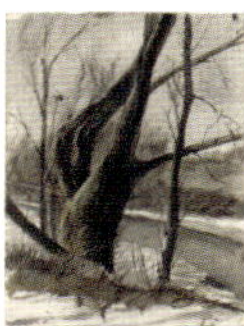

***Thaw*, 1962**
Watercolor on paper, 29⅞ × 21⅜ inches
Mac Weymouth
Plate 38

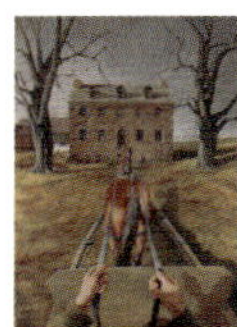

***The Way Back*, 1963**
Tempera on panel, 44¾ × 34¾ inches
Mac Weymouth
Plate 17

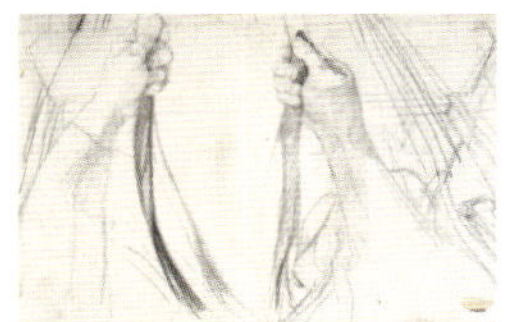

Study for *The Way Back*, 1963
Pencil on paper, 14 × 20 inches
Mac Weymouth
Plate 16

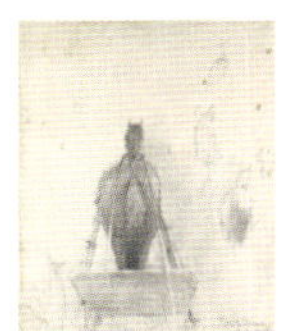

Study for *The Way Back*, 1963
Pencil on paper, 28 × 22 inches
Brandywine River Museum of Art
Gift of the David Taylor Family, 2003
Plate 15

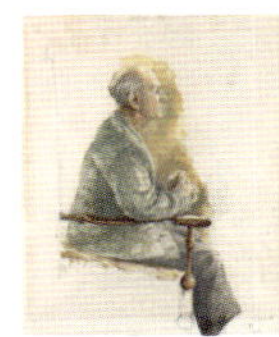

***Buckley*, 1964**
Watercolor on paper, 25 × 21 inches
Brandywine River Museum of Art
Gift of Mac Weymouth, 2017
Plate 23

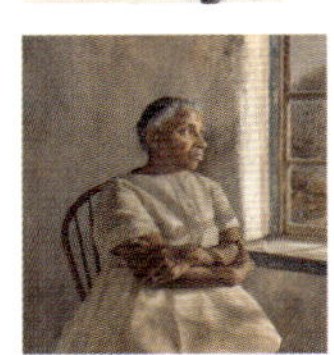

***Gathering Storm*, 1964**
Tempera on panel, 23¾ × 22 inches
Private collection
Plate 19

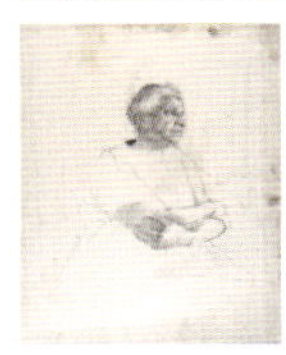

Study for *Gathering Storm*, 1964
Pencil on paper, 28 × 22 inches
Mac Weymouth
Plate 18

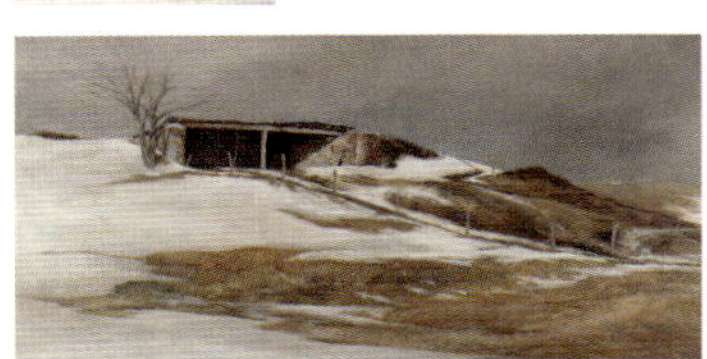

***The Shelter*, 1964**
Tempera on panel, 24 × 50 inches
Blackshear-Campanelli Trust
Plate 22

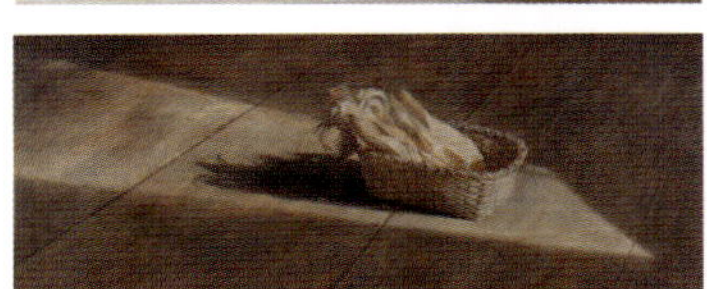

***Corn Basket*, 1965**
Tempera on panel, 14½ × 36 inches
Private collection
Plate 8

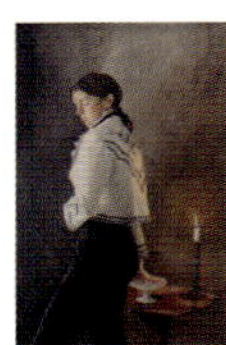

***Portrait of AnnaB*, ca. 1965**
Tempera on panel, 48 × 30¾ inches
Mac Weymouth
Plate 20

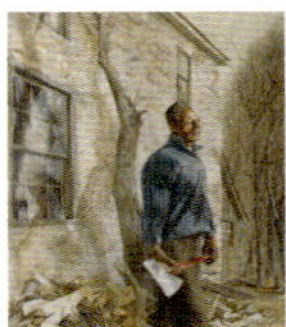

***Eleven O'Clock News*, 1966**
Tempera on panel, 33⅛ × 25½ inches
Brandywine River Museum of Art
Gift of Richard M. Scaife, 1986
Plate 25

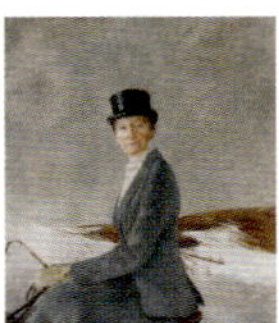

***Mrs. E. Miles Valentine*, 1966**
Tempera on panel, 36½ × 30⅛ inches
Brandywine River Museum of Art
Gift of Mrs. P. F. N. Fanning, 2001
Plate 14

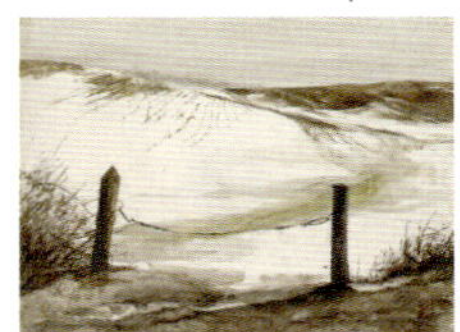

Untitled (Study for *Mrs. E. Miles Valentine*), ca. 1966
Watercolor on paper, 22 × 28 inches
Mac Weymouth
Plate 13

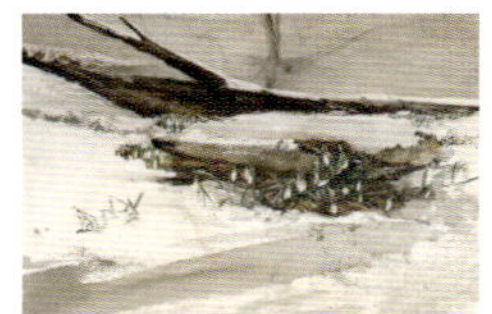

***Snow Drifts*, 1966**
Watercolor on paper, 21½ × 29½ inches
Mac Weymouth
Plate 35

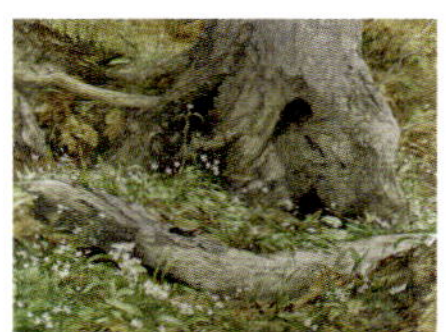

***Tree Trunks*, 1968**
Watercolor on paper, 21½ × 27½ inches
The Metropolitan Museum of Art, New York, NY, U.S.A.
Bequest of Joan Whitney Payson, 1975 (1976.201.26), Image copyright
© The Metropolitan Museum of Art. Image source: Art Resource, NY
Plate 37

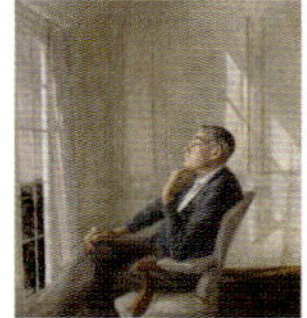

***Portrait of William W. Scranton*, 1969**
Tempera on panel, 31½ × 26 inches
Private collection
Plate 40

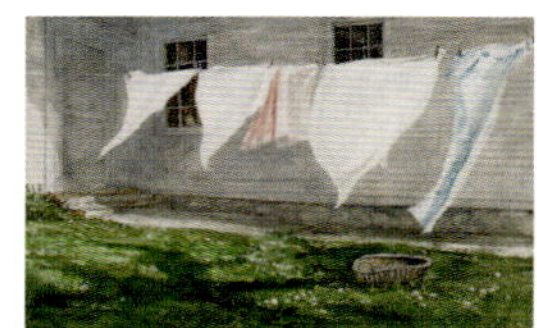

***Clothesline*, 1971**
Watercolor on paper, 19⅞ × 29¾ inches
Mr. and Mrs. Frank E. Fowler
Plate 29

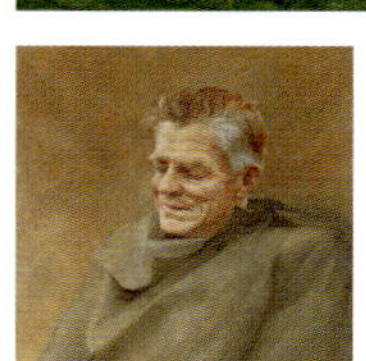

***Henry Belin du Pont, Jr.*, 1971**
Tempera on panel, 18⅝ × 19⅝ inches
Private collection
Plate 41

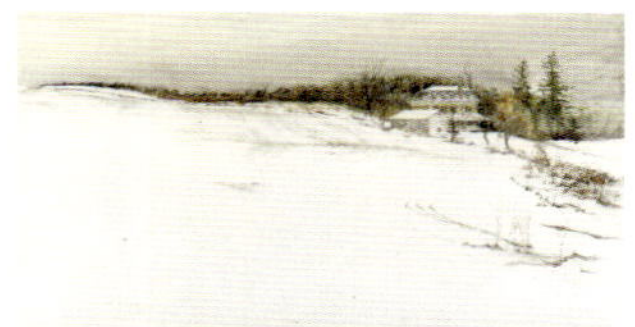

***Robin's House*, 1972**
Watercolor on paper, 21 × 38½ inches
Mr. and Mrs. Frank E. Fowler
Plate 26

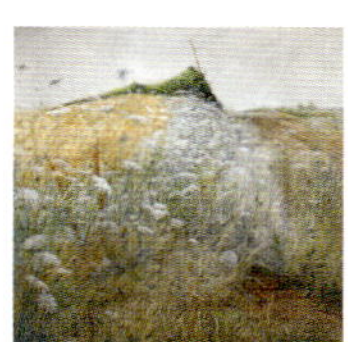

***August*, 1974**
Tempera on panel, 48 × 48 inches
Brandywine River Museum of Art
Gift of George A. Weymouth, 1989
Plate 30

Study for *August*, 1974
Watercolor on paper, 28 × 22 inches
Mac Weymouth
Plate 31

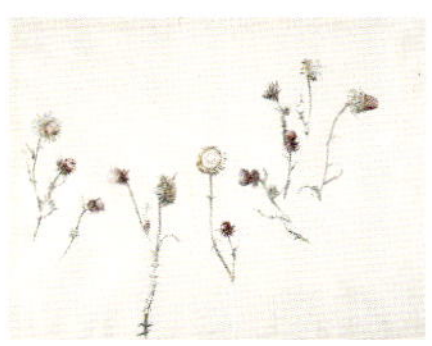

Study for *August*, #1, 1974
Watercolor on paper, 18⅞ × 23⅞ inches
Brandywine River Museum of Art
Richard M. Scaife Bequest, 2015
Plate 32

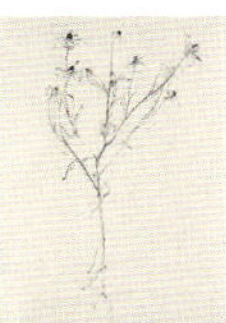

Study for *August*, #2, 1974
Pencil on paper, 24 × 17⅞ inches
Andrew L. Johnson
Plate 33

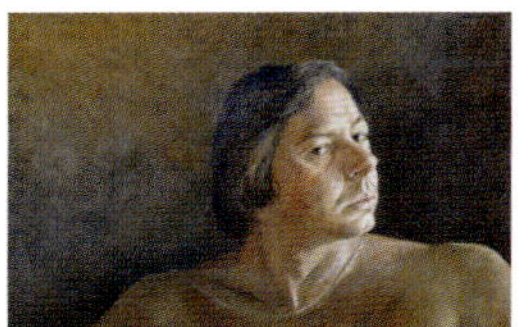

***Montsdeoca*, 1977**
Tempera on panel, 15⅝ × 23⅜ inches
Private collection
Plate 43

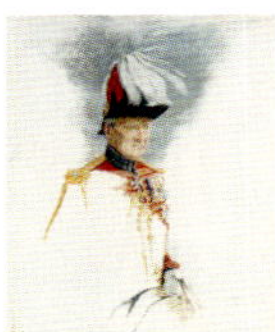

***The Earl of Westmorland, Master of the Horse*, 1980**
Tempera on panel, 44 × 35 inches
The Earl of Westmorland
Plate 61

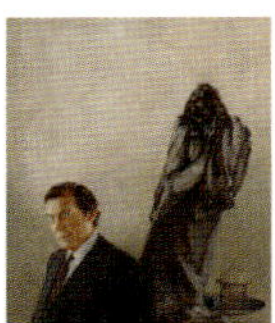

***Edgar Bronfman*, 1980–81**
Tempera on panel, 44 × 36 inches
The Samuel Bronfman Foundation, New York
Plate 21

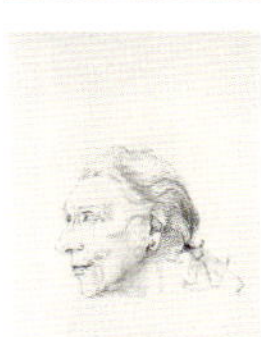

***Countess Westmorland*, 1985**
Pencil on paper, 12 × 9 inches
Mac Weymouth
Plate 27

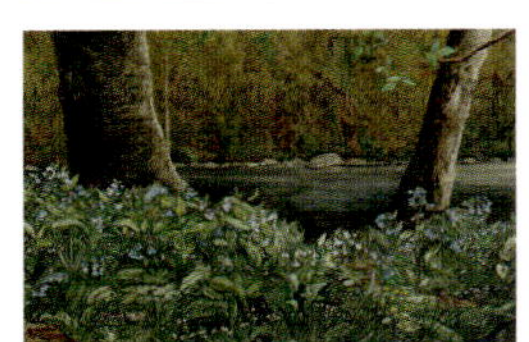

***Indian Hanna*, 1990**
Watercolor on panel, 39 × 59 inches
Brandywine River Museum of Art
Anonymous gift, 2005
Plate 55

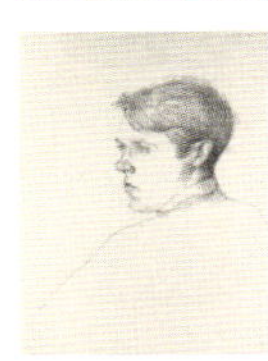

***Mac Weymouth*, 1990**
Pencil on paper, 24 × 18 inches
Brandywine River Museum of Art
Gift of Mac Weymouth, 2017
Plate 28

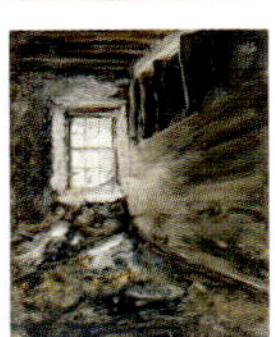

Untitled (*Barn Interior*), ca. 1990
Watercolor on paper, 28 × 22 inches
Mac Weymouth
Plate 47

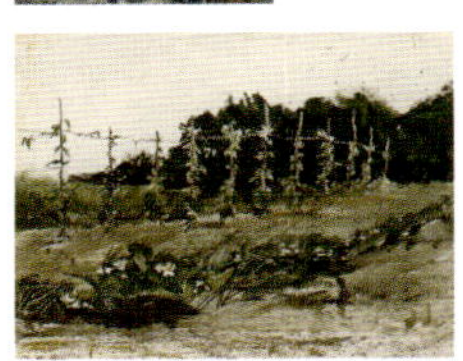

Untitled (*Pole Beans*), ca. 1990
Watercolor on paper, 18 × 24 inches
Mac Weymouth
Plate 36

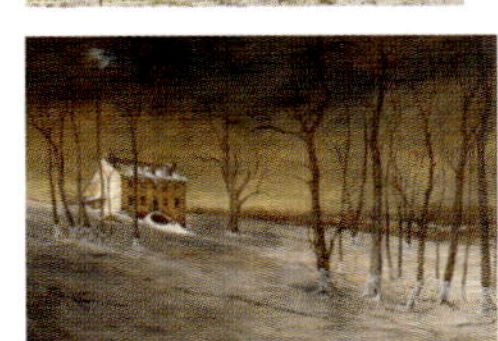

***Ice Shoes*, 1996**
Tempera on panel, 32 × 47 inches
Private collection
Plate 51

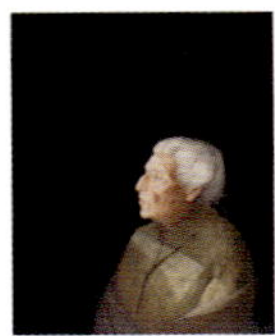

***Baroness*, 1997**
Tempera on panel, 36 × 30 inches
Betsy and Mike Dingman
Plate 44

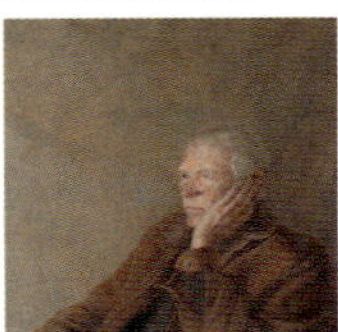

***Michael Wall*, 1997**
Tempera on panel, 24 × 18 inches
Private collection
Plate 12

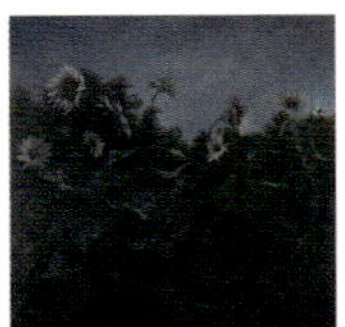

***Night Life*, 2000**
Tempera on panel, 47 × 47 inches
Mac Weymouth
Plate 58

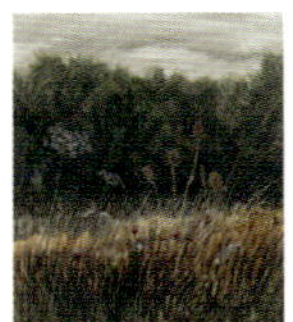

***Teasel*, 2000**
Tempera on panel, 25½ × 20¾ inches
Blackshear-Campanelli Trust
Plate 34

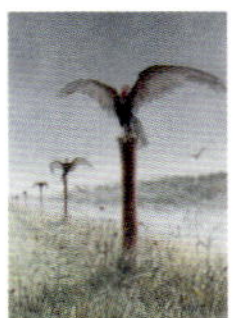

***Party Line*, 2001**
Tempera on panel, 60 × 42 inches
Philadelphia Museum of Art, Purchased with funds contributed by Richard Mellon Scaife and the Edith H. Bell Fund, and partial gift of the artist, 2003. 2003-187-1
Plate 54

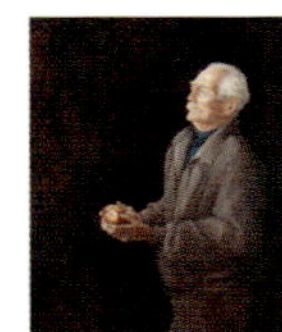

***The Offering*, 2001**
Tempera on panel, 47 × 33½ inches
Private collection
Plate 39

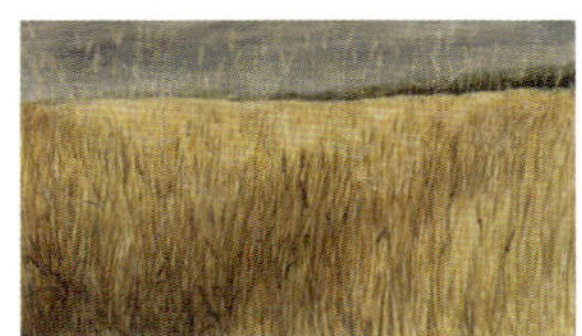

***WWW*, 2002**
Tempera on panel, 21½ × 35 inches
Deborah N. Rush
Plate 59

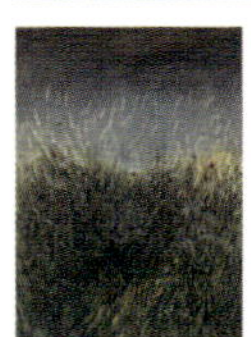

***Website*, 2003**
Tempera on panel, 40 × 28 inches
Private collection
Plate 60

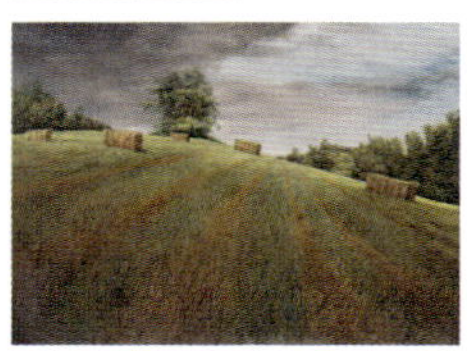

***First Cutting*, 2004**
Tempera on panel, 24½ × 32 inches
Claire Reid
Plate 57

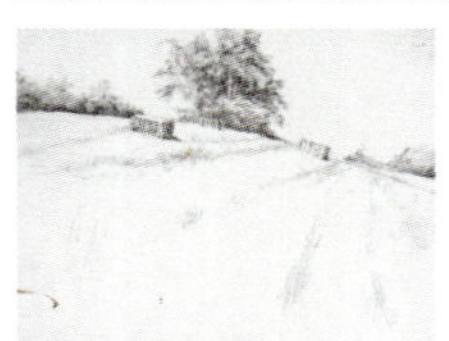

Study for *First Cutting*, 2004
Pencil on paper, 11 13/16 × 13 15/16 inches
Mac Weymouth
Plate 56

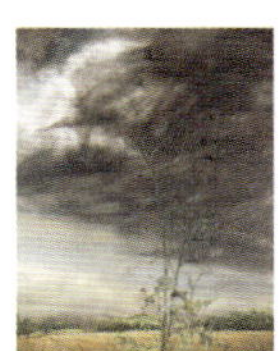

***Storm*, 2004**
Tempera on panel, 40 × 30 inches
Claire Reid
Plate 52

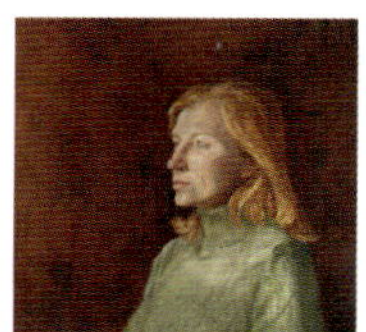

***Portrait of DD Matz*, 2007**
Tempera on panel, 24 × 22½ inches
Private Collection
Plate 42

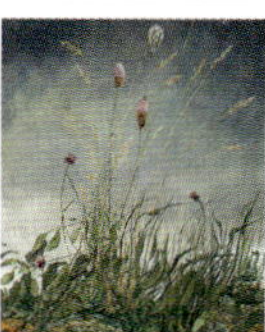

***Before Mowing*, 2009**
Tempera on panel, 23⁵⁄₁₆ × 17¼ inches
The Andrew and Betsy Wyeth Collection
Plate 53

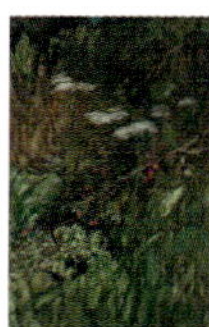

***Under the Fence*, study for *The Crossing*, 2009**
Tempera on panel, 24½ × 17 inches
Jim and Sally Duff
Plate 45

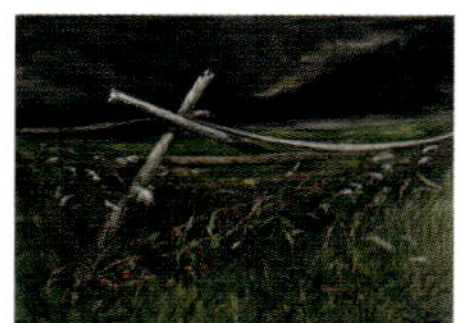

***The Crossing*, 2009–10**
Tempera on panel, 36 × 48 inches
Mac Weymouth
Plate 46

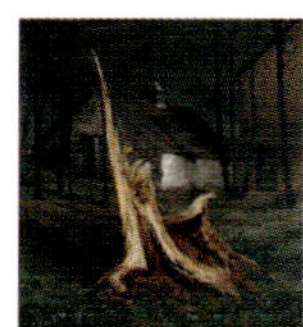

***Requiem*, 2010**
Tempera on panel, 53 × 46 inches
Mac Weymouth
Plate 50

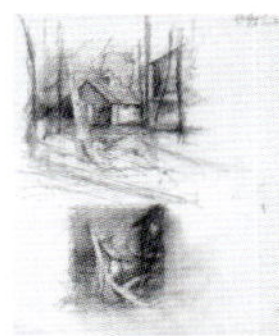

Study for *Requiem*, 2010
Pencil on paper, 17 × 14 inches
Mac Weymouth
Plate 49

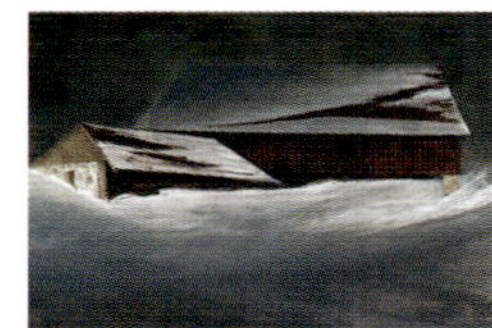

***Rogue Wave*, 2010**
Tempera on panel, 33¼ × 47⁹⁄₁₆ inches
The Andrew and Betsy Wyeth Collection
Plate 48

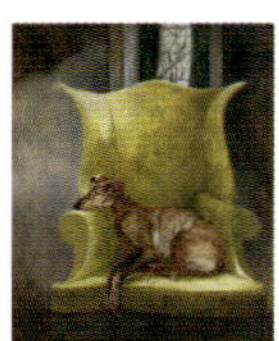

***Melanie in Repose*, 2011**
Tempera on panel, 38 × 27¼ inches
Mac Weymouth
Plate 63

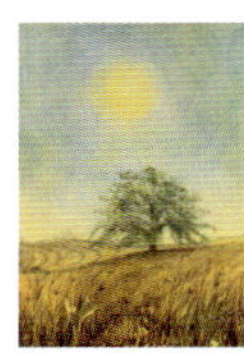

***Swelter*, 2011**
Tempera on panel, 47 × 33½ inches
Private collection
Plate 64

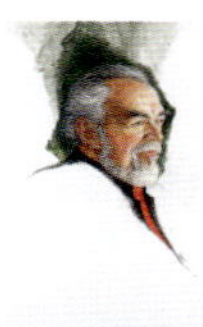

***Portrait of Herbert V. Kohler, Jr. ("The Chairman")*, 2012**
Tempera on panel, 23½ × 17 inches
Mr. and Mrs. Herbert V. Kohler, Jr.
Plate 62

ACKNOWLEDGMENTS

VIRGINIA O'HARA

This exhibition brought together many people committed to honoring George Weymouth's art and aesthetic vision. We are indebted to all of them for their extraordinary dedication. Thanks are due to Carolyn Nicodemus for her skillful assistance to Joseph J. Rishel, the guest curator of the exhibition. We would also like to extend our appreciation to the following individuals who assisted Annette Blaugrund in research for her essay: Mary Warnement, William D. Hacker Head of Reader Services at the Boston Athenæum; Edward Whitley, president, and Holly Taylor, senior account manager, at Bridgeman Images; Diana Thompson, director of collection and curatorial affairs at the National Academy of Design; Richard E. Noble, communications manager, editor, and school historian, and Andrea Upham, administrative assistant, at St. Mark's School, Southborough, Massachusetts; Michael Brenes, archivist at Yale University Library; and Sarah Hagan, fine arts specialist at the Boston Public Library. The Museum would also like to extend thanks to Carlton Cropper for his encouragement and enthusiastic support of this exhibition.

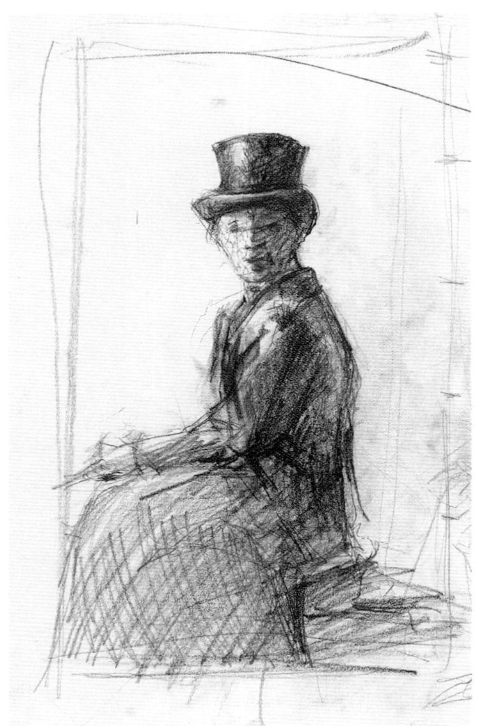

Study for *Mrs. E. Miles Valentine*, 1966
Pencil on paper,
28 x 22 inches
Mac Weymouth

Many staff at the Brandywine River Museum of Art were instrumental in organizing this exhibition. Special thanks are due to Gail Stanislow, former manager of the Brandywine's Walter and Leonore Annenberg Research Center, who sifted through copious archival materials to compile the first detailed chronology of Weymouth's professional career, published in this catalogue. In this endeavor, Stanislow received valuable assistance from Laura Pavona, archivist at the National Gallery of Art; Mary Brooks, archivist at Westtown School in West Chester, PA; and James Dean, founder and director of the NASA Art Program. Mary Cronin, dean of education and public programs, developed programs that enhanced visitors' understanding of Weymouth's achievement. Coordinating the myriad details relating to the loans for, and installation of, the exhibition with consummate skill were Bethany Engel, exhibitions manager; Sara Buehler, registrar; Amanda Shields, associate registrar; and Stephen Ruszkowski, preparator. Christine Podmaniczky, curator of N. C. Wyeth Collections and Historic Properties at the Brandywine, brought considerable expertise to researching Weymouth's involvement in the acquisition of the N. C. Wyeth and Andrew Wyeth studios by the Brandywine River Museum of Art. Thanks are also due to David Shields, the Brandywine Conservancy's associate director of land conservation, for providing information on the history of Weymouth's estate, The Big

Bend, and Rita Razze, Weymouth's long-time assistant at the Brandywine, for providing access to Weymouth's correspondence.

We extend gratitude for the valuable assistance of Dolly Bruni, former assistant to the Andrew Wyeth office and long-time friend of the Wyeth and Weymouth families for her work in compiling important documentation of some of Weymouth's works and their current locations as well as organizing and identifying the numerous drawings in the artist's studio. Thanks are also due to W. Donald Sparks II, Esq., and Beth Ward of Richards, Layton, Finger of Wilmington, Delaware, for their kind cooperation with details relating to the estate of George A. Weymouth.

Mac Weymouth deserves special recognition not only for providing access to research materials relating to his father's life but also for imparting much appreciated insight into Weymouth's artistic practice and for his unfailing goodwill and generosity of spirit. Special thanks also go to Anna B. McCoy, who was invaluable in clarifying details about Weymouth's early years as an artist, horseman and coach driver, and as a founder of the Brandywine Conservancy & Museum of Art. Mary Landa, the Andrew and Betsy Wyeth Collection manager and director of the Andrew Wyeth catalogue raisonné, was extraordinarily helpful in providing personal insights into Weymouth's career and his close and catalytic friendship with Andrew Wyeth.

The Brandywine is especially indebted to the following lenders whose generosity and support have been critical to the success of this exhibition:

Anson and Debra Beard, Jr.
Blackshear-Campanelli Trust
The Samuel Bronfman Foundation
Betsy and Mike Dingman
Jim and Sally Duff
Mr. and Mrs. Frank E. Fowler
Mr. and Mrs. Samuel S. Hobbs and Family
Andrew L. Johnson
Mr. and Mrs. Herbert V. Kohler, Jr.
The Metropolitan Museum of Art
Philadelphia Museum of Art
Private Collections
Claire Reid
Deborah N. Rush
The Earl of Westmorland
Mac Weymouth
The Andrew and Betsy Wyeth Collection

First published in the United States of America in 2018 by

Rizzoli Electa
A Divison of Rizzoli International Publications, Inc.
300 Park Avenue South
New York, NY 10010
www.rizzoliusa.com

in association with

Brandywine River Museum of Art
1 Hoffman's Mill Road
U.S. Route 1, P.O. Box 141
Chadds Ford, PA 19317
www.brandywinemuseum.org

Library of Congress Control Number: 2017950907

ISBN: 978-0-8478-6243-6

For Brandywine River Museum of Art:
Virginia O'Hara, Manager, Walter and Leonore Annenberg Research Center

For Rizzoli Electa:
Publisher: Charles Miers
Associate Publisher: Margaret Rennolds Chace
Editor: Ellen Cohen

Designer: Eileen Boxer, BoxerDesign

Jacket front: *August*, 1974 (detail)
Jacket back: *Baroness*, 1997 (detail)

pp. 2-3: *Charfoot*, 1959 (detail)
pp. 4-5: *Study for August, #1*, 1974 (detail)
p. 6: *Indian Hanna*, 1990 (detail)
p. 9: *Website*, 2003 (detail)
pp. 42–43: *Clothesline*, 1971 (detail)
p. 50: *Field Sparrow*, 1959 (detail)
pp. 60–61: *Michael Wall*, 1997 (detail)
pp. 64–65: *The Way Back*, 1963 (detail)
pp. 96–97: *Portrait of William W. Scranton*, 1960 (detail)
pp. 118–19: *Night Life*, 2000 (detail)
pp. 130–31: *Melanie in Repose*, 2011 (detail)
pp. 134–35: *The Crossing*, 2009 (detail)

2018 2019 2020 2021 / 10 9 8 7 6 5 4 3 2 1

Printed in China

Photo Credits:

Note: BL denotes Blaugrund essay figure, RI denotes Rishel essay figure; CH denotes Chronology figure

Carlos Alejandro: CH figs. 34, 37, 41
© 2018 Andrew Wyeth / Artists' Rights Society (ARS): BL figs. 13, 16, 23, 24
Ann Wyeth McCoy Archives, Brandywine River Museum of Art, the Walter and Leonore Annenberg Research Center: RI fig. 3; CH figs. 9, 10, 15
Beinecke Rare Book and Manuscript Library, Yale Collection of American Literature: BL fig. 5
Brandywine Conservancy & Museum of Art Archives: RI fig. 1; BL fig. 17; all Chronology images not otherwise credited
Brandywine Polo Club: CH fig. 11
Brandywine River Museum of Art: pp. 6, 8; RI fig. 3; BL figs. 3, 8, 9, 12
Brilliant Studio, Exton, PA: pp. 2–3, 4–5, 6, 9, 60–61, 64–65, 96–97, 118–119, 130–131, 134–135, 158; BL figs. 3, 4, 16; plates 1, 4, 5, 8, 9, 12, 14, 15, 17, 19, 22, 23, 26, 28, 32, 33, 34, 36, 38, 39, 40, 41, 42, 46, 48, 50, 52, 53, 55, 58, 59, 60, 63, 64
Richard C. Carter: BL fig. 25; plate 43
The Century Association, New York: BL fig. 11
Christopher Ciccone: plates 52 and 57
The Clark Art Institute, Williamstown, Massachusetts: BL fig. 7
Luc Demers: plate 45
Des Moines Art Center: BL fig. 26
Rick Echelmeyer: BL figs. 3, 4, 12, 19, 20, 22; plates 2, 6, 7, 10, 11, 15, 16, 18, 20, 24, 25, 27, 30, 31, 35, 47, 49, 51, 56, 62; CH fig. 3
Freudy Photos, New York: CH fig. 1
Jacek Gancarz: plate 3
Jim Graham © Jim Graham: RI fig. 5; BL fig. 14, 15; CH figs. 8, 24
Susan Gray © susangrayart.com: RI fig. 4; BL fig. 10; CH figs. 17, 36
Hagley Museum and Library: CH fig. 2
Kit Latham Photographer: CH fig. 35
© The Metropolitan Museum of Art. Image source: Art Resource, NY: BL fig. 21; plate 37
Museum of Fine Arts, Boston: Bl fig. 6
National Academy Museum, New York. USA/Bridgeman Images: BL fig. 18
National Aeronautics and Space Agency (NASA) Art Program, Kennedy Space Center, Florida: RI fig. 6
National Arts Club, New York; C. Zumwalt, photographer. Courtesy National Arts Club. CH fig. 31
Chris Oughtred, North Light Imaging Services: pp. 42–43 (detail), plate 29
Photographic Records Limited, London: plate 61
Rick Rhodes Photography: plate 44
Royal Collection Trust/All Rights Reserved: BL figs. 1 and 2
Bruce Schwarz: plate 21
Yale University Archives: RI fig. 2; CH fig. 4

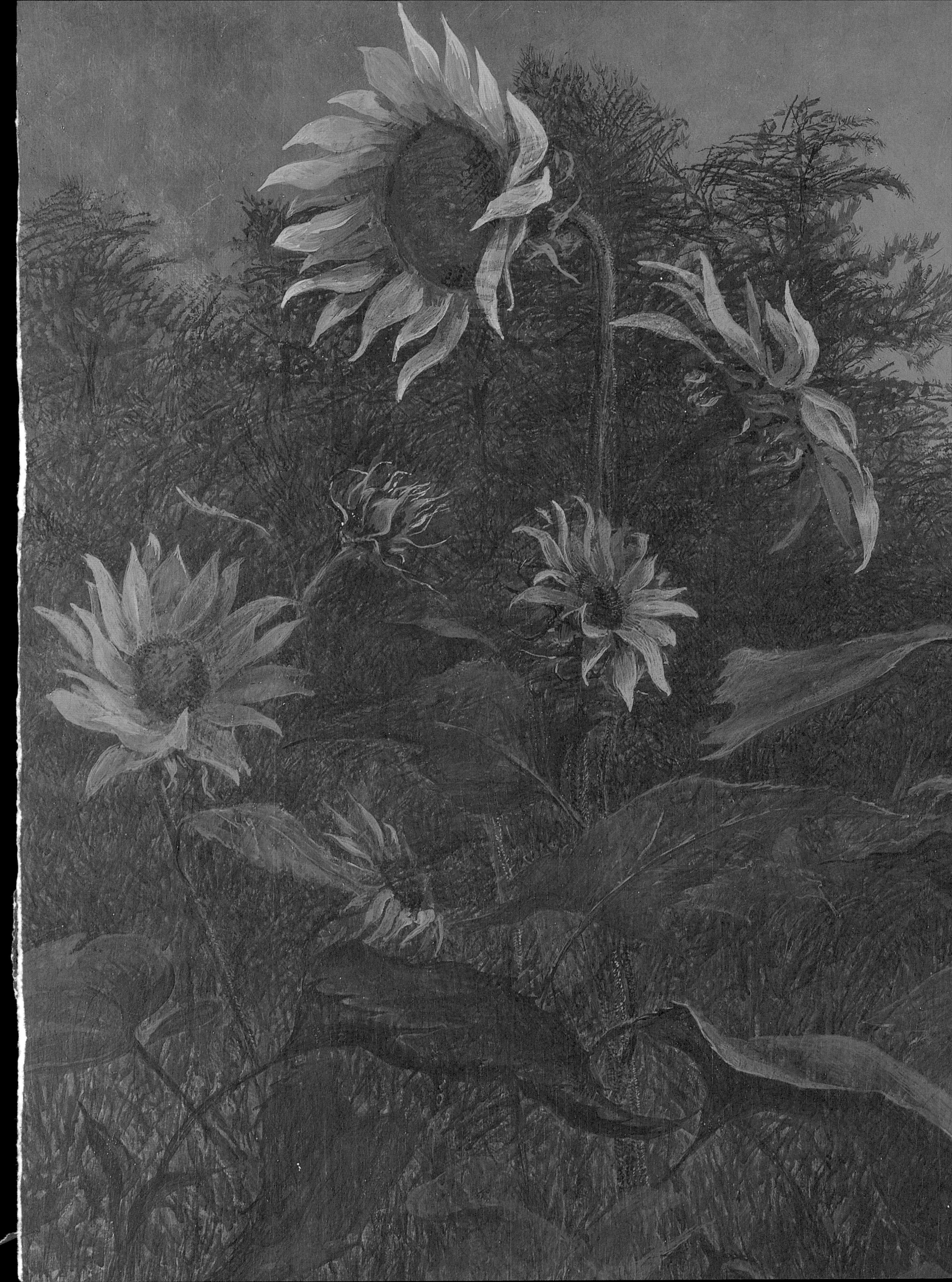

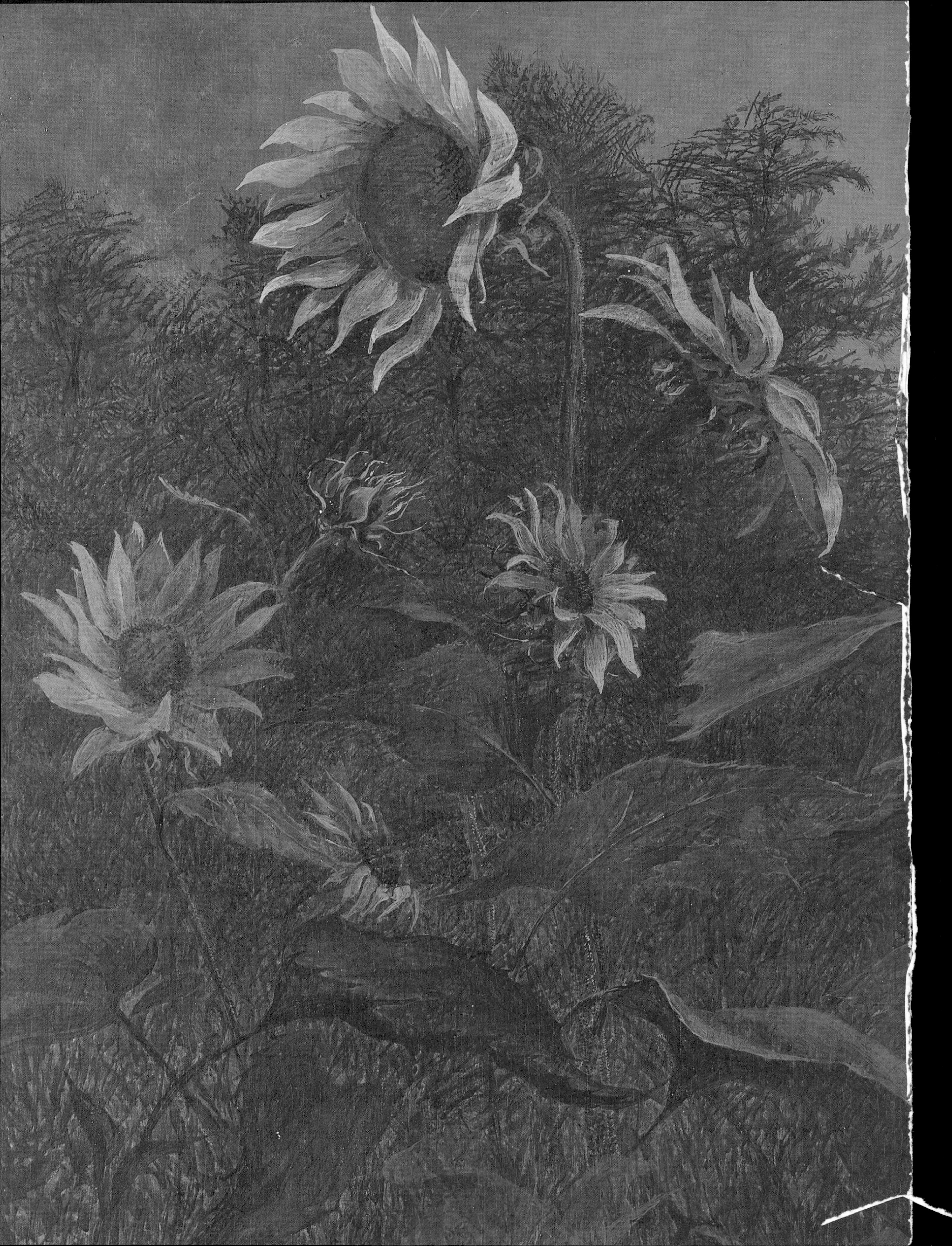